Prisoners' Bodies

States, People, and the History of Social Change

Series editors Rosalind Crone and Heather Shore

The States, People, and the History of Social Change series brings together cutting-edge books written by academic historians on criminal justice, welfare, education, health, and other areas of social change and social policy. The ways in which states, governments, and local communities have responded to "social problems" can be seen across many different temporal and geographical contexts. From the early modern period to contemporary times, states have attempted to shape the lives of their inhabitants in important ways. Books in this series explore how groups and individuals have negotiated the use of state power and policy to regulate, change, control, or improve people's lives and the consequences of these processes. The series welcomes international scholars whose research explores social policy (and its earlier equivalents) as well as other responses to social need, in historical perspective.

1 *Writing the Lives of the English Poor, 1750s–1830s*
Steven King

2 *The People's Health*
Health Intervention and Delivery in Mao's China, 1949–1983
Zhou Xun

3 *Young Subjects*
Children, State-Building, and Social Reform in the Eighteenth-Century French World
Julia M. Gossard

4 *Indentured Servitude*
Unfree Labour and Citizenship in the British Colonies
Anna Suranyi

5 *Penal Servitude*
Convicts and Long-Term Imprisonment, 1853–1948
Helen Johnston, Barry Godfrey, and David J. Cox

6 *In Their Own Write*
Contesting the New Poor Law, 1834–1900
Steven King, Paul Carter, Natalie Carter, Peter Jones, and Carol Beardmore

7 *Looking After Miss Alexander*
Care, Mental Capacity, and the Court of Protection in Mid-Twentieth-Century England
Janet Weston

8 *Friendless or Forsaken?*
Child Emigration from Britain to Canada, 1860–1935
Ruth Lamont, Eloise Moss, and Charlotte Wildman

9 *Fraudulent Lives*
Imagining Welfare Cheats from the Poor Law to the Present
Steven King

10 *Slow Train to Arcadia*
A History of Railway Commuting into London
Duncan Gager

11 *Prisoners' Bodies*
Activism, Health, and the Prisoners' Rights Movement in Ireland, 1972–1985
Oisín Wall

Oisín Wall

Prisoners' Bodies

**Activism, Health, and the Prisoners'
Rights Movement in Ireland, 1972–1985**

McGill-Queen's University Press
Montreal & Kingston | London | Chicago

© McGill-Queen's University Press 2024

ISBN 978-0-2280-2295-4 (paper)
ISBN 978-0-2280-2340-1 (ePDF)
ISBN 978-0-2280-2341-8 (ePUB)
ISBN 978-0-2280-2354-8 (OA)

Legal deposit fourth quarter 2024
Bibliothèque nationale du Québec

Printed in Canada on acid-free paper that is 100% ancient forest free
(100% post-consumer recycled), processed chlorine free

McGill-Queen's University Press in Montreal is on land which long served as
a site of meeting and exchange amongst Indigenous Peoples, including the
Haudenosaunee and Anishinabeg nations. In Kingston it is situated on the
territory of the Haudenosaunee and Anishinaabek. We acknowledge and
thank the diverse Indigenous Peoples whose footsteps have marked these
territories on which peoples of the world now gather.

Library and Archives Canada Cataloguing in Publication

Title: Prisoners' bodies : activism, health, and the prisoners' rights movement
    in Ireland, 1972-1985 / Oisín Wall.
Names: Wall, Oisín, author.
Series: States, people, and the history of social change ; 11.
Description: Series statement: States, people, and the history of social
    change ; 11 | Includes bibliographical references and index.
Identifiers: Canadiana (print) 20240400844 | Canadiana (ebook)
    20240400925 | ISBN 9780228022954 (paper) | ISBN 9780228023548 (OA) |
    ISBN 9780228023418 (ePUB) | ISBN 9780228023401 (ePDF)
Subjects: LCSH: Prisoners—Civil rights—Ireland—History—20th century.
Classification: LCC HV9650.3 .W35 2024 | DDC 323.3/29270941709047—dc23

This book was designed and typeset by Garet Markvoort, zijn digital, in
10.5/14 Calluna with Gotham. Copyediting by Candida Hadley.

For my family, there but for the grace of you

Contents

Figures | ix

Acknowledgements | xi

Content Note | xv

Abbreviations | xvii

Introduction: The Prisoner's Two Bodies | 3

1 'Join Your Prisoners' Union!': A Microhistory of Daniel Redmond and the Prisoners' Union, 1972–77 | 47

2 'A Voice for Prisoners': The Prisoners' Rights Organisation, 1973–76 | 65

3 'A Project against Authority': A Microhistory of Karl Crawley's Disruptive Autonomy | 91

4 'The Beginning of the End': Protest, Rioting, and Revenge, 1979–86 | 109

5 'It Is Doubtful If There Is a Single Prisoner or Ex-prisoner Here':
   The PRO's Sociological Turn, 1977–86 | 130

6 'What We Thought We Had Achieved': Whitaker, Reform, and
   the Legacy of the Prisoners' Rights Movement | 155

   Epilogue: Communicating Bodies | 174

   Notes | 181

   Bibliography | 209

   Index | 233

Figures

1.1 | Annual average daily prison population, 1967–90, and distribution across the prison estate. Also indicating the years new prisons were opened. Graph created by Dr Stephen Roddy. | 32

3.1 | Karl Crawley showing some of the scars left by his numerous operations, Dublin: 1982. Photograph courtesy of Derek Speirs. | 99

4.1 | Rooftop protest over prison conditions at Mountjoy Prison, Dublin: 1984. Photograph courtesy of Derek Speirs. | 116

5.1 | Prisoners' Rights Organisation protest to end civilian detention in the Curragh Military Detention Barracks, Newbridge co. Kildare: 1978. When this march arrived at the Curragh Camp, the photographer, Derek Speirs, was arrested and his film temporarily confiscated. Photograph courtesy of Derek Speirs. | 147

Acknowledgements

I started the research that would become this book in January 2018, exactly six years to the day before completing the final manuscript. More people than I can count have helped me along the way. As a result, it is daunting to write the acknowledgements. If I have left a name off the list, know that it is entirely by accident and I am grateful to everyone who has offered their help. I am most grateful to the people who generously contributed their time and experience to this project, particularly those who participated in recorded oral histories: Michael Donnelly, Tommy Crawley, Eddie Cahill, Wladek Gaj, Máirín de Búrca, Joe Costello, Pat McCartan, Seán Reynolds, and Anne Costelloe. I would like to thank the many people who did not wish to have their experiences recorded but who privately discussed their experiences with me and gave advice about my research. I am also indebted to the many people who helped me contact oral history participants or who gave me access to their private collections of material.

I am profoundly grateful to Professor Catherine Cox for enabling me to come home to Ireland, for introducing me to prison history, and for her generous comments and edits on the numerous drafts of this work. More than that, I am grateful for everything I have learned from her and her tireless support, encouragement, and friendship since 2018. When this manuscript is submitted, I'm looking forward to getting to work on our next collaboration.

I would like to thank Derek Speirs for allowing me to view his incredible collection of prison- and protest-related photojournalism, which spans more than forty years. It has been a unique research resource during this project and I am delighted that he has given me permission to include several of his photographs in the body of the book. I am also extremely grateful to Dr Stephen Roddy, who took an unreadable table of data and turned it into the clear graph in the introduction, and Siobhán O'Brien, who has been such a great help with the publication process.

The research for and production of this book has been generously supported by the Wellcome Trust through both my own Wellcome Research Fellowship '"We are the heroin capital of Europe": Marginal Communities, Health, Identity, and the Opioid Epidemic in Twentieth-Century Ireland' (223588/A/21/Z) and Professor Catherine Cox and Professor Hilary Marland's Investigator Award 'Prisoners, Medical Care and Entitlement to Health in English and Irish Prisons, 1840–2000' (100335I/Z/I3/Z). I would also like to thank University College Dublin for supporting this research with a Seed Funding Award 'Living Inside: Six voices from the history of Irish prison reform' (SFI755), and the School of History there for nearly five years of unwavering support. I was delighted to get to work with such brilliant people as part of the Catherine and Hilary's Prison History Project team, including Sinead McCann, Dr William Murphy, Dr Rachel Bennett, Professor Virginia Berridge, Dr Janet Weston, and many others. I am extremely grateful for the support and friendship that I have found at University College Cork, particularly through the School of History and the Radical Humanities Laboratory, and I am overjoyed to have the chance to make this my academic home once again.

I am grateful to the staff at the National Archives of Ireland, the National Library of Ireland, University College Cork's Special Collections & Archives, and University College Dublin's Archives, as well as Harriet Wheelock and Chiará Morgan at the Royal College of Physicians of Ireland Heritage Centre. I would like to thank Professor Mary Rogan for generously sharing Máirín de Búrca's invaluable blue folder of PRO-related materials and Dr Janet Weston for sharing several oral histories. I am grateful to Emer O'Brien for helping out in a citation emergency. I would also like to thank Kim Redmond for her invaluable research assistance.

I am very grateful to all of the other people who have read, listened to, commented on, and edited this work and its precursors over the years: my parents and brother, Professor Catherine Cox, Dr Miranda Fay Thomas, Dr Verity Burke, Dr Harry Harvey, Dr Alice Mauger, Dr Fionualla Walsh, Professor Hilary Marland, Brian Crowley, James Grannell, Michael Donnelly, the book's three peer reviewers who gave such supportive and constructive comments, both of the editors who have worked on the book, Richard Baggaley and Joanne Pisano, the copyeditor Candida Hadley, and many, many others.

I would like to thank my colleagues, some of whom are my old lecturers, and my new friends at University College Cork for their welcome and encouragement. Including Drs Sarah Bezan, Stephen Roddy, Kylie Thomas, Eugene Costello, Sarah Kerr, Jesse Peterson and Professors Laura McAttackney, Des Fitzgerald, and Adrian Favell from the Radical Humanities Laboratory; and Drs Hiram Morgan, Jason Harris, Jay Roszman, David Fitzgerald, and Maeve O'Riordan from the School of History. I am grateful for the friendship and support of many others as well, including Dr Verity Burke, Dr Alice Mauger, Dr Nicola Kirkby, Dr Fionualla Walsh, Laura Hurley, Dr Billy Ryan, Alexa Wearden, Nicola O'Halloran, and Mairead Crowley.

For their decades of love and support I would like to thank my family and friends: Dr William Wall, Dr Liz Kirwan, Dr Illan Wall, Bríd Spillane, Ruán Wall, Odhran Wall, Dr Miranda Fay Thomas, Janet and Glyn Thomas, Dr Harry Harvey, Eoin Griffin, Dr John O'Donovan, and Stephen Hayes. So much of life is set in train by the relationships that form us, for that reason I have dedicated this book to my family, without whom I cannot know who I would have become.

Content Note

This book contains extensive discussions of imprisonment, hunger strikes, self-harm, drug use, mental health issues, suicide, institutional abuse, child abuse, violent crime, racist language in quotations, and other issues that a reader might find distressing. These topics are dispersed throughout the text from the first sentence to the last, so I implore the reader to be prepared to come upon them unexpectedly as they read.

Abbreviations

AnCO	An Chomhairle Oiliúna (the national industrial training council)
CMH	Central Mental Hospital
COP	Concern of Prisoners
CPAD	Concerned Parents Against Drugs
ECHR	European Court of Human Rights
ICCL	Irish Council for Civil Liberties
IFPA	Irish Family Planning Association
IPRT	Irish Penal Reform Trust
IPS	Irish Prison Service
IWLM	Irish Women's Liberation Movement
MPU	Mountjoy Prisoners' Union
OIRA	Official Irish Republican Army
PIRA	Provisional Irish Republican Army
POA	Prison Officers' Association
PPU	Portlaoise Prisoners' Union
PRO	Prisoners' Rights Organisation
PROP	Preservation of the Rights of Prisoners
PRS/PRG	Prisoners' Revenge Squad/Group
PU	Prisoners' Union
TCD	Trinity College Dublin
TD	Teachta Dála (member of the Irish Parliament)
UCD	University College Dublin

Prisoners' Bodies

Introduction

The Prisoner's Two Bodies

Karl Crowley [*sic*] is a mentally disturbed young man who has made 17 attempts at suicide and who has succeeded in doing severe physical damage to his whole body ... Karl Crowley is held, for the full term of his sentence, apart from the main body of prisoners. He is held in the 'base' which is where the punishment cells are located.
—'12 Years for Picketing', *Jail Journal*, 1975

This book is about bodies – hungry, scarred, isolated, and collective bodies. The prisoner's body, stripped of civil and political rights, and of the normal expressions of agency, becomes a site of communication and resistance. Since the birth of the modern penal system, individual prisoners have used every method, from hunger strikes to self-harm, to express their rejection of 'prison discipline', the legally prescribed internalization of obedience to penal authority. However, these bodily communications become institutional secrets. They take place in locked cells behind high walls and their discussion is protected by medical or legal professional confidentiality and can even be punishable under the Official Secrets Act (1963). In spite of this, for a moment in the 1970s, Irish prisoners found new ways to communicate, which not only instrumentalized their bodies individually but also their collective body.

In a parody of the historian Ernst Kantorwicz's conception of the sovereign bodies of medieval kings, the modern prisoner has two bodies: their 'body natural', the prisoner's body, a physical presence which is legally hidden from the world, and their 'body politic', a conglomerate body of prisoners which, through its conspicuous exclusion from civil society, is a public manifestation of the sovereign power of the state.[1] Ordinary prisoners, that is people whose crimes did not have an overt political motivation, have long used their 'body natural' to resist control within the penal system at an individual level – for instance almost 70 per cent of hunger strikes in early twentieth-century English prisons were by nonpolitical prisoners protesting their subjection to prison discipline or to the material conditions of the prison, but for the most part these took place in isolation.[2] In Ireland in the 1970s, prisoners began to utilise their combined 'body politic' to publicly challenge the fundamental nature of the prison system. They staged protests on prison roofs, imposing a human presence onto a vista designed to conspicuously exclude humans; they smuggled illegal communiques about prison conditions to the media, creating the ordinary prisoner as a subject in the public discourse for the first time; and when they were released from prison, they formed organizations that campaigned on behalf of prisoners, amplifying prisoners' stories and their previously secret acts of bodily communication. This book explores what happens when prisoners' bodies, their secret communications and combinations, are brought into the public sphere.

Themes: Three Red Threads

Three red threads run through this book. The first follows the instrumentalization of prisoners' bodies, this is perhaps the most visible and persistent theme. The book argues that within the prison system, prisoners themselves, on an individual and collective level, instrumentalized their bodies as weapons of protest and tools of communication – for example, through hunger strikes and self-harm, as weapons in riots, or standing on the roof of the prison – as symbols of prisoners' suppressed humanity. On another level, the Prison Officer's Association (POA) instrumentalized the prisoners' collective body as a weapon in their own industrial disputes with the Department of Justice, often isolating hundreds of prisoners at a time in twenty-three hour solitary confinement to highlight the Association's demands. Finally, the Prisoners' Rights Organisation (PRO), a campaign group of activists and former prisoners, discursively instrumentalized prisoners' bodies, in both the individual and collective sense. The PRO publicized individual prisoners' stories, highlighting the health impact of their conditions. They also drew attention to the conditions of the prisoners' body as a whole. They instrumentalized these in order to shape the public understanding of ordinary prisoners and to lobby for changes in public policy and law.

The second thread follows the changing legitimacy of the voices of prisoners, and their representative organizations, in public discourse. Throughout the early and mid-twentieth century, Irish prisoners, except those affiliated with political or paramilitary organizations, were rarely discussed in the public sphere. They were brought into the public discourse in the early 1970s by the advent of the prisoners' movement and the growing prison population. The book explores how, over the next decade and a half, their voices were treated with varying degrees of legitimacy or scepticism. Early coverage of the prisoners' movement in 1972 often treated ordinary prisoners as thoughtless, violent animals, but within a year, some papers became more sympathetic, even publishing direct communiques from prisoners' organizations and interviewing their representatives on the outside. At an official level, there were similar changes in the 1970s. Ministers for Justice in the mid-1970s called the prisoners' organizations 'subversive', but by the early 1980s, ministers from the same political parties were pushing for legislation that the PRO had been involved in drafting.

The final thread follows the representation of ordinary prisoners by their organizations. This book contends that throughout the early and mid-1970s, the prisoners' movement, and particularly the PRO, fought to create the prisoner as a subject within public discourse; they sought to promote the representation of the prisoner as an individual with their own experiences and agency. This was achieved by focusing their messaging on the individual prisoners' 'body natural' – with its hunger, wounds, and ill-health. However, in the late 1970s, the PRO began to objectify the prisoner in the public discourse – highlighting the collective prisoners' 'body politic' as an object of sociological study and data-driven reform. This objectification deepened in the 1980s as public discourse began to focus on the threat of a burgeoning heroin epidemic in Dublin and a perceived nationwide crimewave. This discursive shift vilified the very people the PRO represented and destroyed much of the public understanding developed during the subjectification phase of the PRO's campaign, undermining the support for their research-based advocacy for prisoners.

What Is Communication?

Communication is at the heart of this book: The state communicating its sovereign power by constituting the excluded body of prisoners; activist organizations communicating individual prisoners' stories to raise awareness of prison conditions; prisoners communicating their anger and frustration through hunger strikes and self-harm. So, before we embark on a book about communication, we must discuss what it means – after all, to encompass all of the above-mentioned communications, our definition will need to go beyond simple linguistic communication. Anthropologist and psychiatrist Gregory Bateson and Jurgen Ruesch offer a broad definition of communication which encompasses 'all of those processes by which people influence one another', where influence is understood to include any perception which changes the information that a person has.[3] This definition clearly goes beyond language and must be seen to include any action which is perceived. This incorporates verbal, gestural, or otherwise performed actions, including negated actions, like silence and stillness. Bateson and Ruesch identify four functions that are performed during communication: 'Sending', originating the communication by encoding the message and transmitting it; 'channel', actively passing a message, which can include manipulating the message, for instance, by changing its format; 'receiving', perceiving the communicative action; and 'evaluating', interpreting and assigning importance to its message.[4] Cultural theorist Stuart Hall adds another step in successful communication: 'reproduction'. Reproduction is when a message is rearticulated by the receiver who encodes the message into their actions or frameworks of understanding. This, as we will see in the next section, is at the heart of the concept of prison discipline.[5]

6 | Prisoners' Bodies

Bateson and Ruesch also identified four types of networks in which communication takes place: The intrapersonal, which takes place within the individual; the interpersonal, which happens between two people; the group network, which occurs in a centralized network and in which communication is characterized by two-way patterns from 'one person to many' or from 'many persons to one'; and finally the cultural, which occurs in a decentralized or distributed network and is characterized by communication patterns of 'many to many'.[6] Due to the source-base of this book, which is primarily rooted in the study of the outputs of activist and media groups, we will be primarily focused on the cultural network, which encompasses mass communication: 'A characteristic of these communications is the multiple and often indefinite character of the emitting agency. The communications usually originate in an institution or administrative department, and by the time a speech or a play has been made public it has been worked upon by many persons. It is no longer a message from one individual to another, but is a message from many to many'.[7] Ultimately, however, Bateson and Ruesch note that communication is a dynamic phenomenon which rapidly shifts between different functions and networks, so while we may focus on cultural networks, it will be necessary to examine interpersonal and group networks when possible.[8] This schema allows us to conceptualise communication as more than an individual act; rather, it is a network in which messages are created, altered, repeated, and interpreted by multiple actors. Moreover, it allows us to conceptualise communication as more than simple words; it incorporates gesture, inaction, silence, and perceived intention, all of which are vital to understanding communications by prisoners.

Prison Discipline: Communicating without Words

We can see the necessity of this broad understanding of communication by looking at the function of prison discipline. The Prisons (Visiting Committees) Act (1925), Rules for the Government of Prisons (1947), and Prisons (Visiting Committees) Order (1972) laid out the official channels through which prisoners in the 1970s and 1980s could complain about their conditions. They were entitled to demand to have their food weighed to make sure they get their full allocation;

Introduction | 7

to complain to a prison officer and have their complaint passed on to the governor or the Visiting Committee; to see the governor, at his convenience, to make a complaint in person; and to present complaints to their prison's Visiting Committee in private. The same laws, however, also limited the prisoners' right to complain, specifying that repeated complaints 'with the evident purpose of giving annoyance or trouble, shall be treated as a breach of prison discipline'.[9] Moreover, the very laws that made the governor and the Visiting Committee the only authorities that could hear prisoners' complaints also made them responsible for enforcing prison discipline and punishing inmates. As prisoners and ex-prisoners throughout the period pointed out, this created a situation in which prisoners' complaints, taken through the legitimate channels, were at best structurally discouraged and at worst actively punished. In this context, it is hardly surprising that prisoners sought more visceral ways of registering their complaints, even rejecting the authority of the penal system, which they saw as unsympathetic to their position.

To understand the significance of prison disturbances, or 'mutinies' as they are referred to in the 1947 Prison Rules, we must understand what is meant by the term prison discipline.[10] In common law jurisdictions, prison discipline is at once a clearly distinguished term and a loosely-defined one. Throughout the nineteenth and twentieth centuries, legislation has separated discipline from instruction (1914), correction (1877), regulation (1856), management (1856), and good order (1826).[11] While the latter features of imprisonment are things that are systematically done-to or imposed-upon the prisoner, the case law around prison discipline identifies it as a specific relation that the prisoner must adopt towards the prison.

In 1978, the Irish Supreme Court affirmed that a prisoner 'must accept prison discipline and accommodate himself to the reasonable organisation of prison life'.[12] The performance, or reproduction in Hall's sense, of this acceptance was key to the disciplinary relationship. The same judgement went on to establish that a prisoner may be given the medical treatment that the prison medical officer thinks appropriate but cannot 'demand' treatment and that as long as a prisoner was treated in 'accordance with the regulations, he cannot be heard to complain'.[13] In other words, the ruling insisted that a prisoner may only complain that the regulations are not being strictly adhered to. From this we can see that prison discipline implies a reciprocal enforcement of the prison rules, any other complaints may be seen as a breach of discipline.

Both the laws and the courts' rulings that deal with prison discipline in Ireland speak to a remarkably Foucauldian conception of discipline as a method of producing docile bodies 'that may be subjected, used, transformed and improved'.[14] Discipline is a relation between prisoner and prison that is not solely based on the adherence to the prison's rules (good order), or on their mutual enforcement, but rather the acceptance of the intention of those rules. In short, prisoners must interiorise their own subjection and embody this interiorization in a way that can be understood by the prison authorities. The Rules for the Government of Prisons (1947) lays out the ways a prisoner might breach prison discipline, including a wide array of highly subjective infractions like showing disrespect, idleness, making 'unnecessary noise', giving 'unnecessary trouble', or 'in any other way offend[ing] against good order and discipline'.[15] What is important about these infractions is that they are punishing the perceived intention of the prisoner rather than their actions. An action may be deemed respectful or disrespectful, necessary or unnecessary, depending on how a prison officer, for example, perceives the intention behind it. The 1977 play about life in the Irish prison system, *The Liberty Suit*, touches on the seeming arbitrariness of this:

JONNIE. *Aggressively.* Look it, I'm in here for nothing, remember that, nothing. I'm an innocent victim of Irish law ...
CHARLIE. Going to be hard sitting in your cell for two years telling yourself you're innocent. Much easier if you're guilty.[16]

Within the play's prison logic, the reality of guilt or innocence is irrelevant, to make life bearable Jonnie must accept guilt for things that might not actually be his fault or that he could not control – an acceptance which is key to the performance of prison discipline. It is this acceptance of the arbitrary judgements of prison staff, which, in the disciplinary mindset, prepares the prisoner for reform, a proposition which is laid out in the Prevention of Crime Act (1908) and the Criminal Justice Administration Act (1914) which both describe 'discipline', in the context of detention in a borstal, as 'conducive to his [the prisoners'] reformation'.[17] Sillitoe's *The Loneliness of the Long Distance Runner* offers a clear, albeit fictional, illustration of the role that acceptance of the spirit of the rules plays in prison discipline. The film adaptation, set in a British borstal, culminates in Colin running a cross-country race as the borstal's champion. As he turns onto the final stretch and comes into view of the finish line he suddenly stops, smiles triumphantly at the governor and waves his rival past to victory. The final scene shows Colin back at the lowest level of the borstal system, without his privileges and without the chance of release. He has been broken down to this level not because he transgressed a rule, the race was not mandatory and the other borstal runners who lost were not punished, but because he performatively rejected his disciplinary relationship with the borstal, transgressing the spirit of the rules rather than the rules themselves.

Prison discipline is not homogenous across the prison system, nor is it limited by the walls of the prison. In 1980, the Irish High Court, and later Supreme Court, affirmed that governors of different prisons could adopt a different 'approach to discipline'.[18] This refers to what Foucault would call the 'mechanism' of discipline.[19] The case itself dealt with the imposition of what the prosecuting prisoner called 'military discipline' under the new governor at the Curragh, a military detention barracks used to house troublesome prisoners in the 1970s and 1980s. This included standing to attention while cells were inspected and the degrading use of the word 'prisoner' as a form of address.[20] Although this mechanism varied between prisons, according to each staff's individual explicit and implicit expectations of the performance of respect and obedience, the disciplinary relationship remained the same. Moreover, the Prisoners (Temporary Release) Rules (1960) made it clear that any breach of the terms of a prisoners' temporary release would be 'deemed a breach of the discipline of the prison'.[21] As such, the mechanism of prison discipline, although often appearing homogenous and coincidental with prison rules, can actually be tailored heterogeneously to each individual prisoner's situation. And this extends beyond the walls of the prison, insisting that even outside its walls a

10 | Prisoners' Bodies

prisoner must accept the discipline relationship with the prison and perform an internalised obedience and respect.

Prison discipline is a key concept when thinking about prisoners' protest not only because it is a foundational part of the modern prison system but because it creates a field where all protest is curtailed and, as a result, any action can become protest. Its heterogeneous mechanism means that each prisoner's body is the locus of discipline and its corollary protest. So, if the performance of an internalisation of the spirit of the rules is the standard by which each prisoner is judged, then something as passive as not eating when food is offered, or as personal as self-harm, can constitute a rejection of prison discipline, and with it the entire authority of the prison system. However, there is another side to this. While the individual prisoner's body is a site of discipline and protest, the collective prisoners' body is necessarily a site of mutiny. Any combination of prisoners into a purposeful body poses an inherent threat to the prison system. Indeed, the 1947 Prison Rules identifies all communication between prisoners as a privilege which the governor may withdraw 'in the interests of good order'.[22] Even when prisoners can communicate with each other, many experience the prison system as structurally divisive: 'This old ruse of "divide and rule" is well delineated: culchies are set against jackeens, ordinary against political prisoners, lick-ups against the hards, travelling people against the settled community (in prison!), looneys against the normal – all conflicts deliberately aggravated by the carefully stratified system of jobs and privileges'.[23] By dividing the prisoners' body against itself, the prison retains its power but also imbues every prisoner's actions with the potentiality to communicate protest. However, in the next section we will see that within the cultural network of communication, not all communications are treated equally, and prisoners' protests are not necessarily taken seriously.

Legitimate Voices: Encoding Trustworthiness

In *What is Policy?* sociologist Stephen Ball explains that 'only certain influences and agendas are recognized as legitimate, only certain voices are heard at any point in time within the common-sense of policy'.[24]

Although Ball was describing this phenomenon in relation to policy formation, we see a similar process of legitimization or delegitimization of voices in the realm of public discourse more broadly. Indeed, Stuart Hall highlighted a similar phenomenon in his discussion of the 'professional code', which he saw in operation within mass-communication systems like television. This is a technico-practical code which gives weight to the 'preferred meanings' of the hegemonic code through its production quality, 'presentational values', and the performance of 'professionalism'.[25] This is, in Bateson and Ruesch's terminology, a meta-communication: a communication about communication. It instructs viewers, listeners, or readers of mass-communication on how topics should be presented and addressed, as well as what debates should look and sound like. Hall notes that by controlling the 'structures of access (i.e., the systematic "over-accessing" of elite personnel and "definitions of the situation" in television)', media outlets are able to reinforce ideological reproduction without having to openly enforce ideological edicts on their staff.[26] The other effect of these structures of access is that particular voices come to be seen as the correct, or legitimate, voices to comment on certain situations. Hall gives the example of the television news having 'political elites' comment on and offer interpretations of 'the politics of Northern Ireland or the Chilean coup or the Industrial Relations Bill'.[27] We can see how this gatekeeping system may push certain 'expert' individuals and groups to the fore and, in doing so, validate particular readings of stories. For instance, in the early 1970s, the press emphasized the opinions of doctors and sociologists on growing drug use in Ireland because the issue was primarily related to health and addiction. While in the early 1980s, the arrival of a heroin epidemic and the influence of the international 'war on drugs' had shifted the 'preferred meaning' of the issue to a police function, and the reporting primarily drew on the commentary of the Gardaí and the Department of Justice.[28] However, not all legitimate voices are equal. The professional code weights some voices over others, through production techniques, contextual framing, repetition, and by having other legitimate voices endorse or undermine the message. A newspaper may lend a degree of weight to a person's views by publishing them in the letters-to-the-editor page, but they will invest significantly more legitimacy in an invited article published in the first few pages of the paper; a government minister may be given more or less weight depending on whether they have just been elected with a large mandate or if the government is unpopular and teetering on the edge of collapse; or a sympathetic interviewer may lend legitimacy to an activist discussing prison conditions, while an unsympathetic interviewer may use coded language ('is it realistic to expect...?') or intonations and gestures (a sceptically raised eyebrow) to undermine the interviewee's legitimacy.

Asymmetric Communication

Codes are, as we might expect, not innate human characteristics; rather, they are 'learned perceptions', and they can vary greatly even within a culture.[29] As a result, they are not necessarily processed (encoded/decoded) symmetrically. In his discussion of mass communication, Ruesch describes how this model relies on the assumption that everyone shares the same set of codes and that problems arise when one person has a set of codes which deviate in some extreme way from the codes shared by the rest of their community. 'The person in question may be exceedingly deviant from other people in his communicative habits, and may have his own special rules for interpreting communicative overtones. Yet he unconsciously assumes that these rules are shared, and they are a part of the inevitable and unchanging nature of life. Such an individual is the psychiatric patient'.[30]

This, however, is an extreme example. Hall acknowledges that 'misreadings', in which the receiver decodes a message using a different set of codes to that which the sender used to encode it, are common features of communication.[31] Hall notes that he uses the term 'dominant' rather than 'determined' to describe the order of preferred meanings because it is always possible to 'decode an event within more than one "mapping."'[32] He describes how many messages are decoded using 'negotiated' and 'oppositional' codes, in contrast to the hegemonic code, which is the code that the mass-media message sender inscribed the message with and which prescribes a set of relations between this and other communications.[33] The viewer using the 'negotiated code' accepts the broad totalizations of the hegemonic code but rejects aspects of it at a more local level. For instance, we may consider a reader in 1973 reading about the securitization of the prison system in response

Introduction | 13

to protests and escape attempts by political prisoners. This saw the removal of ordinary prisoners from Portlaoise Prison to make way for the newly segregated political prisoners, as well as the introduction of new restrictions on all prisoners' access to various long-standing privileges, like the ability to receive parcels from friends and families on the outside. A reader operating solely under the hegemonic code would accept that these measures were necessary to ensure the good order of the prison system and that prisoners lost their right to protest when they were committed to prison in the first place. A reader operating under a negotiated code will accept many of these same points but might reject the local implications. For instance, they might accept that an increase in security is necessary in light of the increased risk posed by political prisoners but be angry at the removal of prisoners from Portlaoise because they will now have to make the two hour journey to Dublin to visit their brother in Mountjoy.

By contrast, a reader with an oppositional code entirely rejects the 'preferred meaning' prescribed in the hegemonic code. Instead, they will detotalize the message, stripping it of the broad cultural and political connections that the newspaper reports constructed and instead retotalize it within a different reference framework. This reader might, for instance, entirely reject the necessity of maintaining good order within the system and interpret the securitization and subsequent reorganisation of the prison system solely as a victory for the republican prisoners' campaign to disrupt the functions of civil government. To Hall these 'systematically distorted communications' are not instances of individual misunderstandings or evidence of distinct subcultural aberrations; rather, they are the products of a 'deep-structure process' within the dominant culture caused by the coexistence of discordant fragmentary frameworks of knowledge. This idea draws on Marxist philosopher Antonio Gramsci's conception of the common sense as the 'sedimentation' of fragments of dominant ideas amounting to the 'chaotic aggregate of disparate conceptions'.[34] In Hall's work, the constant piecemeal adaptation, disparate origins, and uneven cultural communication of the common sense enables contradictory fragments to coexist within culture, which are only noticed when they come in contact with each other, producing a systemic misreading of a cultural product.

Hall's papers on encoding/decoding are primarily focused on the reading and misreading of television discourse. As a result, it models a unidirectional form of communication. Bateson and Ruesch's network model is based on a more dynamic process, as we saw earlier, in which information moves back and forth between different nodes along a complex array of vertices. In their model, messages are continually transmitted, received, and retransmitted and, by extension, repeatedly encoded, decoded, and recoded by actors in every function and network, from the intrapersonal to the cultural. Bateson and Ruesch's model offers us the opportunity to examine mass communication as part of a broader network of communication and, in doing so, to explore the process of discourse formation. Throughout this book, I will combine Bateson and Ruesch's network model with Hall's understanding of asymmetric encoding/decoding as I explore how messages are passed between individuals and groups. Some of these people were able to articulate and shape the hegemonic code, while others, like the prisoners, operated outside the commonly accepted structures of discourse production and had their messages repeatedly distorted by more 'legitimate voices'.[35] As such, the source material for this book must be treated carefully and suspiciously.

Retrieving Voices: The Challenges of Asymmetric Communication

The conception of communication laid out in the previous sections pervades every chapter of the book, inflecting its interpretation of different types of source material in various ways. In this section, I will discuss the general application of this approach to the available source material, as well as the types of material that are available. The vast majority of the book's sources fall into four loose categories, each of which can be addressed differently.

The first of these are public sources produced by organisations directly involved with prisons or prisoners which address, or are available to, a general audience. These include the reports, statements, speeches, and other communiques produced by prisoners' advocacy groups, the prison service and Visiting Committees, government departments, and independent committees of inquiry. For the most part,

Introduction | 15

these exemplify a centralised communications network – one coherent, and often corporate, voice speaking to many. These sources are usually the simplest to situate within the broader discourse by examining the mode of publication, the content of the text, its relation to other material, responses to it, reports about it, and any changes in the reception of the author after its publication. A good example of this kind of source is the *Annual Report on Prisons and Places of Detention for the Year 1973*. This was the year, as we will discuss in chapter 1, that the Prisoners' Union activity was at its height – ordinary prisoners in the country's two largest prisons, Mountjoy and Portlaoise, staged labour strikes, sit-ins, hunger and thirst strikes, rooftop protests, and riots and made allegations of violence and abuse against prison officers in both the courts and the press. In spite of all of this, the report minimises the disruption and the term 'Prisoners' Union' is used only once, and then it is used in heavily freighted quotation marks.[36] Indeed disruption of any kind is mentioned only sporadically, and paragraphs in which it is mentioned only account for about 4 per cent of the report. This minimisation speaks to the general refusal by the penal authorities and Department of Justice to legitimise the union by engaging with it – summed up by Justice Minister Patrick Cooney's 1973 statement that he would not recognise the 'so-called Prisoners' Union'.[37] Although the Visiting Committees were statutorily independent bodies, in the few references to disruption in the report we can clearly see the committees' allegiance to the Department of Justice as they refer to the allegations of abuse but dismiss them as 'unrealistic' and the prison activists as 'evilly disposed prisoners'.[38] The latter claim again echoes the minister's suggestion that the union was merely a cover for prisoners who sought to establish themselves as 'mafia bosses'.[39] We can also consider the method of publication itself. Visiting Committee reports are traditionally published within a year (i.e., *The Annual Report on Prisons for 1959* was published in 1960, the 1960 report was published in 1961, the 1961 report was published in 1962). However, the 1973 report was not published until 1976, when the Prisoners' Rights Organisation took the government to the High Court to force its publication.[40] This speaks to the challenges faced by the prison system in the mid-1970s as well as the key role that accurate information played in the campaign for prisoners' rights.

The second category of source is private or semi-private communications. These include government memoranda, private or interorganisational letters, agendas, contributions to closed meetings, collections of raw data, as well as unpublished draft reports or statements, including their marginalia. Given the limited nature of these communication networks, it should, in principle, be easier to analyse these texts. However, due to the highly sporadic nature of the existing archival material, particularly in relation to the prisoners' organisations, it is often challenging to establish the author of specific documents, the nature and evolution of intraorganisational relationships, or even the exact nature of a specific person's role within the organisation. The usefulness of these documents, as well as their ambiguity, is exemplified by a letter written in 1984 by then secretary of the PRO, Sue Richardson, to Concerned Parents Against Drugs (CPAD), a grassroots campaign against heroin-dealing in working-class Dublin communities.[41] The letter takes issue with a suggestion made at a public seminar by CPAD that there were drug pushers on the executive committee of the PRO. Richardson denied this and sought to establish the PRO's bona fides – pointing out that the PRO was established years before the heroin epidemic in Dublin; that it represented all ordinary prisoners equally, including drug users, but is not limited to them; and that although the PRO did not represent political prisoners, it had recently weighed in on several political cause célèbres, like the Nicky Kelly case.[42] The letter goes on to explain that the PRO had consistently called for the establishment of a drug treatment centre for prisoners and that it held the first public seminar on the emerging drug problem in 1981. The letter gives us important insights into the history of the PRO. It speaks, for instance, to the conflict that the heroin epidemic produced for the PRO, which drew much of its grassroots support from the communities worst hit by the epidemic while also attempting to represent equally the interests of all prisoners, including the people that many blamed for the epidemic. It also speaks to the complex political landscape that the PRO were seeking to navigate when it reminds the reader that the PRO had weighed in on the Nicky Kelly case, which related to political imprisonment and had nothing to do with drugs. This clearly sought to establish that the PRO was aware of the growing influence that the Provisional IRA (PIRA) had

Introduction | 17

within the CPAD. Moreover, it also sought to reassure the PIRA that the PRO, whose founders included several members of the Official Sinn Féin from which the Provisionals had acrimoniously split, was not a hostile organisation. Finally, while the letter is very revealing in some respects, it is ambiguous in others. It begs the questions: Who on the PRO committee did the CPAD suspect of being a drug dealer? How did the CPAD respond to this refutation? And what happened at the PRO's public meeting on the 'drugs problem'? Though these are intriguing questions, they are not, unfortunately, answered by the available archives.

The third category of sources this book will use are oral histories. While researching this book, I interviewed people who had been in prison during the prisoners' movement, prisoners' rights activists who played key roles in the PRO's campaigns, and one prison officer who worked primarily in Mountjoy and Portlaoise during the period and as such recalled both the activities of the prisoners' movement and the changing conditions for prison staff. These have proved to be excellent sources, full of rich detail about the internal working of the PRO and about the conditions for both staff and prisoners, and they have confirmed and fleshed out the details of the movement's timeline, which I created through documentary research. As such, I am extremely grateful to my interviewees for their time and candor. There are, however, limitations to this branch of the study. Only three of the people who took part in recorded interviews had spent more than a few months in prison. The relative absence of interviews with people who spent prolonged periods in prison was not a conscious decision but rather a function of the difficulty of finding and making contact with them. Some, like Karl Crawley, whose story is discussed in chapter 3, and Gerry O'Callaghan, a leading PRO activist, died before the beginning of the project; others, like former member of a PRO splinter group called the Prisoners' Committee and current Dublin City Councillor Mannix Flynn, were contactable but preferred not to give an interview; some, like Brendan Walsh, expressed their support for the project but for personal reasons were unable to take part; but the vast majority were simply untraceable. In many ways this untraceability speaks to the red threads that run through this book. The prison system is set up to conspicuously hide people and to remove their voices from public discourse. It is this absence which allows for their problematic representations by government departments, the media, and activist organisations and which makes discursive legitimacy so difficult to achieve even when they can be heard. While acknowledging its limitations, this book will attempt to amplify and legitimise the few prisoners' voices that have survived.

The fourth, and final, category is contemporary publications by people or organisations that were not directly engaged with the prison system. Given the book's focus on public discourse, newspaper articles make up the largest group of sources in the book. Indeed, the timeline of the movement that the book constructs was largely pieced together from nearly 2,500 newspaper articles published during the 1970s and 1980s. These articles give us a rich insight into the day-to-day public activities of, and institutional responses to, various prisoners' rights groups. They also give us, from time to time, brief glimpses of prisoners' voices through interviews or quotations. Most importantly though, they allow us to assess the changing patterns of representations of prisoners and their organisations. These serve as barometers for the discursive legitimacy of the voices of prisoners and their representatives. However, these sources only provide one side of the communicative network (the sender), so there is a risk of missing or minimising the asymmetric decoding of messages, particularly given the emergent nature of the negotiated code about the prisoners' movement. However, the book will mitigate this issue by examining a broad range of newspapers, from the conservative *Irish Independent* to the centre-left *Irish Press*, and by assessing the changing discourse over two decades.

The Literature on Irish Prison History

Imprisonment has an unusual place in Irish history. It is engrained in popular culture – from the early nineteenth century ballad *The Gaol of Clonmel* to the mid-twentieth century *The Auld Triangle*. It is equally engrained in the state's founding mythology. Every member of the first executive council, the Irish Free State's first government, had spent time in prison.[43] Indeed, about 6 per cent of all Irish TDs (Teachtaí Dála, Members of Parliament) have spent time in prison

Introduction | 19

and twenty-eight of the thirty-three Dáils (Parliaments) have included TDs who have been imprisoned – many of whom have held important ministries, from Michael Collins, the pro-treaty Sinn Féin Chairman of the Provisional Government (1922), to Proinsias De Rossa, the Democratic Left Minister for Social Welfare (1994–97). In spite of this, Irish prison history has received only sporadic cover and includes a number of notable lacunae – several important examples of which this book addresses. It is important to note that this book is focused on the Republic of Ireland, which I will refer to as Ireland throughout. The histories of prisons and prisoners in Northern Ireland and the Republic of Ireland were very different during this period. This was not only because of the long-term impact of the different legislative and policy frameworks in the two states, but also because of the disproportionate impact of The Troubles on Northern Ireland, which resulted in a high rate of political imprisonment and political prisoners' protests across the Northern Irish prison estate. A thorough study of ordinary imprisonment in Northern Ireland would be an important addition to the field, but it is outside the scope of the present work.

The only aspect of Irish prison history which might be said to have been thoroughly covered is the topic of political imprisonment.[44] Seán McConville's *Irish Political Prisoners* trilogy alone provides a strong account of the imprisonment of nationalist and loyalist politicals between 1848 and 2000.[45] This trilogy might be seen as the culmination, or at least a summation, of a long tradition of Irish political prison history. This includes numerous studies of specific sites of imprisonment in Ireland like Denise Kleinrichert's research on the HMS *Argenta* prison ship in the 1920s and Dieter Reinisch's examination of politicals' protests in Portlaoise Prison in the 1970s.[46] Others have focused on Irish people who were imprisoned in Britain, like Seán O'Mahony's study of the Welsh Frongoch internment camp after 1916 or Lucy McDiarmid's discussion of Irish revolutionaries in the Holloway Women's Prison in London.[47] Another strand of this history are the numerous biographical studies of specific political activists who spent time in prison, for instance Lindie Naughton's biography of Constance Markievicz, Denis O'Hearn's work on Bobby Sands, and David Fitzpatrick's examination of Harry Boland's life during the revolutionary period.[48] From the perspective of this study, one of the most interesting aspects of this history has been the studies of prisoners' institutional resistance, and particularly hunger striking. There have been several studies of this, including David Beresford's study of the 1981 H-Block hunger strikes, George Sweeney's more general discussion of hunger strikes in the context of what he terms the republican 'cult of self-sacrifice', and more recently, Ian Miller examined how force feeding was used against hunger strikers.[49] Miller, however, looks at a broad range of political prisoners that goes beyond the limits of nationalism and unionism. This built on William Murphy's rigorous examination of political imprisonment in the 1910s and early 1920s, which expanded the framework of political imprisonment to include trade unionists during the 1913 lockout as well as suffragettes and conscientious objectors.[50] This broadening of the idea of the political prisoner speaks to a move in the last two decades to decentre the narratives of national conflict from Irish prison history.

This decentring has been an important development because it has enabled prison historians to refocus not only on other forms of political prisoners but also on what was termed in the 1970s 'ordinary' imprisonment.[51] That is the imprisonment of people whose crimes were not driven by a direct or explicit political motivation. Ordinary prisoners have made up the vast majority of the population of the state's prisons but have traditionally been neglected by the literature. Since 2000, we have seen new vistas of this field opened up by key publications, such as Patrick Carroll-Burke's examination of the origins of the prison system in Ireland, Catherine Cox and Hilary Marland's exploration of mental illness in nineteenth century Irish prisons, and Mary Rogan's study of prison policy in Ireland since independence.[52] Since 2015, in particular, a diverse range of work has been produced by the numerous members of Catherine Cox and Hilary Marland's Prisoners, Medical Care and Entitlement to Health in England and Ireland, 1850–2000 project, of which this book forms a part. This work includes Cox and Fiachra Byrne's examination of children in custody in the 1950s and 1960s, Janet Weston and Virginia Berridge's research on the early years of the HIV epidemic in the Irish prison system, and my own article on the early years of the prisoners' rights movement.[53] Outside of this project, Cormac Behan has also helped to expand this field through his work on penal citizenship and prisoners' right to vote.[54]

Introduction | 21

He has also published numerous papers on the history of the PRO and the Prisoners' Union in Ireland.[55] These offer an interesting overview of several key moments in the prisoners' rights movement, mainly focusing on the 1970s, although 'Putting Penal Reform on the Map' also discusses the gradual penal reform that has happened since the 1980s. This book builds on, and goes beyond, that work, examining the internal politics of the prisoners' movement; the changing relationship between the prisoners' movement and other governmental and civil society organisations; the complex relationship between official and unofficial protests within the prisoners' movement; the diversity of tactics employed by the movement; and its rise, respectability, and fall as a legitimate voice in Ireland's public discourse.

This book expands the field of prison history. It offers the first comprehensive history of the prisoners' movement in Ireland, accounting for everything from individual prisoners' resistance and organised prisoners' protests to the violent campaign of militant ex-prisoners and the legislative successes of the PRO. It also provides the first detailed account of how the prisoners' movement shifted the discourse around penal reform in Ireland. It is the first twentieth-century Irish prison history monograph to fully decentre political prisoners, including them only when their history impinges on that of the ordinaries. This underpins the most important thing that the book does. That is to centre the voices of ordinary prisoners, who were among the most marginalised of communities in twentieth-century Ireland. It firmly focuses on the experiences of ordinary prisoners and their advocates, particularly centring the stories of more than twenty people who spent time in prison, drawing on oral histories, court documents, and the prisoners' own writings.

Structure

Prisoners' Bodies explores the rise and fall of the prisoners' movement in Ireland. It examines both the activities of prisoner-activists inside prison and the activities of activist former prisoners and their allies outside prison. It begins with the formation of the first Prisoners' Union, in 1972, and ends with the decline and discontinuation of the PRO's activities in 1985–86. Excluding this introductory chapter, which lays out the methodological approach of the book and the broad institutional background of the prison system in the late twentieth century, the book is broken into two sections. The first section (chapters 1, 2, and 3) examines the activities of the early years of the prisoners' movement, between 1972 and 1977. The second (chapters 4, 5, and 6) explores the later years of the prisoners' movement, between 1977 and 1985, and its legacy.

Chapter 1 examines the activism of the first prisoners' advocacy group in Ireland, the Prisoners' Union, through the life and activities of the prisoner-activist Daniel Redmond. The union saw early successes and organised the majority of the country's ordinary prisoners through its Portlaoise and Mountjoy branches. However, by transferring the leaders into military custody and severely punishing the other activists, the prison system broke the power of the union. Nevertheless, prisoners continued to organize and held a series of protests and hunger strikes in the Curragh Military Detention Barracks before briefly reestablishing the union in Mountjoy Prison. The chapter explores the organization, tactics, and demands of the union as well as the prison system's reaction to it.

In 1973, a former Prisoners' Union leader was released from Portlaoise and, together with a group of radical law students at University College Dublin (UCD), trade unionists, and others, formed the PRO. Chapter 2 explores the first three years of the organisation's activism and how its tactics changed: initially, they publicised the activities of and advocated for the Prisoners' Union, then they began publicising individual prisoners' stories as a way of building support for general prison reform, then they engaged in various legal battles. The chapter goes on to examine the diverse cast of PRO members who shaped the stances taken by the organization: some straight out of prison, others who had been involved with other civil rights causes, and some politically minded, often well-resourced, students. The chapter ends with an examination of the changing relationship between the PRO and current prisoners through an analysis of the language used in the organization's *Jail Journal*.

In 1975, the PRO organized a series of press conferences to discuss the lives of six prisoners as part of their campaign to humanize prisoners in the public eye and to raise support for prison reform. One of the prisoners was Karl Crawley, a young man who had spent most of his life in penal institutions. Since going to prison, Crawley had waged what his psychiatrist called a 'project against authority' to protest his treatment in prison.[56] Over the next three years, the PRO supported a series of court cases, even going to the European Commission of Human Rights, arguing that Crawley's treatment by the prison system amounted to torture. Chapter 3 offers a microhistory of Crawley's experiences, from his earliest memories, which centred around institutional violence, to his stormy relationship with the PRO. It explores his actions as a conscious decision to challenge the absolute authority of the prison system over his body as well as the result of his institutional, social, and family environment.

From 1979 to 1986, a group of former prisoners perpetrated a series of attacks on prison officers, assaulting them as they left pubs, running their cars off the road, and burning their houses. They felt betrayed by the slow progress of the 'political lobbying or penal reform' of the Prisoners' Union and the PRO. Chapter 4 explores the changing world of the prisoners' protest after the fall of the Prisoners' Union. In the early 1980s, conditions within the prison system were deteriorating. This was partially due to the tense industrial relations between the Prison Officers' Association, the POA, and the Department of Justice, a conflict in which prisoners were used as pawns and periodically locked up alone for twenty-three hours a day. Conditions were also deteriorating because a heroin epidemic had recently swept across Dublin which, combined with the war-on-drugs approach adopted by successive governments, had caused widespread overcrowding in prisons. As tensions heightened, there was a series of protests by prisoners which periodically escalated into riots. The chapter examines one riot in Mountjoy in 1979 which was typical of the period. It then explores the rise and fall of the Prisoners' Revenge Squad and its campaign of violence against prison officers outside prisons. The chapter concludes with a discussion of a riot in Arbour Hill in 1986, arguing that it signified the end of the collective consciousness of the prisoners' movement, which had been fostered by the Prisoners' Union in the 1970s.

In 1979, the PRO organized an independent public inquiry into the prison system chaired by Seán MacBride, the founder of Amnesty International. This set the organisation on a brief ascent to respectability.

24 | Prisoners' Bodies

Chapter 5 explores the changing membership of the PRO from 1977 onwards and the resultant shift in tactics towards a research-driven, sociological approach. This change allowed the PRO to gain legitimacy in the eyes of the media, the public, and politicians and, in the early 1980s, they worked with prominent politicians and civil society organizations to run a successful campaign to close the Curragh Military Detention Barracks and an almost successful campaign to abolish the death penalty. Ultimately, however the PRO was overtaken by the changing discourses around crime, and drugs, in particular, in the mid-1980s and their respectability began to fall away.

The concluding chapter of this book discusses the establishment and findings of the Committee of Inquiry into the Penal System, chaired by T.K. Whitaker in 1984–85, and the legacy of the prisoners' rights movement. The committee's report marked the official acceptance of many of the core ideas of the prisoners' rights movement and resulted in the effective dissolution of the PRO, whose organisers believed that their work was done. However, thirty-six years have passed since the publication of the report and, in spite of its recommendations, the population of the prison system is double what it was in 1985. Nearly 10 per cent of committals in 2019 were for nonpayment of fines (Whitaker recommended that carceral sentences be reserved for only the most serious offences), prisoners still spend sixteen hours a day in their cell (Whitaker recommended this be reduced to twelve), only half of all prisoners live in single cells (Whitaker recommended that all prisoners should have private cells), and some prisoners still 'slop out' – meaning they have no in-cell sanitation (Whitaker recommended that prisoners should have access to a toilet, wash basin, and fresh water at all times). The final chapter asks how the system reached this point and examines the national and international forces that shaped it over the last three and a half decades.

The Politics of Names

This book is punctuated by the stories of people who spent time in prison, and during my research and writing I have often questioned the ethics of using protagonist's real names. On one hand, the stories often touch on the mental and physical health of prisoners, and there is a well-established literature on the importance of protecting the identities of patients in the history of medicine. This has been the approach adopted by various historians who have written about closely related subjects. Janet Weston and Virginia Berridge, for instance, chose to anonymize the subjects of their study on AIDS in English and Irish prisons, giving them pseudonyms in public outputs.[57] However, the cohort of people dealt with in this book are qualitatively different in that many were activists in prison, campaigning for improved conditions, while others waged personal battles against the authority of the prison system. There is, of course, a long tradition of historians writing about imprisoned political activists – from antiapartheid leaders to suffragettes. To anonymize the subjects of these studies, even where they were in acute health crises like Irish republican hunger strikers, would do them a disservice.

I have decided to proceed without anonymization for two reasons. The first is that, although I have developed many of their stories through archival research, all of the prisoners' names used in this book were widely available in newspapers. Moreover, every named prisoner signed public letters which were later published, gave interviews themselves, or had close friends and family who gave interviews or held press conferences on their behalf. In that respect, the study is distinctly different from traditional history of medicine work. The subjects of the work would have had no expectation of anonymity and in most cases actively publicised their names and experiences. The second reason draws on the growing literature which questions the process of the reanonymising people within marginalized groups, whose marginalization was marked by systematic anonymization.[58] Anonymising processes were widespread across Ireland's carceral state in the mid- to late twentieth century. For instance, many of the prisoner-activists in this book grew up, at least in part, within the industrial school system. Christine Buckley, a survivor of St Vincent's Industrial School in Goldenbridge, Dublin, recalled that at Christmas, 'Some of the kids had to learn off their names, because they didn't know their names, because you had a number ... and you'd be reminding little kids that their name was such-a-name because when Santa would call out the name from the parcel they wouldn't know'.[59] The effects of institutional anonymization might seem less extreme for adult

26 | Prisoners' Bodies

prisoners, most of whom were, presumably, not at risk of forgetting their given names, but prisons often obscure their inmates' agency and identity through anonymity. Throughout the 1970s and early 1980s, the pages of the *Jail Journal* were littered with complaints that, on committal, a prisoner 'loses his identity as a human being and as a citizen of the state'.[60] I concluded that it was important not to contribute to this identity loss by stripping people's names from their protests, resistance, or attempts to communicate. This book will unearth and reconstruct both.

It is for similar reasons that I have chosen to eschew the use of the term 'sic' when quoting prisoners and activists. At several points in the book I will quote from the correspondence of or interviews given by prisoners and activists. In order not to erase the identities of the authors I have let these quotations stand as they were originally written or spoken. Some of these are in regional dialects while others use nontraditional spelling. Most of the dialect words used are self-explanatory – for instance, the second person plural pronoun 'yous' – however, there are a handful of words which the international reader might not be familiar with. For instance, the word 'culchie' refers, usually in a playful or derogatory way, to someone from a rural area. I have provided a brief explanation of these in the footnotes. Similarly, where nontraditional spelling is used, it is generally a phonetic spelling of a local pronunciation, for instance 'family' is written as 'famely' in one prisoners' correspondence, manifesting a three-syllable pronunciation with a stress on the second syllable turning it from a soft 'i' to a hard 'e'. As such, these spellings could be seen as dialect features and, thus, and expression of the writer's identity. In light of this possibility, I believe it would be inappropriate to treat them as errata. To do so could be read, at best, as patronizing or, at worst, as a deliberate attempt to undermine the legitimacy of the writer's voice – which, considering the centrality of communication and its embodiment to this book, would be counterproductive.

Absent Bodies: A Note to the Reader

This book centres on communicative bodies, both natural and politic, that decry prison conditions and the nature of the penal system.

It explores the history of the prisoners' rights movement through the experiences of ordinary prisoners and their allies. Twenty-two named prisoners' stories illustrate the book, and many more prisoners appear as unnamed parts of the prisoners' body politic. However, between 1972 and 1985 nearly thirty-six thousand people were sentenced to prison in Ireland. Because of this, it is imperative that this book should be haunted by silent bodies, unnamed people who did not take part in the prisoners' collective communication and whose individual communications went unrecorded or remain irretrievable.

Perhaps the most obvious absence in this book is that of imprisoned women. This is not the result of an intentional choice, or indeed unintentional bias, but it is a reflection of the lack of extant evidence of a prisoners' rights movement among the women in prison. In the 1972–85 period there were two places where women were imprisoned in Ireland, one in Limerick Prison and one in Mountjoy Prison in Dublin. Both were very small institutions. The average daily population of women in Mountjoy fluctuated from just thirteen in 1978 to twenty-nine in 1985, while in Limerick it fluctuated from less than six in 1974 to seventeen in 1985.[61] The women's sentences also tended to be short, with an average of 68 per cent of women's committals each year being for six months or less.[62] These small numbers and short sentences would have made it hard to build the momentum for a prisoners' movement, and even harder to sustain it once the prison's authorities decided on its suppression. So, it may be that the movement never took root in the women's sections of the prisons. On the other hand, it is also possible that the movement did take root but has left no lasting evidence. One of the PRO's earliest press releases mentioned that women were 'discriminated against in prison' and a contemporary article in the *Jail Journal* claimed that women in prison were not allowed writing implements, suggesting that 'it must be to prevent them smuggling out incriminating notes'.[63] Smuggled notes from the men's prisons were a driving factor in the early years of the PRO, and the inability for women to get notes out may explain why women's concerns so rarely featured in the organisation's activism. An absence which is particularly conspicuous given the prominence of feminist activists like Máirín de Búrca and Margaret Gaj within the PRO. This lack of smuggled material, however, would not explain the absence of references to sustained protests in the annual Visiting Committee reports or the various government memoranda about unrest in the prisons, which do often pass comment on unrest in the men's prisons.

Whatever the reason, imprisoned women were one of many groups who left little or no evidence of their overt challenges to the prison system. As a writer, I must content myself with periodically discussing the reasons that some people might not have engaged with the prisoners' rights movement and highlighting the places where such people are represented in an indirect form. However, as a reader, I must ask you to allow yourself to be haunted by their absence and to allow their ever-present absence to stand for the penal system's elision of prisoners' experience and the exclusion of prisoners from discussions around their own lives and conditions.

Expanding the Prison System

Before we begin our exploration of prisoners' protests it is important that we understand the situation and conditions of the Irish prison system. In the eighteenth and nineteenth centuries, Ireland was the focus of many formative experiments of the modern prison system. These included what became known as the 'Irish convict system', under which convicts were kept in a solitary system for eight months and then awarded marks, earning them privileges, based on their behaviour in association with others.[64] The Irish penal estate grew throughout most of the nineteenth century, peaking at around four thousand inmates in the 1870s (between seventy and eighty prisoners per a hundred thousand people).[65] Between then and the 1920s, the prison population fell precipitously and the average daily prison population in Ireland normally hovered between four hundred and seven hundred for most of the first half of the twentieth century, excluding periods of internment.[66] After the end of the Second World War, the prison population reached a highpoint of 777.[67] It steadily declined for sixteen years until 1958, when it was below four hundred (around fourteen prisoners per hundred thousand head of population).[68] Due to the historic decline in the prison population, governments spent most of the first decades of independence closing Ireland's ageing prisons, including Dundalk (1854–1931), Galway (1811–1939), Waterford

Introduction | 29

(1861–1943), and Cork and Sligo (both 1823–1956). These closures were welcomed by self-congratulatory exchanges in the Oireachtas (Parliament and Senate):

> Sen. Walsh: It is very satisfactory to note that this Bill [closing Cork and Sligo prisons] is required in order to reduce the number of prisons needed in the country. It is satisfactory to realise that this steady reduction in prisons has been going on for a number of years and that the number of prisons now required is so small ... The fact that there is only an average of eight prisoners in Sligo, which caters for a number of the northern counties, as against 400 for the whole country, shows that Donegal, for instance, is the most crimeless county in the whole State. That is not to be wondered at because the reputation we have in the North for being law-abiding citizens is very well known.[69]

Apart from these closures, there was little change in the prison system until 1956, when Ireland's only borstal was moved to a section of the women's prison in the Mountjoy Prison complex.[70] This marked the beginning of a period of penal reform in Ireland. The borstal was replaced by St Patrick's Institution in the Criminal Justice Act (1960). This officially brought the treatment of young people, aged seventeen to twenty-one, in line with the treatment of adults and in many cases shortened their sentences, formerly between two and four years under the borstal system.[71]

By 1960, Ireland was left with four penal institutions: St Patrick's Institution in Dublin for sixteen- to twenty-one-year-olds, Portlaoise Prison for adult male prisoners in the midlands, Limerick Prison for adult men and women in the mid-west, and Mountjoy Prison for adult men and women in Dublin. These prisons had space for over twelve hundred adult prisoners, more than two-and-half times the average daily prison population. However, the principal buildings were almost all more than a century old: Portlaoise was opened in 1830 and extended in 1851–53, 1879, and 1898–99; Mountjoy was opened in 1850 and the women's prison, which became St Patrick's, was finished in 1858; and Limerick was opened in 1821, expanded in 1835–36, and altered to allow separate confinement in 1848–50.[72]

30 | Prisoners' Bodies

From 1958 to 1972 the average population increased in all but three years.[73] Initially this was gradual, rising 33 per cent in the first eight years of the 1960s, from 461 (1960) to 615 (1968). As the *Annual Report on Prisons for the Year 1963* pointed out, much of this early growth reflected a changing culture of sentencing, including the increase in custodial sentences for young people. To a lesser extent, it also reflected the growing proportion of people with longer sentences in prisons. For instance, although there was a slight drop in committals between 1962 and 1963, the number of sentences lasting longer than six months increased.[74] However, after 1968, the increase in the population became more rapid. In the four years between 1968 and 1972, the population rose a further 70 per cent from 615 (1968) to 1035 (1972), bringing the prison population close to the prison estate's capacity. This increase corresponded with the outbreak of open hostilities in Northern Ireland and the rise in politically motivated crimes in the Republic; however, this was certainly not the only reason for the increase. The *Annual Report on Prisons and Detention Centres for the Year 1972* shows a notable increase in committals for all kinds of crimes, including drunkenness, which increased more than 50 per cent from 113 (1969) to 180 (1972), and simple larceny, which went up nearly 75 per cent from 264 (1969) to 457 (1972). Moreover, in this period, the total number of young people being committed almost trebled from 274 in 1969 to 782 in 1972.[75] Indeed, Garda statistics show a widespread increase in recorded offences during the late 1960s, with the number of indictable offences passing twenty thousand for the first time in 1967. By 1970, that number had risen to thirty thousand, and it had almost reached forty thousand per year by 1972, which compounded the ongoing trend for longer sentences (see figure 1.1).[76]

The population stabilised in the 1970s, with the average daily prison population rising by only 10 per cent between 1972 (1,035) and 1979 (1,140). As the prison population approached its capacity in the late 1960s and early 1970s, more rehabilitationist non- or semi-carceral sentences became popular for more minor offences. As a result, the percentage of the prison population convicted of serious crimes, and violent offences in particular, rose. For instance, in 1967, 33 per cent of committals to prison were for violence against the person or property offences with violence; by 1977, this had risen to over 45 per cent. This

Introduction | 31

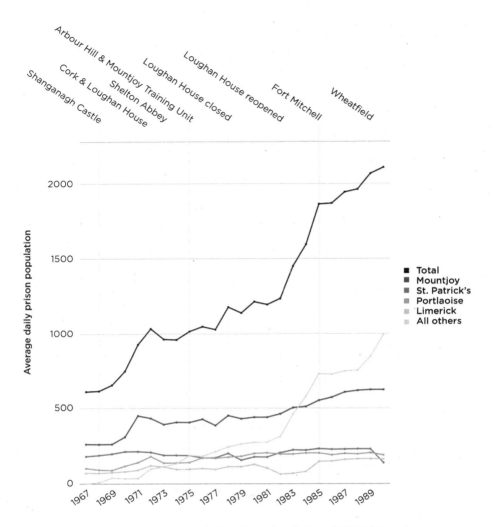

Figure I.1 Annual average daily prison population, 1967–1990, and distribution across the prison estate. Also indicating the years new prisons were opened.

trend can also be seen in the growing number of long sentences. In 1967, 24 per cent of committals to prison (509 people) were for more than six months, but by 1978, this had more than doubled to 51 per cent (1,139). The percentage of short sentences also fell dramatically, with sentences of four weeks or less making up 22 per cent of all committals in 1968 and just 12 per cent a decade later in 1978. The growing proportion of long sentences had a cumulative effect on the prison population. While the number of committals grew by just 20 per cent in the decade between 1968 and 1978, the average prison population grew by almost 92 per cent.

Many of these trends, however, were reversed in the 1980s, during which the average daily prison population began an inexorable rise which would continue, in all but four years, until 2013. Between 1981 and 1985 the population increased 56 per cent to 1,863.[77] The bulk of this growth was driven by the growth in petty crime associated with the heroin epidemic as well as the move away from a noncarceral rehabilitative consensus. This saw the proportion of people committed to prison with no prior convictions rise sharply from an average of 34 per cent between 1955 and 1979 to a peak of over 57 per cent in 1985, and a corresponding rise in the number of short sentences.[78]

Unlike the optimistic reports of the early 1960s, the annual prison reports of the 1970s reveal a system struggling to keep its head above water. The annual report for 1971, which was not published until January 1974, for instance, was accompanied by memorandum to the government explaining, 'The delay in preparing the 1971 report is attributable to the severe pressure on prison staff which resulted from riots and general disturbances in the prisons during 1972 and 1973. Preparation of the report for 1972 is well in hand and it should be available in a few weeks'.[79]

The 1973 report commented, 'It is only fair to say that more progress could have been made were it not for the persistent efforts at disruption by groups of prisoners', while the 1975 report described how 'facilities at Mountjoy Prison were strained to the limit', and the 1978 report noted that the 'consistently high number of men in custody made it difficult to keep them all fully employed'.[80]

During the period 1972–85, the government made concerted efforts to alleviate the material pressure on the system. In the early 1960s, the country's prison infrastructure had not been significantly modernised since the formation of the state and what little modernisation had taken place focused almost exclusively on Mountjoy. In the 1970s, the modernisation programme was extended across the country. This included a major spending programme that saw the annual expenditure on Irish prisons rise more than 2180 per cent from £602,028 in 1971 to

£13,125,906 in 1979.[81] In light of the growing prison population, finding new space to relieve the overcrowding became imperative. One of the major expenditures for the system in this decade was the construction or conversion of the first new prisons in the history of the state – Shanganagh Castle (1969), Shelton Abbey (1972), Cork Prison (1972), Loughan House (1973), Arbour Hill (1975), and Fort Mitchell on Spike Island (1985).[82] The decade also saw the repurposing of the Curragh Military Detention Barracks to take civilian prisoners (1972).

The 1960s, 1970s, and 1980s saw rapid expansion of the prison system. The population grew more than 400 per cent from 1960 to 1985, the number of prisons rose from four to ten, and the prison budget rose more than twenty-fold. However, the changes of these three decades were more than mere adjustments in scale. These decades also saw profound changes in the function and makeup of the prison system.

Reform

Imprisonment has been one of the most common recourses for the courts since the late eighteenth century, but the justification for this has been far from stable. By the 1980s, it had become commonplace for those discussing criminal justice in Ireland to comment on the fact that there was no clear rationale behind the Irish prison system. In 1985, eight possible justifications for the prison system were outlined in the report of the Joint Working Party, a collaboration between the Irish Council of Churches, an organisation which includes most of Ireland's non-Catholic Christian churches, and the Irish Commission for Justice and Peace, part of the Irish Catholic Bishops' Conference. These justifications were: 'humane containment', 'treatment and rehabilitation of offenders', 'social control and protection, deterrence of crime', 'punishment of offenders', 'enforcement of justice', 'redressing of injustice', and 'restitution to victim'.[83] Of these eight, the only one which had been definitively and recently endorsed by the Department of Justice was 'humane containment'.[84] This was the stated aim of the department, as outlined in its 1981 *Prisons and Places of Detention: Survey of Objectives*.[85] However, it was, as the Joint Working Party observed, a 'means without an end'.[86] It established the prisons' aim as the deprivation of prisoners' liberty while otherwise respecting their human dignity and rights. Although this determined how prisons aimed to treat their inmates, it did not offer a justification for their imprisonment.

One of the justifications for imprisonment which had had a longer and more formative influence on the late twentieth-century Irish penal system was the 'rehabilitative ideal'.[87] Rehabilitation had been a long-standing influence on the penal system. As Victor Bailey argues, the report of the Gladstone Committee on Prisons (1895) was often seen as the starting point of the modern 'rehabilitative ethic' in the penal system in the United Kingdom, although arguably its roots, in education and moral reform, stretch significantly farther back.[88] While the Gladstone report did not address the situation in Ireland, it did influence the development of the Irish prison systems. By the mid-twentieth century, the rehabilitative ideal was, in many ways, a distillation of the modernist project. It was built on a fundamentally materialist conception of human behaviour in which the material and psychological conditions which produced deviant behaviour could be scientifically identified and therapeutically manipulated 'in the interests of his [the convicted person's] own happiness, and satisfactions and in the interest of social defence'.[89] The means to this end changed over the course of the twentieth century. Education and employment training were key features of rehabilitation throughout the period, but as the decades wore on, the approach expanded and developed into a more rounded form of what Garland called 'penal welfare'.[90] This approach sought to soften the boundaries of the prison, integrating it into the civilian welfare state by developing transitional models that included the introduction of welfare officers who found jobs and other social supports for prisoners on the outside, conditional and day release programmes, and 'aftercare' programmes which sought to help released prisoners reintegrate into the community. However, the rehabilitative ideal was not without its detractors. On the political right, commentators depicted it as 'soft on crime', reducing the deterrent effect of the criminal justice system, and ineffectual, pointing to the inability to identify any sustained measurable success.[91] The left, on the other hand, saw it as paternalistic, normative, and discriminatory against social minorities and objected to the use of indefinite sentences which vested pseudo-judicial authority in prison officials.

Introduction | 35

Indefinite sentencing, in particular, became a key issue for both the British and American prisoners' rights movements.[92]

The late 1970s and 1980s saw the rise of a new punitive approach to imprisonment, exemplified by the American war-on-drugs legislation which introduced mandatory minimum sentencing for drug possession (1986) and later three-strikes laws (1994), under which people received a mandatory life sentence on their third conviction. This approach reversed the rehabilitationist attempt to reduce the carceral role of the criminal justice system in favour of a harsher sentencing model intended as a deterrent to crime. Although, as Rogan notes, the Irish governments of the 1980s did not have the 'stomach' for the harsh punitivism of either Reaganite America or Thatcherite Britain, the rapid increase in the prison population and the changing sentencing patterns certainly demonstrates a shift away from rehabilitationism.[93]

In Ireland, the 1960s and early 1970s had been the most intense period of rehabilitationist activity in the twentieth century. There had been a pronounced tendency towards rehabilitative penal reformism in the Irish civil service since the 1950s, but it had been largely restrained by a lack of both finances and political will.[94] In 1957, Fianna Fáil came to power and, although the party was still led by an 'old guard', many of whom had fought in the War of Independence and the Civil War, the party now had a young, vigorous, faction of first time TDs with an inclination towards liberal reforms. Charles Haughey was, as historian T. Ryle Dwyer described him, 'the epitome of the men in the mohair suits who were changing the face of Fianna Fáil'.[95] As the minister for justice (1961–64), he established an Inter-Departmental Committee on Juvenile Delinquency, the Probation System, and the Institutional Treatment of Offenders and Their After-Care. The committee included representatives from the Departments of Justice, Health, Education, and Industry and Commerce and was tasked with drawing up plans for a more rehabilitative prison system. Following the committee's advice, Haughey introduced a number of rehabilitative reforms including expanding the parole service and introducing more educational opportunities, job training, and aftercare services.[96] Throughout the period, the annual Visiting Committee reports commented on the 'substantial progress' made towards penal reform through the provision of new educational and vocational training facilities, as well as the development of facilities for prisoners on work day release and the establishment of aftercare committees comprised of businessmen and trade unionists who placed ex-prisoners in employment.[97] The reports demonstrate a clear sense of pride and optimism permeating the system. However, Haughey was transferred out of the Department of Justice in 1964 and although the new minister, Brian Lenihan, was also committed to the principle of rehabilitation, he lacked Haughey's vigour and the pace of reform slowed. Although there may have been plans to introduce these reforms across the country, by 1964, they were still limited to Dublin. Indeed, although probation and temporary release played a key part in many of the new ideas, it was 1969 before any full-time probation officers were appointed outside of Dublin.[98] This geographical inequality persisted and, by 1978, four of the country's six hostels for recently discharged prisoners or people on probation were in Dublin, and the remaining two were in Cork and Waterford, leaving the cities of Limerick and Galway, not to mention the entire North and West of the country, with no residential aftercare facilities. Indeed, although there was still a degree of enthusiasm for rehabilitative reforms within the prison system – for instance, the POA sought social worker training for its members in order to expand their rehabilitative function, and the annual Visiting Committee reports of the late 1970s emphasise their growing success integrating welfare roles into the prisons – after Haughey left the department in 1964, the political drive behind these reforms began to dissipate and progress slowed.[99]

In light of the declining political interest in penal reform and the material challenges faced by the prison service, the main focus in the 1970s was on alleviating the pressure on the system. However, between 1972 and 1982, some small steps were taken towards continuing the reforms started in the 1960s. New industrial training programmes were introduced, new prison and welfare officers were hired, the prison diet was varied, and a new 'intensive supervision' programme was introduced for prisoners on early release.[100] However, in spite of these steps, the drive for rehabilitation seemed to slow down as the decade wore on. At the beginning of the period, the Fianna Fáil minister for justice Dessie O'Malley (1970–73) described rehabilitation as 'my primary task', and, at the start of his term, O'Malley's successor Patrick Cooney (1973–77) described it as 'the whole basic aim of penology' in mid-1974.[101] However, by the end of that year Cooney, who was firmly situated on the right-wing of the Fine Gael party, had lost his

Introduction | 37

commitment to rehabilitation, telling the Dáil, 'No institution and no system can rehabilitate anybody ... rehabilitation is and cannot be the only consideration'.[102] When Fianna Fáil came back to power in 1977, their policy had moved away from the rehabilitative focus of the 1960s, and the new minister for justice Gerry Collins (1977–81) mentioned rehabilitation in the Dáil only a handful of times, never directly endorsing it. When Fine Gael came back to power in the early 1980s, their minister Jim Mitchell (1981–82) explicitly declared that 'rehabilitation has to come second' to security.[103] Finally, in his brief tenure, Fianna Fáil's minster for justice Sean Doherty (1982) said little about rehabilitation, but in a Private Members debate, one of his party colleagues, Ben Briscoe TD, commented in support of the government, 'There is too much emphasis on rehabilitation. I am in favour of rehabilitation if it comes right, but it can only come right through punishment'.[104] The ambiguity around the role of rehabilitation in prisons extended into the legal system, and legal scholars Raymond Byrne, Gerard Hogan, and Paul McDermott's 1981 review of the case law on the objectives of the prison system concluded that judges have repeatedly contradicted each other, with some indicating that the role of the system is to punish and others saying that it is to rehabilitate.[105] The same year, the Irish Council of Churches published a report which concluded that 'there is no one dominant conceptual framework ... The prison buildings, legislation, sentencing options, etc. reflect a mixture of the concepts of retribution, punishment, humane containment and psychological rehabilitation, a situation which leads to confusion and worse'.[106]

By 1985, the very idea of rehabilitation seemed to be considered a thing of the past, even among groups sympathetic to its aims. The interdenominational Joint Working Party's report's note about it began: 'In the recent past, the belief was widely held in a number of countries that the objective of prisons was to engage in treatment of offenders ... assisting them to lead a "good and useful life."'[107]

The 1960s and the 1970s saw a good deal of reform in the prison system, but it still faced profound challenges. Throughout the period, educational and medical provision remained basic, in spite of their rehabilitative importance. Education had been an important part of the prison system since the nineteenth century, and since 1947, every prison was required to provide classes in reading, writing, and arithmetic for four hours a week to eligible prisoners.[108] By 1972, however, this requirement had been largely neglected. The Prison Study Group, a group of academics based at University College Dublin in the early 1970s who conducted the first investigation of the prison system in almost three decades, reported that neither Mountjoy nor Portlaoise had trained teachers and basic literacy classes were provided by uniformed officers; in Limerick these classes were provided on a voluntary basis by a retired nun. What is more, these meagre facilities were only available to a small number of prisoners who cannot read. For instance, in Mountjoy, only thirteen of the prison's average population of 416 attended classes regularly.[109] Work programmes and training schemes were also very limited, in spite of Haughey's reforms. For instance, in September 1973, of the 268 prisoners working in Mountjoy over 60 per cent passed their time sewing mailbags and mats, chopping wood, and cleaning the prison, while only 10 per cent were involved in trades. Similarly, in Portlaoise, only 6 per cent were involved in trades, while over 60 per cent of working prisoners were employed on the prison farm and gardens, in cleaning duties, or cutting turf, tasks which the predominantly urban prisoners saw as provocatively irrelevant to their lives.[110]

As Weston and Berridge have described, the medical provisions were also limited and medical professionals played no role in prison management.[111] Each adult prison had a daily visit from a medical officer who dealt with minor complaints, while any major tests or operations necessitated that prisoners be transferred to a civilian hospital, where they would remain in chains and guarded by several prison officers. In spite of estimates that as many as 50 per cent of prisoners needed some form of mental healthcare, psychiatric provision in prison was extremely limited.[112] In 1972, the Department of Justice employed a full-time medical officer for Mountjoy who was a trained psychiatrist, and there was also a visiting psychiatrist who came to the prison once a week to see an average of six prisoners. In 1973, the number of visits was increased to three a week, but even still the psychiatrist's main role was to provide prescriptions rather than social, occupational, or talking therapies.[113] Neither Limerick nor Portlaoise had any psychiatric services at all and prisoners' crises were either dealt with as disciplinary matters or by transfer to the Central Mental Hospital (CMH) in Dundrum.[114] The CMH was not a prison, but it was the main provider of intensive psychiatric care to prisoners. In 1972, 70 of the hospital's

Introduction | 39

120 patients were 'criminal lunatics', usually referred to as 'justice patients'.[115] Although prisoners were meant to be committed to the hospital by a psychiatrist, the fact that Mountjoy was the only prison with one meant that, in practice, many prisoners saw a psychiatrist for the first time after they had been transferred to the CMH. For the most part, these committals were brief, with prisoners hospitalised until their crisis abated and then immediately returned to prison. Even as the main psychiatric service provider to prisoners, the Prison Study Group report noted, 'The psychiatric treatment in Dundrum is very limited. There are no facilities for rehabilitation'.[116]

Political Prisoners and The Troubles in the Republic of Ireland

Since the foundation of the state, there had been prisoners who believed that the political motivation for their offence entitled them to different treatment from 'ordinary' prisoners. At various times, protests by these 'political' prisoners have had a significant influence on the prison system. This is particularly true of the 1970s.[117] In the 1970s, the politicals only ever made up between 13 per cent (1975) and 17 per cent (1981) of the prison population.[118] In spite of this, however, they have dominated media, and indeed historical, reporting of prisoners' issues.

During this period, the republican prisoners treated prison protests as 'war by other means', and orchestrated a long, drawn-out campaign whose 'main objective is to make the jail inoperable', as one spokesman for the POA put it.[119] Throughout the 1970s and 1980s, there was a more or less constant stream of protests. These included riots and several high-profile hunger strikes in 1975, 1976, and 1977.[120] Their protests focused on achieving 'political status', which they felt should grant them rights similar to those of prisoners of war, including exemptions from wearing prison uniforms, from prison labour, and from association with 'ordinary' prisoners. As well as protests for political status, the politicals' 'war by other means' included a series of dramatic escapes.[121]

In October 1973, two PIRA volunteers hijacked a helicopter and landed it in the middle of a football match in Mountjoy's exercise yard where three senior PIRA officers got on board before it took off again.[122] After this, all political prisoners were concentrated in Portlaoise Prison, where there were several more, less successful, escape attempts in 1974 and 1975. These stopped after one volunteer was shot dead and several more injured during an attempt in Portlaoise.[123] This loss dampened the PIRA's enthusiasm for trying to escape from the increasingly militarised prison, and there were no more significant attempts until 1985, when twelve PIRA prisoners tried to blow open the outer wall of Portlaoise with a homemade bomb that failed to explode.[124]

In reaction to the regular protests and escape attempts, the government and the prison administration created an especially restricted regime at Portlaoise. In 1973, armed soldiers were brought in to patrol the outer walls and roofs of the prison, where they remained a permanent fixture until the 1990s. To prevent smuggling, the prison also banned the food parcels that prisoners' had traditionally received from friends and families on the outside.[125] However, in spite of these restrictions, the government and prison authorities did make important concessions to the politicals. The governors of Portlaoise and Mountjoy both met delegates of political prisoners to negotiate the end of particular protests, which was a major concession in an institution which treated any form of association as a privilege. Moreover, the government's policy of concentrating politicals in Portlaoise, as harsh as the regime there was, seemed like the concession of de facto political status, as it gave them the freedom from association with 'ordinaries'; they also won the right to wear their own clothes and to not partake in prison labour.[126] While the campaigns by the political prisoners dominated considerations in Portlaoise and had ramifications throughout the prison system, forcing increases in the security precautions and eroding the morale of prison officers, after 1973, they had limited direct effects on the 'ordinary' prisoners who made up the vast majority of the prison population and who were the sole inhabitants of most of the state's prisons. The one exception to this was the Curragh Military Detention Barracks.

In May 1972, after a riot in Mountjoy, the state began transferring disruptive prisoners to the Curragh using a special piece of legislation called the Prisons Act (1972).[127] This act enabled them to transfer

Introduction | 41

civilian prisoners to military custody to relieve overcrowding in the prison. During the relevant Dáil debates, one Labour TD, Dr David Thornley, described the act as 'internment by backdoor methods';[128] however, it turned out to be more than this: the new act allowed any prisoner, ordinary or political, to be transferred into military custody to relieve overcrowding or other strains on the prison system or if the prisoner needed special security arrangements. This paved the way for the Curragh to be used as a punishment camp for disruptive people from other prisons.[129] The first transfer of thirty-four prisoners at the end of May included both politicals, like Thomas McMahon, who had acted as a spokesman for the Mountjoy rioters in 1972, and career criminals with no organisational affiliations, including Michael Fardy, who later went on to be the secretary and press officer of the PRO.[130] Indeed, as the 1970s wore on, the proportion of politicals was reduced and, by 1978, only four of the thirty prisoners in the camp were political prisoners. It was seen by many as a 'dumping ground for misfits and undesirables', containing a disproportionately high percentage of prisoners with psychiatric complaints and people convicted of sexual offences.[131]

Throughout this period, relations between the political and ordinary prisoners remained tense. The largest organisation of the politicals, the PIRA, saw themselves as the inheritors of a long and apparently noble tradition of political imprisonment and so believed they were a class above ordinary prisoners. They argued that as prisoners of war they should not be forced to associate with ordinary prisoners and refused to live on the same landings as them. This, in turn, stoked resentment among the ordinaries. It is notable that unlike the civil rights and Black Power movements in the US, most of the Irish political prisoner organisations did not seek to find common ground with the ordinaries, with the exception of the activists from Saor Éire, as we will discuss in later chapters. Prior to their transfer to Portlaoise in 1973, the politicals' activities had had direct and immediate effects on ordinary prisoners. Their protests and escape attempts led to restrictions on parcels and mail coming into the prison, restrictions on visitors, and disruptions to the everyday life of the prison, including lockdowns and cell searches. However, after the 1973 transfer, the politicals' activities had very little direct impact on the ordinaries. Isolated in Portlaoise and the Curragh, or in manageably small numbers

42 | Prisoners' Bodies

under close observation in other prisons, the politicals were not able to disrupt the ordinary running of most of the civilian prisons. However, their sustained disruptions in Portlaoise did have several important, if indirect, impacts on the day-to-day lives of ordinary prisoners. The first of these involved growing security concerns within the prison system. These revolved around the control of protests inside the prisons, the detection of smuggling, and the prevention of escapes. In many cases, 'security concerns' necessitated the resolidification of many of the prison walls; this meant the introduction of armed soldiers as sentries on the walls of Portlaoise and Limerick Prisons, where female politicals were held. However, although security and rehabilitation are uncomfortable bedfellows, both Mary Rogan and Shane Kilcommins note that some rehabilitative reforms continued throughout the period of securitisation in the 1970s.[132] The second of these impacts was the sapping effect that the campaign had on the prison officers' morale. When Seán Reynolds, a prison officer based in Mountjoy, was seconded to Portlaoise in 1975 to repair some riot damage, he recalled being pulled aside by a political prisoner: 'Our lives were being threatened ... I was told the house I lived in and the street I lived in, told they could have me shot'.[133] The threat posed by the politicals compounded over a decade of tense industrial relations and heightened tensions with prisoners, both ordinary and political, who often suffered during prison officers' disputes with the Department of Justice. Although these impacts had an important cultural influence on the prison system, the politicals' ability to directly affect the broader prison system was limited.

'School for Revolution:' The Attica Prison Rebellion and Irish Public Discourse

The Irish prisoners' movement did not emerge from a vacuum. Prisoners have offered resistance to institutional power since the formation of the modern prison system. However, it was not until the mid- to late 1960s that prisoners around the world began to organise themselves into coherent groups that could coordinate their protests and conduct complex campaigns for reform. The prisoners' movements in the US and the UK were particularly influential in Ireland. In this

Introduction | 43

section, I will discuss how these movements were reported on by the Irish press and the kind of narratives Irish prisoners might have been exposed to by this reportage.

The American prisoners' movement emerged primarily from the civil rights movement and the disproportionate rate of imprisonment of Americans of colour. In the 1960s, imprisoned civil rights and black power activists argued that prisoners were a 'convicted class' and that the reason for their imprisonment was fundamentally political.[134] Armed with these ideas, civil rights and Black Power organisations expanded the common ground between political and ordinary prisoners.[135] In a letter from prison in 1970, George Jackson, a leader of the Black Panther Party whose book *Soledad Brother* (published in Ireland in 1971) was highly influential on the prisoners' movement, wrote,[136] 'These prisons have always borne a certain resemblance to Dachau and Buchenwald, places for the bad niggers, Mexicans, and poor whites. But the last ten years have brought an increase in the percentage of blacks for crimes that can clearly be traced to political-economic causes. There are still some blacks here who consider themselves criminals – but not many'.[137]

Throughout the early 1970s, prisoners' unions began to emerge across the US, including in 'North Carolina, Michigan, Delaware, Rhode Island, Massachusetts, Maine, Wisconsin, Washington, and the District of Columbia'.[138] From the outset, the Irish newspapers recognised the political implications of these unions. One 1970 article in the *Irish Times* referred to the American prison system as a 'school for revolution', and warned that if a young draft resister 'goes to prison a radical ... he is likely to leave it a revolutionary'.[139] However, the amount of coverage that prison activism received was limited, until the Attica Prison Rebellion in September 1971.

The rebellion at the Attica Correctional Facility near Buffalo, New York, was a response to poor prison conditions and institutional racism. The prisoners elected a committee who issued a list of twenty-seven demands, concluding, 'We demand, as human beings, the dignity and justice that is due to us by right of our birth'.[140] In the course of the four-day rebellion, forty-three people died, thirty-three prisoners and ten prison officers, thirty-nine of whom, including seven officers, were killed by the security forces when they stormed the prison,

44 | Prisoners' Bodies

dropping tear gas into the prison yard and blindly opening fire into the smoke.[141]

The Irish reportage of this riot combined sympathy with a generalised disapproval of criminality. Most papers used validating language like 'rebellion' and 'protest' from the outset.[142] Some were tentative when reporting the sensational story, announced by the authorities to justify storming the prison, that the prisoners had cut the throats of the hostages and even castrated one.[143] Within two days of the end of the rebellion all of the major papers had corrected this story and reported that the hostages had been killed by gunfire, probably originating from the security forces.[144] A week after the end of the rebellion, the centre-left *Irish Times* published an opinion piece by the American journalist Anthony Lewis which compared the Attica prisoners actions to those of the American revolutionaries of the eighteenth century and concentration camp inmates revolting against Nazi guards. Lewis went on to ask, 'When the channels of access to political influence are open to everyone in a society, then violent means cannot be justified. But is there such a perfect society anywhere?'[145] Less than a week later, even the conservative *Sunday Independent* had published a sympathetic opinion piece, by another American journalist, Joseph Kraft, which asked, 'Isn't radicalisation inevitable when large, impersonal organisations try to regimen members of a minority group lately come to a sense of its own rights?'[146] Meanwhile, nationalist newspapers, like *The Corkman*, drew heroic parallels between 'patriot soldiers', like Michael Fitzgerald, who died on hunger strike in Cork Gaol during the Irish War of Independence, and the Attica prisoners, who proclaimed, 'If we cannot live as people let us at least attempt to die as men'.[147]

The rebellion at Attica dragged the possibility that ordinary prisoners could have legitimate concerns and critiques of the prison system into Irish public discourse for the first time. It also established the roots of two key narratives that would gradually play out in Irish prisons over the coming decade. The first was that the Attica prisoners were just demanding the 'dignity and justice' that was owed to all human beings. This would be an influential line of thought that we will repeatedly see echoed in the words of Irish prisoners and activists on the outside. The second was that prisons could become sites of radicalisation unless politically conscious activists are segregated from

Introduction | 45

prisoners who have been socially and economically marginalised. We will see this narrative be brought out every time prisoner-activists are isolated in solitary confinement or the Curragh and regularly when representatives of the Department of Justice and the prison service speak to the press.

Conclusion

This chapter has introduced the structure and general themes of the book. It has also laid out the methodological approach the book has taken, situating prisoners' bodies as communicative objects at its centre, and explored the powder keg that the Irish prison system had become by the 1970s. The prison estate was antiquated, understaffed, and overcrowded. The prison officers were engaged in a long, drawn-out, industrial war with the Department of Justice. The new ideas and enthusiasm that drove the reforms of the 1960s had quickly dissipated, leaving many reforms half-completed and resources unequally distributed across the country. Even the raison d'être of the prison system was becoming increasingly unclear. In the next chapter, we will explore the beginning of the ordinary prisoners' movement in Ireland, its rise within the prison walls, the attempts by various prison administrations to stamp it out, and the work of prisoner-activists to keep it going.

1

'Join Your Prisoners' Union!'
A Microhistory of Daniel Redmond and the Prisoners' Union, 1972–77

Introduction

The first organisation set up to campaign for general penal reform in twentieth-century Ireland was the Portlaoise Prisoners' Committee, which would become the Prisoners' Union at the beginning of 1973. In this chapter, I will explore the rise and fall of the Prisoners' Union through the experiences of one of its leaders, Daniel Redmond. In many ways, Redmond's story was typical of the prisoner-activists of the period. He came from a working-class background and spent time in St Patrick's for comparatively minor offences as a juvenile before graduating to armed robbery and ending up in Portlaoise. His life was marked by poverty, migration, homelessness, and repeated incarceration. His activism arose organically from these experiences of powerlessness and deprivation rather than any overtly ideological commitment. The chapter follows his life through four phases. The first, from 1964 to 1972, follows his early life and his emergence as a 'hard man' figure in Dublin. The second, from 1972 to 1973, follows the initial formation of the Portlaoise Prisoners' Union, its attempted suppression, and the emergence of the Mountjoy Prisoners' Union. The third period, in 1975, follows the attempt by the prisoner-activists to keep the union alive after they had been transferred to the Curragh Military Detention Barracks. The fourth and final period, in 1977, covers a short-lived revival of the Prisoners' Union in Mountjoy.

As well as offering a history of the prisoners' movement, this chapter also points to the presentation of masculinity in prison, a theme which will permeate the book. 'Hardmanship' is an idea which recurs in many of the stories in this book, from the organising work of Michael Fardy with the Prisoners' Rights Organisation (PRO) to the individual disruption of the prison system of Karl Crawley. The figure of the hard man was ubiquitous in Irish culture in the 1970s and 1980s. On the grand political stage, Liam Cosgrave, the leader of the Fine Gael party, was called the hard man who held the 1973 coalition government together.[1] A minister for the environment complained that 'the drunk person ... has been looked on in Ireland as something of a folk hero or "the hard man".'[2] In interrogations, Gardaí sometimes threatened, 'You're a hard man, but we'll soon knock that out of you.'[3] Countless footballers, hurlers, and boxers were called hard men in the press. Even the frog race at the 1970 Listowel Garden Harvest Festival was won by a frog called 'The Hard Man.'[4]

The hard man represents a particular figure of exaggerated hegemonic masculinity – heterosexual and homosocial, not necessarily likeable but certainly commanding of respect. Unlike in Hilary Young's characterisation of hard man culture in late twentieth-century Glasgow, in Ireland the hard man was not an everyman figure. Rather he was, as the minister for the environment observed, a kind of 'folk hero': a living caricature in whom the ordinary traits of hegemonic masculinity were exaggerated.[5] He was a conglomerate hard-drinking, hard-fighting sportsman who provided for his family and who was too proud to seek any sympathy about his difficult life. As we will see throughout this book, the hard man features heavily in Irish prison life in the period, and as such, he is an important figure in our consideration of prisoners' activism.

Becoming a 'Hard Man' (1964–72)

Daniel Redmond first came in contact with the prison system in 1964 when he was nineteen years old and was sentenced to six months in

St Patrick's juvenile institution for stealing £12–4–0 from a garage in Cabra, on the north side of Dublin city.[6] Two years later, in 1966, he was remanded on bail for the robbery with violence of a string of bookies and a draper's shop.[7] However, he absconded to London before his trial. At twenty-five, in 1970, he was down on his luck – 'unemployed, no fixed address' – and was convicted of stealing £143,000 in jewels from an eighty-three-year-old woman in her home in Notting Hill, London. He was also convicted of possession of a shotgun, a pistol, and two revolvers.[8] Firearms would become a trademark of his later career. In 1971, by now married with five children, he returned to Ireland and settled in the recently constructed, but already socially disadvantaged, county Dublin suburb of Ballymun. In November that year he was arrested, along with his younger brother Kevin, for the armed robbery of £4,144.38 from the Dublin Corporation offices. Their getaway included a car-chase across Dublin city, during which they fired a shotgun at the pursuing squad-cars. The two brothers were released after a bail hearing in May 1972, and, just three months later, they and a third man, Desmond Kinsella, raided an armoured car that had been bound for the Eastern Health Board and stole £8,648.[9] Kevin Redmond was given a four-year sentence, and Kinsella, who pleaded guilty, got three. Daniel, however, was sentenced to seven years, largely on the evidence of a garda who said that he was the ringleader of the operation.[10] By this stage, Redmond had clearly proven his credentials, he was the archetype of a 'hard man' – daring, violent, unafraid of the law, and a promising young leader in the criminal fraternity.

In the early 1970s, Redmond began to develop as an activist, advocating for the rights of ordinary prisoners. Redmond's armoured car raid was tried in the Special Criminal Court, a juryless court intended primarily to prosecute paramilitaries, although it was increasingly being used against Dublin's semi-organised crime gangs. At the end of his trial, Redmond addressed the court and demanded a jury trial, telling the judge, 'I am not political, far from it'.[11] Three months later he was back in the Special Criminal Court for his part in shooting at a garda in the course of an earlier robbery and, having written to the Attorney General and the Court Registrar demanding an explanation of why he would not receive a jury trial, he told the court, 'I am not going to recognise this Court until I get an answer. As far as I am concerned this Court is just a Tory assembly'.[12] This is our first evidence of his attempts to resist the structures of penal authority in a coherently articulated way.

'I Am Not Political, Far from It': Daniel Redmond and the Prisoners' Union (1972–73)[13]

Redmond arrived in Portlaoise Prison in 1972. At that time, the prison population was mainly made up of ordinary prisoners, but there were also eight politicals. These came from at least three different denominations (Provisional IRA [PIRA], Official IRA [OIRA], and Saor Éire) – representing only a small fraction of the prison's average population of 179. The political prisoners at Portlaoise had been agitating for some time. Much of this agitation had taken place at a low level, and it peaked with a twenty-day hunger strike by an OIRA prisoner in July 1972. However, not long after Redmond arrived at Portlaoise there was a rapid development of militancy among ordinary prisoners. On 13 and 14 November 1972, around half the population of Portlaoise Prison staged a sit-in, refusing to return to their cells or to take part in prison labour. Their representatives, the Prisoners' Committee which seems to have included Redmond, presented the governor with a list of complaints about conditions of cells, the lack of recreational facilities, and the quality of the food. This protest demanded improvements in the conditions of all prisoners, rather than any particular category, which clearly distinguished them from the earlier protests of political prisoners. After the second day of protests, the prison's Visiting Committee placed seventy-nine prisoners on a punishment diet.[14] Although this was supposed to be reviewed after twenty-eight days, one prisoner recalled it continuing for fifty-seven days, earning the committee the moniker of 'the bread and water committee'.[15] In addition, the prisoners were 'held in cells [for] 23 hours a day with no papers, no visits, no letters and no tobacco'.[16] A letter from the Prisoners' Committee to the *Irish Times* also described 'barbaric' unofficial punishments which included prison officers beating Daniel Redmond unconscious with batons because he had 'acted as a spokesman for the prisoners and the warders ... [had] him marked as a ringleader'.[17] A few days after this letter reached the *Irish Times* a recently released prisoner, Sean Whelan, publicly sent his statement about their treatment to Amnesty International, which had just launched its high-profile global anti-prison-torture campaign.[18]

In the aftermath of the protest, several prisoners, including Redmond, went on hunger strike to protest their punishment and eleven prisoners attempted suicide.[19] Although a representative of the Visiting Committee dismissed the suicide attempts flippantly – 'A couple of prisoners had scratched arms'[20] – they seem to have been far more serious than that. Daniel's younger brother, Kevin, was one of the men who attempted suicide and was transferred to the Central Mental Hospital (CMH), where he stayed for more than four months, suffering from a breakdown.[21] In all, eight prisoners were removed from Portlaoise to the CMH in just under a month beginning on 21 November, a week after the punishment regime began, and ending on 18 December.[22] This was five times higher than the average number of removals for the first ten months of the year (1.6 people per month), and a full twenty-four times higher than the monthly average the previous year (four people in all of 1971).[23]

From this first protest we see the resistant action of both the collective prisoners' body and the individual prisoners' bodies. By combining and acting as a single body, to present the prison with demands outside of the official, individuated channels, the Prisoners' Committee not only breached prison discipline but one of its leaders was charged with inciting the 'prisoners to revolt and cause mutiny'.[24] When the prisoners were put on twenty-three hour lockup, there were no further opportunities for them to continue as a combined body, and so they began individual protests in which they exercised a radical autonomy over their own bodies. By refusing food and by wounding themselves, the prisoners became an embodied rejection of prison discipline and its internalised power relation, because they were rejecting the ability of the prison to punish them. Threatening a prisoner with a restricted diet will not work if they are already on hunger strike, and a prisoner who self-harms so seriously that they must transferred to hospital cannot be confined to a solitary cell.

When the punishment regime was lifted in early January, the *Irish Independent* reported that some of the Portlaoise prisoners' demands had been met, 'They were given new beds, toothbrushes, toothpaste and new hand basins', but that they were still angry.[25] As soon as the punishment diet was over, they came together again. On Sunday, 28 January, eighty-seven prisoners formed the Portlaoise Prisoners' Union (PPU). Elections were quickly organised and a committee, including a president, two secretaries, and eight shop stewards, was formed.[26] Many of these appointments were short-lived. According to one activist, the prison authorities intimidated members, forcing the first president and five members to resign. On top of this, the first two secretaries, Simon O'Donnell and Hugh Meenan, were transferred to the Curragh Military Detention Barracks in March 1973; this made way for the appointment of Daniel Redmond as the union's secretary.[27] In spite of the losses, the PPU had grown to ninety-three members by the end of March. Nonetheless, the union made several false starts. In early February it smuggled out a letter warning of, or perhaps threatening, an impending riot.[28] In late February it called for a hunger strike unless facilities were improved and the victimisation of PPU members ended.[29] There is no evidence that either of these threats materialised.

The minister for justice, Patrick Cooney, simultaneously denied the existence of the PPU and claimed that it had been established by 'subversives', the euphemism for the wide range of physical-force republicans.[30] As we discussed previously, the politicals had been active in the prison system since the late 1960s, but their relationship with the ordinaries was often tense. The PIRA held itself separate from ordinary prisoners, insisting they occupy different landings in prisons until 1973, when they were all moved to Portlaoise. There were some similarities and connections between the PPU and the politicals. The PPU deployed similar tactics to those that had been used by generations of political prisoners, including labour strikes, sit-ins, and hunger strikes.[31] However, it would be easy to overstate these tactical similarities and draw conclusions about the influence that the politicals had on the ordinaries. Given the unbalanced power relationship between prisoners and the institutions, and the limitations it puts on prisoners' tactical options, prisoners' protests around the world often look similar. Moreover, the tradition of prisoners using their bodies as weapons of protest was deeply inscribed in Irish culture by stories of prison escapes during the War of Independence and the deaths on hunger strike of people like Thomas Ashe and Terence MacSwiney.

Indeed, prisoners' protests are so deeply inscribed in Irish culture that historian George Sweeney even suggested that hunger striking, in particular, was part of a longer mythology which stretched back to pre-Christian Ireland.[32] However, there were also more concrete links between the ordinary prisoners and the republican movement. In their early months, the PPU smuggled out communiques through Saoirse, an organisation campaigning for the release of OIRA prisoners which controlled one of the few illicit lines of communication.[33] In addition, one of the PPU's first secretaries, Hugh Meenan, seems to have been a political prisoner, and it was a source of considerable frustration to the prisoners that the governor would meet Meenan as a representative of the politicals but refused to do the same when he was representing the ordinaries.[34]

In 1974, a memorandum, prepared by the Department of Justice to make the case for continued segregation of prisoners in the Curragh, claimed that prisoners from the revolutionary socialist and republican organisation Saor Éire had originally fomented the PPU's campaign.[35] However, the PPU members always disputed these accusations. In May 1973, an early PPU secretary, Simon O'Donnell, emphasised that the union was not politically affiliated, claiming that of the first ninety-three members only four had political affiliations; O'Donnell himself and another man were members of the Maoist, antinationalist British and Irish Communist Organisation and the two men 'had sympathies with' Official Sinn Féin, while all of the other members of the union had no affiliations.[36] Certainly Daniel Redmond and Noel Lynch, the union's secretary and president during the most intense period of their campaign, were 'far from' political, to use Redmond's own turn of phrase. This is not to say that they did not want to change the prison, or even conditions in society in general, but they had no part or interest in the 'national struggle', which delineated what was thought of as political imprisonment in Ireland at the time, and the crimes for which they were sentenced were not politically motivated.

Initially, the union's demands were practical and primarily focused on the bodily needs of the prisoners rather than broader structural reforms. The union's initial demands were for recognition of the union, an extra hour's exercise each day, and for overcoats. These demands were not only rejected by the prison, but the prisoners were punished for making them. Those who wanted overcoats were moved from working in 'fairly warm sheds' to 'pulling carrots with bare hands in the icy mud', others were threatened with a punishment diet unless they left the union. Later, in February 1973, seventy prisoners were refused recreation until they left the union, while the union's president was punished for speaking to a group of prisoners.[37] In addition to these official punishments, union members alleged that there were regular punishment beatings from prison officers.[38]

Over the next few months their demands became more structural and widespread. As the union's campaign began to gather momentum, it smuggled a list of eleven demands out to the Prisoners' Rights Organisation (PRO) which later printed them in the *Jail Journal*. These included:[39]

> An impartial parole board with an elected union member sitting on same to ensure fair play for all ...
> The present biased, sadistic and hypocritical Visiting Committee to be instantly dissolved and be replaced by a Committee of sociologists, social workers, law students and trade union representatives, plus an elected PPU member, to ensure fair play ...
> The immediate abolition of all dietary punishment, solitary confinement and physical and mental harassment.
> We now seek the recognition of the PPU by Trade Unions and the Minister of Justice.[40]

These structural demands were accompanied by more familiar and immediate demands about the improvement of educational and recreational provisions and the facilities for visitors.

The PPU's campaign began in earnest six months after the initial protest. As in the silent protest, the combined prisoners' body acted to physically disrupt the functioning of the prison. On the morning of 23 May, the PPU members staged another sit-in, demanding an immediate meeting between their representatives and the minister for justice. The governor called in Garda reinforcements to move the prisoners back into their cells. At midday, before the Gardaí had time to enter the prison, the prisoners voluntarily returned to their cells. This time the focus of the punishment was on the four 'ringleaders' who received dietary punishment and were denied recreation, while the other protesters only forfeited their weekly food parcel privilege.[41] Unlike the previous actions, this protest attracted significant public attention, thanks to the publicity of the newly formed Ad Hoc Committee for Prison Reform, which acted as the PPU's voice outside the prison. The prisoners' position was widely reported, as was the speech by Minister for Justice Patrick Cooney to the Prison Officers' Association (POA) in which he claimed that the PPU was being run by 'a small group of violent long-term prisoners' who were 'not interested in "prisoners' rights" or anybody else's rights, but in projecting themselves into a Mafia-like position as power bosses within the prisons'.[42]

Although both the November 1972 and May 1973 protests were met with harsh punishment and informal retaliation from prison officers, by September, Noel Lynch and Daniel Redmond, president and secretary of the PPU, were able to claim limited victories. In a letter smuggled out on toilet paper, they announced that their protests had resulted in a new dietary programme and the beginning of the construction of a new toilet block.[43] This letter, the only one to be published in a national newspaper, was the PPU's first and last public declaration of success. Even this modest boast may have been too much of a challenge to the prison authorities. On 13 September, five days after the letter was published, prison officers came to move four leaders, including Lynch and Redmond, to the Curragh Military Detention Barracks.[44] Officially the transfer was to relieve overcrowding, but the timing and the selection of prisoners suggest other motives. The men barricaded themselves into their cells. The authorities instituted a bread and water diet for the leaders, and a widespread sit-down protest began, during which fourteen prisoners climbed onto the roof.[45] Over the next two days, prisoners took shifts sitting on the roof in groups of five, entertaining themselves by singing and shouting at passers-by.[46] While this was happening, two other protests broke out in Mountjoy. One was a hunger strike for political status by PIRA prisoners; the other was the first protest by the recently formed Mountjoy Prisoners Union (MPU). This new formation claimed to represent all the prisoners in Mountjoy and that they were protesting for 'more humane conditions for prisoners and to highlight the lack of proper educational, medical and recreational facilities in the prisons'.[47]

It remains unclear whether there was any coordination between these three protests, but the Portlaoise protests were widely reported, so we can be confident that the MPU was aware of what was happening in Portlaoise.

When the last prisoner climbed down from the roof of Portlaoise on 15 September, the PPU leaders were not immediately removed from Portlaoise, but they were punished for their 'mutiny' with a bread and water diet – which they protested, as they had done in December 1972, with a bodily rejection of prison authority in the form of a hunger and thirst strike. The PPU tried to publicise this a week later when Richard Power, one of the leaders, appeared in court in Waterford applying to have a wallet returned to him.[48] The court appearance gave him the opportunity to publicly announce that he and two other PPU leaders had been put on a punishment diet and that, in protest, they had undertaken a hunger and thirst strike. The judge, deciding that the application was vexatious, adjourned the proceedings 'until you are on full food or dead' and prejudged the case: 'I will strike it out then'.[49] While the protests had established prisoners' conditions as a subject for public debate, this did not mean that prisoners had a legitimate voice in that debate, and the hardships of individual prisoners continued to fall on unsympathetic ears.

Later in September, the leaders of the PPU were quietly moved to the Mountjoy 'B Base', basement solitary confinement cells. On arrival, the organisers, described in a Department of Justice memorandum as 'extremely resourceful agitators', made contact with the general population of prisoners through their ventilation windows. From this point on, the distinction between PPU and MPU is no longer significant and I will simply refer to both groups in the aggregate as the Prisoners' Union (PU). Within a month, the PU in Mountjoy attempted another protest, similar to that in Portlaoise.[50] With the help of the PRO, the prisoners smuggled out a letter on 6 October reiterating their demands for the abolition of dietary punishment and solitary confinement; extended visiting times, recreational time, remission, and a parole system; improved education, trade courses, and medical and psychiatric care; and official recognition of the PU.[51] After handing over the letter, twenty prisoners tried to climb onto the roof but were prevented from doing so by prison officers. The press' tendency to distrust prisoners can again be seen in the *Irish Independent*'s report on the incident, which was called 'Knives Used in Jail' and reiterated the POA's claim that officers had been attacked with 'bars, bricks, trays, pots of hot tea, broken delph[sic], pieces of steel piping and knives', injuring twelve.[52] The article did not mention the PRO's claim that the prisoners had not used violence. Two weeks later, the PU smuggled out another letter accusing prison officers of 'severely beating' twenty-seven prisoners, ten of whom had to be hospitalised, and calling for an inquiry into the events. Later that month, the PRO claimed that these twenty-seven prisoners had also been put in solitary confinement.[53] On 11 November 1973, the PRO released a statement that twenty-five leaders of PU had been moved to the Curragh Military Detention Barracks.[54]

The PU's activities did not end with collective prison protests. In 1973, when he arrived at Mountjoy, Daniel Redmond allegedly told a fellow inmate and former neighbour from Sillogue Road in Ballymun, Patrick Beirnes, that 'we won in Portlaoise by assaulting prison officers, threatening prison officers, and dragging prison officers through the Courts'.[55] Beirnes went on to become the chairman of the Mountjoy Prisoners' Union.[56] Around at the same time, the POA became increasingly concerned about the 'frame ups' and 'persecution' of its members as part of a perceived '"smear campaign" controlled by the Portlaoise Prisoners' Union'.[57] In 1973 and 1974, prisoners took several cases against prison officers. Redmond was involved with two typical cases: in April 1973, he accused six prison officers of assault and actual bodily harm following the Prisoners' Committee protest, and in November 1973, he sued the governor of Mountjoy for illegally withholding letters that he had tried to post.[58] He and Patrick Beirnes also accused a deputy chief officer at Mountjoy of indecently assaulting Beirnes.[59] The courts did not uphold any of Redmond's complaints, and indeed in 1975, he and Beirnes were sued, albeit unsuccessfully, for libel over the indecent assault accusation. However, while the complaints were not upheld, the tactic was successful at disrupting the ordinary running of the prison and bringing the ordinary working of the prison system into the realm of public debate. These disruptions not only included the time and preparation that dealing with such legal cases entailed but also the institutional humiliation of having the governor of the country's second largest prison and six of his officers publicly remanded on bail.[60]

Hunger Strikes and the Prisoner's Union in the Curragh (1975)

When the union leaders were transferred to the Curragh Barracks in November 1973, their number included not only Daniel Redmond, the secretary of the union, and Noel Lynch, the president, but also many of Daniel's old comrades. There was Patrick Beirnes, who had taken a sexual assault case with Redmond against the prison officer in Mountjoy. There was Peter Anthony Downey who, along with Redmond, had allegedly been beaten up and had his teeth kicked out in his cell as a suspected ringleader of the November 1972 protest.[61] Thomas Holden, who also claimed to have received 'a kicking' from prison officers after the November 1972 protest and again in December 1973, and who, along with Redmond, was charged with assaulting a prisoner who would not take part in the Prisoners' Committee protests.[62] At the trial, Holden gave evidence against Redmond, alleging that Redmond had been involved in the attack and Holden had just tried to break up the fight; this may have led to a coolness between the two.[63] Finally, Kevin Redmond, Daniel's younger brother, was also transferred to the Curragh. Once the union activities settled down, many of the prisoners were released or transferred back to civilian prisons. By April 1974, only three of the twenty-five PU activists remained in the Curragh: Daniel Redmond, Noel Lynch, and Patrick Beirnes.

The beginning of 1975 was marked by a series of high-profile hunger strikes at Portlaoise, which was, by this stage, solely occupied by politicals, except for a handful of ordinaries employed in cooking and cleaning for the politicals who refused to do prison labour. In January and February, twenty republican prisoners went on hunger strike demanding the segregation of political prisoners from the few remaining ordinaries. Around this time, the Department of Justice confirmed that six ordinary prisoners in Portlaoise had gone on hunger and thirst strike and, although the department refused to say what their demands were, the strikers managed to smuggle out a statement saying their strike would continue until 'they have been granted segregation [within Portlaoise] and until all other republican demands have been

58 | Prisoners' Bodies

agreed to in writing.[64] Three of the ordinaries, who supported the politicals' demands, lasted six days on hunger and thirst strike, and two days after the end of their strike a settlement was reached between the politicals and the government giving them de facto, although not de jure, political status.[65]

Meanwhile, the situation was also tense in the Curragh. A week after the settlement of the strike in Portlaoise, Patrick Beirnes was released from the Curragh, and he contacted the PRO. He announced that twelve ordinary prisoners in the Curragh had begun a hunger strike.[66] The *Irish Independent* reported the names of eleven of the PU strikers, including three of the activists from Portlaoise – Thomas Holden, Richard Power, and Noel Lynch.[67] It is possible that Daniel Redmond was the twelfth, unnamed, hunger striker, given his involvement with PU protests and his experience of hunger striking in the past. However, he may also have been keeping out of it. In October 1974, he had told a court that 'he had learned his lesson' and that he now passed his time building miniature cabinets in the Curragh which he sold on the outside to support his family.[68] The hunger strikers, whose statement claimed that they had the support of all twenty-nine prisoners in the Curragh, made four demands. They wanted the improvement of visiting conditions. There were only three visiting boxes, for twenty-nine inmates, which meant that sometimes visits were reduced to fifteen minutes.[69] They wanted 'the cessation of intimidation and provocation' including the night-time parading of '"moon-men" troops in riot gear and carrying batons and shields' as well as troops in riot gear searching cells by night.[70] They wanted an improvement in the prisons' diet and the establishment of a 'comprehensive parole system'.[71] In addition, the prisoners complained that the materials for their handicrafts, like the miniature cabinets that Redmond built, had been removed.[72]

The strike began on 23 February, 1975. The strikers were locked in their cells for all but thirty minutes each day and were refused visits or newspapers.[73] Several strikers dropped out in the first few days and by the twenty-seventh, the number had dwindled to five, including Holden and Lynch.[74] After a week, the PRO, who were representing the prisoners on the outside, announced that Christy Kelly, a striker with a back injury, had been refused medical attention by the authorities at the Curragh.[75] The strike ended after eight days and the press noted: 'There has been no change in the conditions' at the Curragh.[76] Indeed in January 1976, ten months after the end of the hunger strike, the secretary of the PU in the Curragh published a statement in the PRO's *Jail Journal* which reiterated and detailed their complaints about intimidation by the military police and guards, including alleged assaults and threats to frame prisoners for attempting to escape, shoot them, and leave them 'hanging across the wire'.[77] This statement may have been written by Redmond. Several of the turns of phrase are similar to a letter published by Lynch, as president, and Redmond, as secretary, during the 1973 protests. For instance:

The most frustrating aspect of our few demands is that they are for basic human rights, nothing more. (1973)[78]

Many of the prisoners are incarcerated there because they asserted that prisoners were human beings entitled to basic human rights. Surely that is no reason to treat them like animals? (1975)[79]

The use of the title secretary, rather than president, suggests that the second letter was written by Redmond rather than Lynch. Ultimately, the PU at the Curragh was always doomed to failure. Without the critical mass of people necessary to constitute a threatening collective body, or the threat that the protests would spread to the wider prison population, the individual rejections of penal authority could be locally managed and nationally ignored.

A New Prisoners' Union in Mountjoy (1977)

By May 1976, Redmond had been transferred back to Mountjoy and he remained there until late 1977. While Redmond was there, there was a fresh outbreak of PU activity. This began on Saturday, 5 March 1977, when a prisoner swallowed several three-inch nails. He was the tenth person to attempt suicide at the prison in just two months.[80] George Royale, who was in Mountjoy for armed robbery and who later went on to be a leading member of the PRO, began a hunger strike

60 | Prisoners' Bodies

to protest the conditions that had led to these attempts.[81] Three days later, fifty members of the PU refused food in a one-day hunger strike. Twelve prisoners continued their strike throughout the week, and the following Monday, they were joined again by fifty to sixty prisoners on another one-day hunger strike.[82] Royale continued his strike until 17 March. In a court appearance during the strike, he claimed that he was on strike because he was being treated like a 'security prisoner' and that 'the hunger strike and the series of attempted suicides were the result of the ill treatment of prisoners'.[83] The union offered a more schematised view of this in the PRO's publication *Jail Journal*: 'The prison conditions in Mountjoy are ... the direct result of the decision of Mr Cooney, the Minister for Justice, to view all prisons as security institutions primarily and all prisoners as security risks ... They are provided with food but denied mental and emotional sustenance'.[84] Once again, we see hunger striking being used as a rejection of the prison, but this time it was an embodied rejection of the psychological conditions of imprisonment. The hunger strikers' denial of food mirrored the prison's denial of prisoners' mental and emotional needs.

The strikers issued seven demands to resolve these problems, including the restoration of library and educational services, permitting prisoners to receive reading material and luxuries from outside the prison, an end to solitary confinement, and 'that the prison officers cease their ill-treatment of prisoners'.[85] There are, of course, clear lines of continuity between these and the PU's demands in Portlaoise and Mountjoy in 1973, and the hunger strikers' demands in the Curragh in 1975, but most of the demands for structural reform, like the abolition of the Visiting Committees, had been abandoned. Even in their reduced form, the strike does not seem to have achieved any of its aims.

The second major flare up happened on the evening of 17 July, when a body of 100 to 150 prisoners came together and staged a sit-down protest in the yard.[86] When this was broken up by prison officers, fourteen prisoners made their way onto the roof of the recreation building and began throwing slates.[87] Prison officers attempted to subdue the fourteen 'ringleaders' in what the press referred to as a 'vicious hand-to-hand battle' resulting in the hospitalisation of three officers and three prisoners.[88] The PRO later claimed that at least one prisoner was thrown off the seventeen-foot high roof.[89] The Department of Justice said that in its view there was 'no particular reason' for the disturbance, but the PRO claimed that the dispute was over prison conditions, including 'the lack of education and training facilities', echoing the demands made by the hunger strikers in March.[90] The department characterised the protests as the work of 'a small number of prisoners who are well known as prisoners who try to organise disruption ... and then, with the assistance of people outside the prison, try to secure maximum publicity'.[91] The PRO, the 'people outside' to whom the department referred, offered a different interpretation, describing a 'legitimate and peaceful demonstration' organised by the PU which was brutally suppressed by 'untrained and unskilled' prison officers.[92] As well as the hospitalisation of some of the leaders, others were confined to the B Base punishment cells for more than two months.[93] This was the last, failed, attempt to establish a union inside prisons in Ireland. However, as we will see in later chapters, it was not the end of prisoners' protests.

Daniel Redmond: Coda

When Daniel Redmond was first transferred from Portlaoise to Mountjoy in 1973, he told another prisoner 'we won in Portlaoise and we will win here'.[94] Four years later his prediction had not come true. The union had been removed from Portlaoise (1973), broken in Mountjoy (1973), ignored in the Curragh (1975), and its last gasp was to be extinguished in Mountjoy (1977). The final nail in the coffin came in the form of the annual Visiting Committee report on Mountjoy in 1977 which only vaguely alluded to the union activities as 'the frivolous complaints' of 'malcontents' and a 'mini-riot which ... cost several thousand pounds in roof repairs'.[95] The report found the facilities in the prison 'to be quite satisfactory'.[96]

Redmond was released from Mountjoy at the end of 1977 but was not out of prison for long before he was picked up for another armed robbery and sentenced to fifteen years. This time he was transferred to the Curragh almost immediately.[97] He does not seem to have been involved in any further disturbances. In 1985, the Supreme Court suspended the remaining eight years of his sentence. The court heard that he was working as an instructor for An Chomhairle Oiliúna, the Irish

62 | Prisoners' Bodies

industrial training authority, and he had 'a good, stable relationship with a woman'. A Garda detective inspector even told the court that 'he is leading an honest and upright life'.[98] By this stage, Redmond was forty years of age and had spent around a third of his life in Portlaoise, the Curragh, and Mountjoy. When he left prison, he went to begin his new life in Clondalkin, a southwestern suburb of county Dublin. Since then, for nearly forty years, he has remained free.

Conclusion

Ordinary prisoners, in Ireland and abroad, have long risked their health by using their bodies to protest. In Ireland, however, there was a parallel tradition of imprisoned political activists which dominated the public representations of prisoners' protests. These prisoners were treated as martyrs by the Irish republican tradition and their single-mindedness and idealism was venerated. The PU leaders undertook hunger and thirst strikes, and they faced punishment diets and extended periods in solitary confinement. They were allegedly threatened and severely beaten, and they organised a union which persisted, on and off, in the face of this hardship for more than four years. In light of this, it is difficult to believe the government's claims that the activists were only interested in developing their own power within the prisons and that they were not committed to the aims of the union and the reform of the prison system. However, Redmond's story, and indeed the story of most of the PU leaders, highlights something that would become a crucial and troubling issue for the PRO, as we will discuss in chapter 6. It highlights that involvement in serious activism does not preclude people from involvement in serious crime. By not living up to the hagiographic expectations of purity set by the republican tradition of prisoner-activists, the PU were left open to accusations that they were exploiting the prison system with the intent of becoming 'mafia bosses'.[99]

At every stage, the PU used the individual and collective bodies of the prisoners to not only protest their conditions but to embody a rejection of penal discipline. Simply by constituting themselves as a single, coherent body – by meeting as a union or staging a sit-in – the prisoners manifested a rejection of the prison's divisive order and heterogeneous discipline. By demanding reforms that reached beyond the implementation of the Rules for the Government of Prisons, they became a mutiny. By individually refusing food or by doing injury to themselves they refused the prison's power to punish them through either diet or confinement. Prison discipline is, as we saw in the last chapter, a means of producing docile bodies ready for rehabilitation, and the PU and its members challenged this, instrumentalizing individual and collective bodies against the very foundations of the prison. Bodies became both the medium of communication and the message being communicated. In the next two chapters we will see how, outside the walls of the prison, the PRO also used prisoners' bodies to communicate their demands – sometimes amplifying the communications of prisoners and the PU and sometimes creating their own messages through the figurative and literal use of prisoners' bodies.

2

'A Voice for Prisoners'

The Prisoners' Rights Organisation, 1973–76

Introduction

The fifth United Nations (UN) Congress on the Prevention of Crime and the Treatment of Offenders opened in Geneva on 1 September 1975 with some unexpected drama. The congress grew out of the League of Nations' International Penal and Penitentiaries Commission and had run conferences every five years since 1955. The participants included representatives of governments and civil administrations around the world, as well as experts, advisors, and nongovernmental organisations representing the range of legitimate voices involved in debates about criminal justice and penology. Over the years, the conference had adopted groundbreaking resolutions including the Standard Minimum Rules for the Treatment of Prisoners (1955) and recommended the development of distinct police services for juvenile crime (1960).[1]

As the inaugural meeting of the 1975 congress convened at the Palais des Nations, two photographers made their way past the press cameras at the front of the assembly and unfurled a banner that read 'Prisoners' Rights Organisation'. Thinking it was part of the opening ceremony, the assembly began to clap. For two minutes the photographers spoke about 'the degrading and inhuman conditions in Irish prisons'.[2] By the time the security guards finally managed to eject them they had distributed 500 leaflets, which claimed that Irish prisons were 'among the most repressive in Europe', and 150 copies of a publication called *Jail Journal*.[3] The would-be photographers were Pat McCartan, a young solicitor who went on to become a TD and judge, and Brendan Walsh, a former prisoner who went on to become an actual photographer. Both were founding members of the Prisoners' Rights Organisation (PRO). Outside the Palais, McCartan and Walsh held an impromptu press conference with the assembled international press, here and in the PRO's publication *Jail Journal*, they explained that the protest had two aims.[4] The first was to embarrass the Irish delegation in front of the international community by raising awareness of Irish prison conditions. The second was to highlight that while prisoners 'were the people under discussion' at the congress there was no delegation of prisoners or ex-prisoners.[5] In their article about the protest in *Jail Journal,* they boasted about the 'huge publicity created', that it resulted in articles about Irish prison conditions in 'the national newspapers of Switzerland, Spain, Germany, France and England' and a television report on the Canadian National Broadcaster.[6] In Ireland however, the event was entirely overshadowed by the funeral of the late-president Éamon de Valera, which was the main news story in Ireland in early September 1975. While the funeral certainly overshadowed the event itself, there were several reports on the congress, including about Israel's withdrawal prior to the opening session and the resolution to define and ban torture.[7] In spite of these reports, however, across all the national and regional newspapers, I have only been able to find a single short article about the PRO's protest sandwiched between reports about a failed coup in Ecuador and the election of a new canon at Saint Patrick's Cathedral.[8]

What emerges clearly from this event and its reporting, or lack thereof, is the deep-rooted exclusion of prisoners and their representatives from the discourse about prisons. The congress, which brought together nearly a thousand legitimate voices on criminal justice and penological issues, ejected Brendan Walsh, one of the few people there who had actually spent time in prison. This speaks to the challenges faced by prisoner- or ex-prisoner-led penal reform organisations internationally, as well as in Ireland. In this chapter, I will explore the PRO's early attempts to gain legitimacy for their own voices and those of prisoners.

The Prisoners' Union (PU), discussed in the last chapter, was the first reform organisation focused on ordinary prisoners' rights in twentieth-century Ireland. However, between 1973 and the mid-1980s, the PRO became its most vocal and successful. It explicitly rejected the categorisation of prisoners into "'political" and "non-political"', arguing that political motivation should not result in 'preferential treatment or otherwise'.[9]

The history of the organisation can be divided into three distinct phases. The first three years, 1973–76, were marked by frenetic street-level organisation. In this period, the PRO tried to build support among prisoners, former prisoners, and their families. The tactics focused on street demonstrations and legal battles. The second stage of the organisation's development, 1977–80, was marked by what might be thought of as a sociological turn. In this period, the PRO focused on changing government policy through conducting and publicising their research on conditions in prison and within the communities the majority of prisoners came from. Moreover, this period was marked by a series of splits, as the more militant members, who thought the PRO was losing sight of the needs and concerns of ordinary prisoners, attempted to form their own organisations. Finally, the third phase was marked by the organisation's declining importance as the Catholic Bishops' Council (1983) and later the Whitaker Report (1985) took up the case for reform and the press began to focus on these more traditionally legitimate voices. The splits which began in the late 1970s deepened and the organisation ultimately disintegrated.

This chapter focuses on the PRO's first three years as they built up a following and achieved a degree of legitimacy in the public discourse. The chapter establishes what the PRO's aims were and the tactics they used to achieve them. It discusses the group's membership and where its activists and its support came from. Finally, the chapter explores how the PRO effected the public discourse about 'ordinary' prisoners in Ireland in the period.

The Prisoners' Rights Organisation | 67

What Did the PRO Do?

At the height of the PU's campaign in May 1973, a group of radical University College Dublin (UCD) law students, called the Law Students Union for Action, organised a meeting about prison conditions. They invited Máirín de Búrca, an Official Sinn Féin organiser who had recently been imprisoned, and Brendan Walsh, who had spent time in prison for bank robbery.[10] After the meeting, the speakers and some of the activists formed the Ad Hoc Committee for Prison Reform.[11] At the centre of the committee was Tom Bourke, a thirty-nine-year-old Limerickman who had spent a third of his life in British and Irish jails. In Portlaoise Prison, which he had left two weeks before the press conference at which they announced the formation of the committee, Bourke had been angered by the lack of education and training opportunities. He had been refused permission to do an accountancy correspondence course and instead spent over two years working in the tailors' shop making prison uniforms, a skill not transferable to his previous life as a house-painter.[12] Bourke had become involved in the PU at its formation and quickly became the union's secretary. Alongside him, the committee included Conal Gibbons, then a law student at UCD; Pat McCartan, also a law student at UCD and the secretary of the National Civil Liberties League; John Kearns, an organiser with the Amalgamated Transport and General Workers' Union; Matt Merrigan, Irish district secretary for the same union and a former Labour Party candidate for the Dáil; and Maura Bates, a solicitor.[13] The committee quickly grew and, on 12 July, they held a public meeting reforming themselves as the Prisoner Rights Organisation.[14]

The PRO quickly published a six-point programme. The first demand was that the prisons should be moved towards a 'rehabilitative rather than punitive' function.[15] The second was for eleven rights for prisoners ranging from the right to form a union to the right to 'proper medical care, including psychiatric treatment'.[16] Third was the demand for prisoners' dependants to be supported by the state. Fourth was for 'adequate preparation for release' including education and assistance with housing, employment, and marriage counselling.[17] Fifth was the destruction of all criminal records five years after the person leaves prison.[18] Finally, sixth was that the prison system should be administered by a board representing a 'cross-section of the community with knowledge of and an interest in the welfare of prisoners', this was to include an ex-prisoner, a serving prisoner, and a trade union organiser.[19]

This programme was clearly based on the eleven demands of the PU, outlined in the previous chapter. There are distinct lines of continuity, including the demands for improved educational facilities, changes to the system of visiting rights, the right to join the PU, and the inclusion of trade unionists, current and former prisoners, social workers, and other interested parties in the prison system's administrative and oversight boards. However, the PRO had developed these demands beyond improvements to the current system and reshaped them into a programme for systemic reform which included changing the prison system's raison d'être, restructuring the administration of the system at a fundamental level, and reframing how the justice system interacted with wider society by limiting the long-term impact of a conviction and enabling the system to address the perceived root causes of recidivism: poverty, lack of opportunities, and the absence of support when readjusting outside prison.[20] Although the PRO was acutely conscious of the social inequalities that underpinned a lot of crime, they made a conscious decision at the beginning to focus on the 'immediate necessity' of relieving the conditions in the prison system.[21]

The PU was not the only influence on this six-point programme. The Irish Women's Liberation Movement (IWLM) had published its own six-point programme, the *Chains or Change* manifesto, in 1970. Both manifestos deal with similar themes, including the establishment of specific rights, an entitlement to housing, improved access to employment, and support for single parent families. This continuity may have been the result of the fact that the IWLM and the PRO shared several influential activists including Máirín de Búrca and Margaret Gaj, both of whom were founding members of the IWLM while also taking leading roles in numerous activist causes from the 1960s onwards. There are also clear lines of comparison between the two organisations' tactics, not least in their picketing of institutional targets and their publications (*Fownes Street Journal* and *Jail Journal*). The PRO also drew on the ideas of Preservation of the Rights Of Prisoners (PROP), the British prisoners' organisation. The list of prisoners' rights that the PRO proposed in the first issue of *Jail Journal* clearly drew on the Charter of Rights promulgated by PROP, including general political rights that one might expect from any civil rights campaign, like the right to vote in local and national elections and the right to join trade unions, and more specific rights tailored to prisoners' needs, like the right to have all criminal records destroyed after five years and the right to legal representation and to call witnesses at prison disciplinary hearings.[22]

In its first two years, the PRO focused on picketing institutional targets to highlight general problems and to demand change. On 29 July, just over two weeks after the organisation was formed, fifty protesters held a picket outside Mountjoy Prison calling for an end to the 'mental and physical torture' of the current penal system. According to one journalist, the organisation threatened that this was 'the first salvo in a campaign which would become nation-wide within the next few weeks'.[23] A month later, twelve PRO activists picketed a dinner dance in Kildare that Minister for Justice Patrick Cooney was holding for American delegates of the International Police Association. Picketers called on the minister to follow through on the 'radical noises' he had made while in opposition.[24] In September, forty activists picketed the Department of Justice in Dublin to protest poor psychiatric provision in prison.[25] In October, they went to County Laois to picket Portlaoise Prison, protesting the general prison conditions.[26] In spite of their early enthusiasm for a nationwide campaign of pickets, once the PU had been suppressed inside the prisons, the organisation's demonstrations became far less frequent. Throughout 1973–74, they continued to sporadically picket institutional targets like the Department of Justice and Mountjoy Prison to highlight events like the hunger strike of eleven former PU members in the Curragh Military Detention Barracks, where they had been isolated for their union activities. Perhaps the most spectacular of these institutionally targeted protests was the 1975 protest at the UN Congress on the Prevention of Crime and the Treatment of Offenders in Geneva, described at the outset of this chapter. However, throughout this period, the PRO protested institutional targets, using the pickets to highlight individual prisoners' stories and using these stories, in turn, to illustrate broader trends within the prison system. The earliest editions of the *Jail Journal* include articles, with titles like 'Prison Statements' and 'How to Win Friends', that were written by PU members and justified their union activities through their own experiences in prison. Other articles like 'The Women's Prison: The Facts and the Horror', 'A Prisoner Looks at Crime', and 'Mountjoy and Pentonville' were by ordinary prisoners without any particular activist credentials and examined the conditions in prisons. Many articles aimed to establish, for people with no experience of prison, the basic living conditions and patterns of life in prison. In the first three issues of the journal, one writer described, through his own experiences, the living conditions in Daingean Reformatory, a reformatory school for children between twelve and seventeen years old; Portlaoise Prison, the high security adult prison; and 'Dundrum', the Central Mental Hospital (CMH) where prisoners with serious psychiatric diagnoses were treated. Another former prisoner wrote 'Working Parole' to describe his experience, including the social and institutional challenges, of transitioning out of prison.[27] Other articles like 'Mountjoy Riots', 'Prison Statements', and 'Reply to Prison Officers' aimed to offer a counternarrative about prisoners' protests to that presented by the state and by prison officers.[28] While these articles advanced the PRO's aim of giving voice to prisoners, many of the most important stories that they told emerged from elsewhere, notably coroners' reports.

In October 1973, the PRO won a major publicity coup when they were given permission to be represented at the inquest into the death of Joseph Kavanagh. Kavanagh was a thirty-eight-year-old farm labourer with no criminal convictions who lived with his two brothers in County Wicklow.[29] He had been a patient at the local psychiatric hospital, but in the preceding week he had stopped attending the clinic and taking his medication.[30] In July 1973, he was arrested for assaulting his aunt, Patricia Doyle.[31] After just over a week on remand in Mountjoy he hanged himself in his cell using his bedsheets.[32] At the inquest, the PRO demanded a full inquiry into the circumstances surrounding the death and the lack of psychiatric care in Mountjoy.[33] Moreover, because they had been included in the inquest process, they seem to have accrued a degree of legitimacy. Almost every national and most major regional newspapers that reported the death also reported on the PRO's demand for an inquiry.[34] While most of these news reports

The Prisoners' Rights Organisation | 71

ultimately endorsed the coroner's conclusion that an inquiry was unnecessary and that the inquest would suffice as an inquiry, the PRO had clearly earned the right to be heard on these matters.

The PRO's tactics shifted in 1975, bringing together their experience of picketing, their use of individuals' stories to highlight broader structural issues, and their experience with the coroner's court. This change was prompted by a cluster of suicides and attempted suicides in custody. On 14 April, an eighteen-year-old man from Dublin's south inner city, Kevin Kenna, set fire to himself in his cell in St Patrick's, the institution for juveniles that was part of the Mountjoy Prison campus.[35] He was rushed to the Mater Hospital, across the road from St Patrick's, where he was treated for severe burns. Kenna's father later complained to the press, through the PRO, that he had not been informed that his son had been hurt for three to four days.[36] The next day, 15 April, Leo Byrne hanged himself with his own shirtsleeve in the Bridewell Garda Station in Dublin.[37] He had been arrested when a woman reported that he had assaulted her after an evening's drinking in the Legal Eagle pub, beside the Four Courts.[38] Less than two weeks after Byrne's death, on 28 April, John Donnellan, a fifty-year-old man died in Mountjoy Prison. Donnellan was a farmer from Lisdoonvarna, County Clare, who had previously had psychiatric trouble. During his time at Mountjoy, he wrote to his wife to tell her that he planned on going on hunger and thirst strike and to ask her to claim his body when he died so he could be buried in his hometown.[39] A few days before his death he had been put in 'the pad', Mountjoy's padded cell, for 'making a general nuisance and tearing up bedsheets'.[40] After he was returned to his cell, he hanged himself using a torn pillowcase.[41] Finally, a little over two weeks after that, on 15 May, John McCarthy, another eighteen-year-old man in St Patrick's Institution, hanged himself in his cell.[42] McCarthy was from the Traveller community and his family lived in Limerick. He had a 'long history of convictions' dating back to when he was ten years old, and was a month and a half into an eight month sentence for stealing a car and related traffic offences. At the time of his death, he would have been eligible for release in less than two months.[43] His death came as a shock to both prison officers and the other inmates.[44] In his statement to the coroner, Denis Donoghue, the governor of St Patrick's, wrote about McCarthy: 'I knew the

72 | Prisoners' Bodies

deceased personally. I would say he was an outgoing type. He had no psychiatric history that I am aware of. He was the type of person one could not associate with self-destruction. The recent publicity given to a recent hanging may have prompted him to some prank or experiment which misfired with tragic consequences'.[45]

The governor's final sentence was clearly aimed at the PRO. It echoed comments made five days previously, by Minister for Justice Patrick Cooney, who told the press that the PRO's agitation and awareness raising activities were 'particularly harmful and dangerous with possible serious effects on the mentality of prisoners ... suicides of this type had epidemic-type overtones and it was a scientific fact that they could be repetitive ... A top psychiatrist has already warned that depressed prisoners could be caught up in a death-wish syndrome under which they might be spurred to take their own lives because of the notoriety achieved by the deaths of others'.[46] The coroner's file on McCarthy's death includes three leaflets from the PRO calling for a full public inquiry and announcing their planned picket outside the home of the civil servant with responsibility for prisons, Richard Crowe. Handwritten at the top of the pamphlets were the inscriptions: 'Circulated by post', 'Subsequent to John Donnellan's death in Mountjoy', and 'Circulated outside John Donnellan's inquest and outside Mountjoy'.[47] It is unusual that prisoners' inquest files would include evidence of this nature, most only contain statements by witnesses and doctors' reports. The coroner clearly believed that the PRO's publicity campaign about the death of John Donnellan had been effective at achieving notoriety and was at least willing to entertain the idea that it had influenced John McCarthy's suicide.

This cluster of suicides prompted a shift in the PRO's tactics. Initially they attended the coroner's inquests into the deaths and, as they had done at the inquest for Joseph Kavanagh in 1973, demanded a full public inquiry. However, they quickly moved beyond this approach, instead targeting the people operating the apparatus of the penal and judicial system. They targeted the 'Red Mass', which is held each October near Dublin's Four Courts to mark the beginning of the legal year. Their leaflets highlighted what they perceived as the unjust use of the prison system, for instance imprisoning 'beggars and alcoholics',[48] suggesting that the members of the legal professions attending the mass

The Prisoners' Rights Organisation | 73

were hypocritically paying mere 'lip service' to natural justice. They concluded: 'It is difficult to believe that Jesus of Nazareth would bless the act which condemned a mentally disturbed young man to a living hell in prison or a bureaucracy which forced suicide on four people and then sought to evade responsibility by claiming "accidental death" or "brain storms". It would, in our opinion be more fitting to open the Irish Law Year with a Black Mass'.[49]

At the beginning of May, before John McCarthy's death, the PRO began circulating the pamphlets mentioned above, which announced their intention to picket the home of Richard Crowe, the senior civil servant at the Department of Justice with responsibility for the prison system. Michael Fardy later told the High Court that this was the natural escalation of their picketing of institutional targets.[50] The pickets, which were to take place for two hours at midday every Saturday, demanded two things: 'A full-scale public inquiry into prison conditions in general and the prison psychiatric facilities in particular' and to bring into the public view the role of senior civil servants who exercise 'complete dictatorial power over the lives and deaths of prisoners'.[51] After the death of John McCarthy, however, their demands shifted from exposing the role of civil servants to demanding the resignation of Richard Crowe.[52] The first picket took place on Saturday, 3 May 1975 and was attended by eight PRO members: Pat McCartan, Brendan Walsh, Máirín de Búrca, Frank Crummy, Jo Ann Gibbons, Michael Fardy, Wladek Gaj, and Joe Costello.[53] They carried placards reading: 'Cooney and Crowe Judicial Murderers' and 'Cooney and Crowe Murderers By Neglect'.[54] A week later, on the Friday, 9 May, Crowe won a High Court injunction against the PRO, temporarily forbidding further picketing.[55] In defiance of this order, three unidentified activists and six of the original picketers, all but McCartan and Crummy, returned to picket Crowe's home on 10 May.[56] In response to this, the High Court made the injunction against McCartan and Crummy permanent and awarded costs against them while granting an interlocutory injunction against the other six until a hearing was convened.[57] After a second stern warning from the High Court, the picket on Crowe's home was abandoned and the following Saturday the PRO were to be found picketing outside institutional targets once again, in this case Mountjoy and St Patrick's Institution.[58] The pickets alone

74 | Prisoners' Bodies

might not have gained much notoriety, indeed we have seen that even spectacular protests by the PRO, like their disruption of the opening of the UN's Congress on the Prevention of Crime and the Treatment of Offenders, often received little or no press attention in Ireland. However, the picket on Crowe's house offered the PRO a new way of communicating. The High Court injunction and the PRO activists' later court appearances attracted widespread press attention. The previous year, in May 1975, there were forty-two articles in the four major national newspapers, the *Irish* and *Sunday Independent*, the *Evening Herald*, the *Irish Press*, and the *Irish Times*. By comparison, in May 1974 there had been a single personal ad about a discussion group held by the PRO.[59] Indeed, between May 1974 and March 1975, before Kevin Kenna attempted suicide in St Patrick's, there was an average of just two articles a month about the PRO in the same four newspapers. Of the forty-two articles in May 1975, twenty-four articles were directly about the picket or related court appearances, each making reference to the PRO's demands and the recent spate of suicides in prison. These included two in-depth profile pieces. One, in the *Sunday Independent,* was called 'Ex-prisoner Is Scourge of the Irish Penal System'.[60] It was written by the well-known feminist journalist June Levine and was based on a friendly interview with the then secretary of the PRO, Michael Fardy. The second was over half a page in the *Irish Times*, entitled 'Momentum Added to Prison Reform Campaign', which included a verbatim interview with two unnamed former prisoners now active in the PRO and some evocative drawings of Mountjoy by Wladek Gaj, the son of PRO founder Margaret Gaj.[61]

In June 1975, the PRO found a new story and a new target. A little over two weeks after the inquest into the death of John Donnellan, on 3 June, the PRO held a press conference with Nora Donnellan, his wife; Christina Kenna, the mother of Kevin Kenna, who had set fire to himself in St Patrick's Institution; and Bernadette Crawley, the mother of Karl Crawley.[62] On 19 June, the same day as the final inquest of the suicide cluster, the PRO picketed outside the Central Criminal Court in Dublin.[63] This time it was not about an inquest but about the trial of Karl Crawley for assaulting a garda. We will deal with the full story of Karl Crawley in greater depth in the next chapter, here it suffices to include the description of him given in the special issue of

The Prisoners' Rights Organisation | 75

the *Jail Journal* in autumn 1975, which tied his story in with the cluster of suicides:

> Karl Crowley [*sic*] is a mentally disturbed young man who has made seventeen attempts at suicide and who has succeeded in doing severe physical damage to his whole body ... Karl Crowley is held, for the full term of his sentence, apart from the main body of prisoners. He is held in the 'base' which is where the punishment cells are located. He is exercised in handcuffs and is handcuffed for his visits which take place in a special room ... Karl Crowley is not the only retarded prisoner in our jails but he is by far and away the most viciously treated.[64]

A few weeks later, on 8 July, the PRO again picketed the court where Crawley's trial had reconvened.[65] This time one of the activists slipped into the court and hid leaflets under the Bibles on the jury's benches.[66] The leaflets argued that Crawley needed care in the CMH but, because they mentioned that he was currently serving three years, the judge deemed them to be prejudicial and adjourned the trial. Six PRO activists on the picket, including Máirín de Búrca, Margaret Gaj, and her son Wladek, were arrested and charged with 'interference with the course of justice' under the Offences Against the State Act, an act intended to deal with the IRA and other 'subversive' threats to the state.[67] Ten days later, the activists were convicted and sentenced to twelve months in prison.[68] The PRO condemned the decision as a 'savage sentence' intended to 'prevent fair comment and peaceful protest'.[69] The six appealed the decision and, in November, although the conviction was upheld, the activists were given the benefit of the Probation Act, so they never served a night in prison.[70] Like the picket at the home of Richard Crowe, the ensuing legal battle lifted this picket, and Crawley's case, into the public view once more. Newspapers reported on Crawley's later acquittal, on his transfer to Meath Hospital after swallowing seven pieces of metal and a pipe cleaner and how the prison officers had not believed him for five days, and they reported when his mother told journalists about his conditions and how he 'was a real Mammy's boy'.[71] Indeed, over the next four months, between them, the national newspapers, mentioned above, published almost one story a week about Crawley's case and his mental and physical health.

76 | Prisoners' Bodies

The following year, it was widely reported in the press when Crawley, with the aid of the PRO, took a High Court case to be released from Mountjoy. In the course of the case, it emerged, and was widely reported, that during his most recent sentence Crawley had been moved to the CMH eleven times and that, while in Mountjoy, he was kept in solitary confinement in the basement and handcuffed every time he left his cell.[72] Also widely reported was the evidence of the medical director of psychiatry at the Eastern Health Board, Dr Brian McCaffery, who stated that in spite of not being 'legally insane' under the M'Naughten rules, which determine whether a person can be held legally responsible for their actions, Crawley 'is not able to resist his impulsive actions ... whenever he is confronted with what he would interpret as authority figures getting at him'.[73] McCaffery concluded that Crawley needed treatment in a 'special Psychiatric Unit in a top security facility' and, as the CMH was 'geared towards a different type of psychiatric population', there were no appropriate facilities for Crawley.[74] McCaffery's comments allude to his view that the CMH was 'geared towards' the needs of patients with 'psychopathic' disorders, while Crawley was more 'in touch with reality' and intent on using his intelligence and prodigious physical resilience and climbing skills, which allowed him to scale the stone walls of the prison, to resist the prison authorities.[75] This final point, regarding the lack of appropriate facilities for people like Crawley, became the headline of the story for many major newspapers. For instance, the *Irish Times* led with 'Republic's Institutions "Not Suitable" for Man Whose Release Is Sought;' the *Irish Independent* led with 'No Place for This Prisoner;' and the *Cork Examiner* with '"No Place" for Man Who Swallowed Spoons'.[76]

Acting on Crawley's behalf, Patrick McEntee, a barrister with an international reputation for defending civil and political rights, argued that Crawley's treatment in Mountjoy amounted to torture and that the state could not continue it.[77] The court found against Crawley. In his judgment, the president of the High Court, Justice Thomas Finlay, later chief justice of Ireland, argued that Crawley's treatment, although not ideal, was an attempt to keep him from further injuring himself: 'I am quite satisfied that the purpose and intention of the restrictions and privations surrounding the prosecutor's [Crawley's] detention are neither punitive nor malicious ... I must construe the entire concept of torture, inhuman and degrading treatment and punishment

The Prisoners' Rights Organisation | 77

as being evil not only in its consequences but evil in its purpose as well. It is most commonly inspired by revenge, retaliation, the creation of fear or improper interrogation. It is to me inconceivable to associate it with the necessary discharge of a duty to prevent self-injury or self-destruction'.[78]

However, the press' reporting of this judgment demonstrated how much the public discourse around prisoners had changed since the beginning of the prisoners' rights movement. In his judgment, Justice Finlay noted that 'it is not the function of the Court to recommend to the executive branch of the state what is desirable or to fix the priorities of its health and welfare policy', but he made it clear, albeit indirectly, what he thought the executive should do.[79] The newspapers' echoed this sympathetic tone, reporting that the president of the court remarked that he had to hand down this judgment 'no matter where his sympathies might lie' and suggesting that the state may have a duty to build a specialised facility to care for people like Crawley.[80] The press noted how the judgment had been given in spite of 'the harshness of the privations which he [Crawley] had undergone, and, to a lesser extent, continued to suffer'.[81] The press also spent significantly longer discussing Crawley's case than that of the state, repeatedly suggesting that while the judgment was final it was not ideal and that reform was needed in the psychiatric care of prisoners.[82] This was an important step forward in the public legitimation of the PRO, who had made the reform of psychiatric care of prisoners one of their central and most regularly repeated demands.

Who Were the PRO?

As already mentioned in relation to the IWLM's influence on the PRO's six-point programme, activists' backgrounds play an important role in shaping a group's tactics and aims. Among the principal activists in the PRO there were three main routes into the organisation. First, there were those student radicals who became interested in prisons through their studies; then there was a host of well-known left-wing and civil rights activists who had become interested in prisoners' rights after being involved in other causes; and finally, the last group were people who had become activists in prison or because of their time in

78 | Prisoners' Bodies

prison. This last group made up about half of the organisation in the early years.[83]

It is striking how many people involved with the PRO have gone on to hold major public offices. Committee members like Mary Ellen Ring, Pat McCartan, Conal Gibbons, and Joe Costello later became High Court, Circuit Court, and District Court judges and a minister of state, respectively, and at least three others went on to be TDs. Ring even went on to chair the Garda Ombudsman.[84] Similarly, Michael D. Higgins, who sat on the Commission of Inquiry into the Prison System that the PRO convened in 1979, became a senator (1973–77 and 1983–87), TD (1981–82 and 1987–2011), government minister (1994–97), and the president of Ireland (2011–25); Mary Robinson, the barrister who worked with the PRO on the Karl Crawley case, was also a senator (1969–89) and went on to become the president of Ireland (1990–97) and UN High Commissioner for Human Rights (1997–2002). This is an indication of the degree of legitimacy eventually achieved by the PRO, but we can also see it as an indication of the number of PRO activists who came from a professional or middle-class background. All of the activists mentioned above held, or were studying for, university degrees while involved in the PRO, an uncommon opportunity in Ireland at the time: in 1971 only 5 per cent of Irish men and 3.5 per cent of Irish women ever attended university – by 1981 this had risen to just 9 per cent and 6.5 per cent, respectively.[85] Students and graduates from UCD in particular, like Ring, McCartan, Gibbons, and Costello, played formative roles in the organisation. This cluster may have been the result, however indirect, of the work of the Prison Study Group, the interdisciplinary research group at UCD in the early 1970s which collected and compiled data on the Irish prison system and, in 1972, published the first independent report on the prison system since the 1940s.[86]

Other activists found their way into the PRO through their involvement in other civil rights causes. Máirín de Búrca, for instance, had been involved with Sinn Féin since she was sixteen years old. In 1969–70, the party split between the 'Officials', with whom de Búrca sided, who pursued a nonviolent, all-Ireland, Marxist political agenda, and the 'Provisionals', who favoured physical-force nationalism. Soon after the split, de Búrca became the general secretary of Official Sinn Féin.[87] In 1971, she spent a week in prison and the experience stuck with her, prompting her to join the PRO when it was formed in 1973. Sue Richardson followed a different path into the organisation. Having changed her name from Sarah Poulikos, Richardson fled to Dublin from the UK in 1972. She had been wanted by Scotland Yard in connection with her involvement in the Angry Brigade, an English militant anarchist group that planted twenty-five bombs over the course of the 1970s, targeting property rather than people. When Richardson left London, four members had recently been sentenced to ten years for conspiracy to cause explosions in the UK. In Ireland, she became active in the Dublin Anarchist Group and from there found her way into the PRO.[88]

These activists did not focus exclusively on prisoners' rights. Apart from Sinn Féin and the PRO, in the 1970s, Máirín de Búrca was an active member of numerous groups including the Irish Women's Liberation Movement and the Irish Council for Civil Liberties. Sue Richardson remained active in the Dublin Anarchist Group throughout her time in the PRO and was sentenced to three years in 1979 for her part in a bank robbery, which was suspected to be the work of a militant organisation, although this went unconfirmed as Richardson never named her co-conspirators. Frank Crummy, who took part in the PRO's picket on the home of the civil servant Richard Crowe, was a director of the Irish Family Planning Association (IFPA) which ran sexual health clinics and agitated for the liberalisation of the laws banning contraceptives.[89] In 1976, the year after the Crowe pickets, Crummy was involved in another well-known act of civil disobedience when the IFPA started selling a booklet about family planning methods which had been banned by the censor.[90] Finally, Margaret Gaj, who was one of the six PRO activists sentenced for picketing Karl Crawley's trial, was ubiquitous in Irish civil rights movements in the 1960s and 1970s. She was a founding member of the IWLM; a leader of the Dublin Housing Action Committee; and an active member of the anti–Vietnam War group, Irish Voice on Vietnam; and the anti–corporal punishment organisation, Reform. Gaj's Restaurant, on Lower Baggot St. in Dublin, was such a popular meeting spot for student radicals and political activists that it was under regular surveillance by the Garda Special Branch and she once jokingly advertised the café under the strapline 'all the best spies eat at Gaj's'.[91]

The PRO, however, was not just made up of these social activists. Throughout its existence, the organisation included an array of former prisoners and their families, some of whom took prominent, although often short-lived, roles in the organisation. For instance, Michael Fardy was key to the organisation's development in the mid-1970s, when he was the PRO's secretary. He established a 'one-man advice bureau' called Concern of Prisoners (COP), was named in the high court injunction that ended the PRO picket at the home of Richard Crowe, and was convicted under the Offences Against the State Act for picketing outside Karl Crawley's trial. Like Bourke, his role was also formative but short-lived and after 1975, Fardy seems to have had little to do with the organisation.

Prisoners also came to the organisation through different routes. After years of bouncing between prisons in Ireland and the UK, Fardy had been involved in the Mountjoy riot of 1972 and had spent time in the Curragh. In 1973, he met several PU activists when they too were transferred to the Curragh, and together they went on a series of hunger strikes to protest declining conditions. It was this long process of politicisation in prison that led him to join the PRO on his release.[92] On the other hand, George Royale, who became a PRO committee member in the early 1980s, told journalist Vincent Browne that a single event had made him join the PRO. In 1976, in the middle of the night, while he was in Garda custody in Dublin's Bridewell he heard 'screams and shouts coming from the tunnel under the station'.[93] When Royale complained to a garda, he was told to 'keep his mouth shut'.[94] He said that what he heard, and the reaction of the garda he had spoken to, drove him to join the PRO.[95] He later discovered that he had overheard Brian McNally being tortured – McNally was one of five people wrongfully arrested for the Sallins Train Robbery (1976) and sentenced to between nine and twelve years based on confessions given under duress.[96]

Many of the former prisoners who became involved with the PRO were, what might be called, 'hard cases', with multiple convictions for possession of firearms, armed robbery, and assault. As already mentioned, Fardy had been in and out of prison for over a decade after his debt collecting business folded, and Bourke and Royale had similarly long lists of convictions. Moreover, many returned to crime after a

The Prisoners' Rights Organisation | 81

stint of activism with the PRO. Fardy, who, while he was the secretary of the PRO, told a journalist that he often fantasised about committing the perfect crime, was convicted of driving the getaway car for a bank robbery in 1979.[97] In the late 1980s Royale was sentenced to four years for robbing a Cash and Carry shop in Wexford and an additional two years for planning to kidnap a Limerick jeweller in 1985.[98] Other former prisoners had had less prominent careers and were more akin to 'the unfortunates' that Fardy mentioned as making up the majority of the people who consulted his COP information bureau.[99] Many rank and file members of the PRO found their way into the organisation through repeated, and often intergenerational, trauma. One such member was Michael Donnelly, who attended PRO marches in the early 1980s. Donnelly grew up in Monto, a working-class area of Dublin's north inner city. His father, who had himself been traumatised during his time at the Marlborough House juvenile detention centre, was physically abusive throughout his childhood. At the age of five, Donnelly was raped for the first time by a man who ran a local Catholic youth club.[100] This abuse continued for eight years until his father sent him away to sea at the age of thirteen.[101] By the age of seventeen, Donnelly was regularly using opiates, initially Diconal and later heroin, to cope with the trauma, and this led him into conflict with the law. In 1980, at the age of eighteen, he was sentenced to six months in St Patrick's for assaulting a garda.[102] The following year, he was sentenced to three years in the adult prison in Mountjoy, and he spent the next fifteen years in and out of Mountjoy, Arbour Hill, Portlaoise, and Limerick Prisons.

From his first moments in St Patrick's, Donnelly found that imprisonment was a traumatising, and re-traumatising, experience: 'When I went in the doctor said to me "drop your trousers and bend over and cough" and to me that didn't make sense. You know, like, if you're doing an examination you put a stethoscope to your chest, you don't bend over or cough and he's looking up your bum. It's very perverted, well I felt it was, as someone who was coming from trauma. That triggered the ghosts of the past'.[103] It quickly became clear that the prison itself was a dangerous and violent place. He found that the prison officers sought to intimidate prisoners and push them to their psychological limits. Donnelly, at the time, had trouble regulating his reactions due

82 | Prisoners' Bodies

to his past trauma. He also felt like the 'new kid on the block', because it was his first time in prison, and that all the other prisoners were watching him for weakness.[104] Eventually, he lashed out at a prison officer. This heightened the cycle of institutional violence and reaction. He spent prolonged periods in the B Base solitary confinement cells, forced to exercise with his hands cuffed behind his back. Donnelly described how, during this time, officers would bang their batons threateningly as he walked past them to the wing's toilets to empty his 'piss pot' in the mornings, they would hose him down with cold water in his cell in the middle of winter, and they would keep him waiting for days before giving him the methadone that he needed. Donnelly also recalls that the prison officers would often inflict extreme violence on prisoners: 'I think the final straw for me was getting batings, constantly getting batings, constantly dragged out of the cell, constantly being bet'.[105] Prison officers would often wear balaclavas during these punishment beatings so they could not be reported to the governor by name. Donnelly also remembered that some officers in Mountjoy would go to The Hut, a pub in Phibsboro, on their dinner break only to return drunk and violent. In one particularly vicious attack, Donnelly claims, a group of officers pulled him out of his cell and beat him until he fell to the ground, then one of the officers sexually assaulted him with a brush handle.[106]

Prison officers were not the only enforcers of prison discipline. Donnelly found that the prison medical officers could function as part of the prison's disciplinary system as well. Having been identified as a 'difficult prisoner', Donnelly was put on regular doses of the anti-psychotic medication Largactil, which was often used as a sedative in many mid- and late twentieth-century institutions. He was also sent by the prison medical officer to 'the drum' (the CMH) and the Richmond Hospital, where he was given electro-convulsive treatment.[107] According to Donnelly, the medical officer would also use the padded cell as punishment. He remembers the doctor sending him to the padded cell for four days at a time and if he acted aggressively when the cell door was opened the doctor would, without examination, say 'you can stay for another day, and another day, and another day'.[108] Like many others, Donnelly used self-harm to cope with the tension, violence, and his own unresolved trauma. However, Donnelly claims that even this was weaponised against him. When I interviewed him, he described being brought to the prison medical officer to have a wound on his forearm sewn up, and he said that the doctor threatened, '"I'm going to leave you with a scar you'll never forget" and he put the stitches in so wide apart that it left me with a horrific scar'.[109] Since then, Donnelly has been able to cover many of his wounds with tattoos, but the large jagged scar that the prison doctor left is still prominent decades later and, looking at it during our interview, he reflected, 'I have to live with that' and 'May god forgive them, they were animals'.[110]

In 1983, when he was released from Mountjoy for the first time, Donnelly knew a few people from his local area who were involved with the PRO. As well as his violent treatment, due to the Largactil he had been given by the prison medical officer, Donnelly's weight had more than doubled to twenty-five stone while he was in Mountjoy. So, when he got out, he went to the PRO office on Buckingham Street, a few roads away from where he lived, to discuss his situation. The PRO took Donnelly's accusations extremely seriously and introduced him to a writer from *Magill Magazine*. *Magill*, under the editorship of Vincent Browne, had published a number of important exposés of institutional abuse in Ireland in the late 1970s and 1980s, and in 1983, they discussed writing another one about how Donnelly had been treated – perhaps following on from the article about the life of Karl Crawley which had been published the previous year. However, in the end, Donnelly decided not to go ahead with the article for his own safety. 'At that time I had a charge, and I knew if I had to go back into prison after doing an article I'd be vindicated but I wouldn't be able to do my time. They'd be coming at ya, and that's the way they do, they come at ya once you go against ... If the system gets its hand slapped, then you get a hand slap, and they'll never forgive ya'.[111]

Donnelly was, in many ways, a typical member of the PRO – trapped in a cycle of trauma, social deprivation, and imprisonment. He did not have prior political convictions, and he gravitated towards the PRO because it was one of the few organisations that took his experiences seriously and which sought to represent people like himself.

Throughout the 1970s and into the early 80s the PRO commanded a strong support base, particularly among former prisoners, their friends, and families. However, this support base was relatively fluid,

84 | Prisoners' Bodies

and many activists drifted into the group for a short time before moving on to other things, while others, like Donnelly, engaged with the organisation episodically as they moved in and out of prison. There are no extant membership lists of the organisation, so estimating its exact strength and changing composition is challenging. However, between May 1973 and May 1974, they took in £17.75 in membership fees, suggesting that they had as many as seventy-one active members (regular membership being 25p), a further £44 was being taken in associate members' donations ('for people who are sympathetic but who cannot be fully involved' but are willing to donate at least £1), and they had sold 2,647 copies of their magazine *Jail Journal*.[112] By 1976–77, their membership had grown significantly, with their membership fees and donations totalling £102, and they sold more than eighty-seven hundred copies of *Jail Journal*.[113] By 1979, they were regularly selling two thousand copies of each bimonthly issue of the magazine.[114] The PRO's regular protests were generally attended by about a hundred marchers and occasionally many more. This may not seem terribly big, but it compares favourably with the regular marches organised by other groups, including Official Sinn Féin, Macra na Feirme (a farmers' organisation), and public service unions.[115] The support base that came to the marches was firmly rooted in the prisoners' families and friends, and photos of their protests feature children carrying slogans like 'the Gardaí murdered my daddy'.[116] Beyond the people who came to the protests, the PRO fostered support among a wide array of groups. In the winter of 1976–77, they attempted to organise a conference for prisoners' representative organisations from Europe and America.[117] This international conference does not seem to have come to fruition, but they were much more successful when organising support among Irish civil society organisations. In 1977, they were able to present a petition for a full inquiry into the prison system to the Dáil. The petition had been signed by over ten thousand people and it was accompanied by a list of organisations that had passed motions supporting the petition, including urban district councils in Letterkenny (County Donegal), Carrickmacross (County Monaghan), Midleton (County Cork), Youghal (County Cork); the Waterford and Wexford councils of trade unions; and even the culturally and politically influential Gaelic Athletic Association.

A Passive Voice?

Up until now, this chapter has focused on how the organisation communicated. Initially, these communications took the form of institutional pickets, then later, high-profile legal battles. At the same, the PRO elaborated the details of its message through the *Jail Journal* and press conferences. I have also discussed the membership of the organisation – a mixture of experienced civil rights campaigners and former prisoners. In this section, I will look in more detail at what exactly the PRO was communicating, the narratives they were creating, and how those narratives were received by different groups.

In its first months, the PRO represented itself, in many ways, as an adjunct of the PU, and much of the organisation's energy went into conveying the radical agency of the organised prisoners as a means of emphasising their relatability and the reasonableness of their demands. Their message is encapsulated in the editorial that opened the very first issue of *Jail Journal*: 'The union leaders have been beaten up, put in solitary, threatened and promised a soft time if they give up the union. All this has failed, as the attempts to break up ordinary trade unions failed in the old days, and for the same reasons; the prisoner [sic] have genuine grievances and are ready to fight for them'.[118] This sentiment was echoed throughout the first issues of the *Jail Journal*. An article about protests in Mountjoy stated 'the vast majority of prisoners who are engaged in the protests are intelligent, non-violent, and are of good behaviour'.[119] This was supported in articles by prisoners, like 'How to Win Friends' which described how a prisoner-activist, Richard Power, benevolently gamed the system in Portlaoise to have another prisoner transferred to Limerick Prison to be closer to his family.[120] This language of agency was reinforced in other articles of the period, for instance, an article about prisoners' mental health issues called 'The Good Life' in which a former prisoner describes some of the people he met during his brief spell in Portlaoise, including one man who was 'serving ten years and he has fought hard to maintain his sanity'.[121]

During late 1973 and 1974 there was a subtle, but significant, shift in the language used by the *Jail Journal*. The articles gradually moved from describing what prisoners did in prison to describing things that happened to prisoners. To see this, we may compare an article about Daingean Reformatory in the first issue of the journal in 1973 and another on the conditions for visiting prisoners in an issue of the journal published at the end of 1974. While both articles focus on the treatment of the inmates in the two institutions, the article about Daingean repeatedly expresses the kind of limited, and often transgressive, agency the inmates were able to enact; for instance, 'After twelve months in the bake-house I asked (Lewy the Lip [the prefect]) for a job in the air', or 'We were going mad for a smoke, so we decided to get into the Beak's office [to steal cigarettes]'.[122] By contrast, the article about visiting conditions hardly contains a trace of this agency and at times actively negates it: 'He is powerless'.[123] This sense of powerlessness pervades the *Jail Journal* from 1974 onwards, both in articles by and articles about prisoners. An article called 'Working Parole', for instance, described the attempts by a prisoner, in the final three months of his sentence, to be granted day release from the prison to find a job.[124] An overwhelming sense of impotence pervaded the article, which described a litany of rebuffs from different offices of the prison service until the welfare officer finally became involved and he was able to apply for work outside the prison. However, once he had made this application, the welfare officer ignored him, leaving him once again powerless to effect anything, 'I left everything in his [the welfare officer's] hands. After that for the next five and a half weeks I had to serve I had no more contact with Welfare Officer O'Brien, or any other Welfare Officer. I was not told the result of the job details he was supposed to follow up'.[125]

Another article from the same year, called 'Sub-Citizens', describes how a prisoner 'loses his identity as a human being and a citizen of the State'.[126] The article went on to encourage members of the PRO in prison to request copies of the prison rules, which they were legally entitled to, and when the request was denied or the prisoners victimised, they should contact the PRO 'immediately'.[127] By the mid-1970s, the PRO's new message was clear: prison makes a person into an 'unwilling recluse', it strips them of any power, and sometimes even of their agency, but their powerlessness is deserving of sympathy and compassion and the PRO will act on their behalf.[128] By 1975, in an internal document, they described the function of the organisation: '(Since)

Prisoners (~~were~~) are refused the right to act on their own behalf or to demand their own rights. We therefore believe(~~d~~) that it (~~was~~) is necessary for people outside prisons to act (~~on their behalf~~) for them'.[129] By this time, even former prisoner-activists who did not identify themselves with this narrative of powerlessness were reinforcing it, seeing themselves as the exception that proves the rule. Michael Fardy, for instance, in his interview with the *Sunday Independent*, bragged to the journalist about 'the games he has played' with the prison system and how his personal discipline made him a match for the system but concluded that 'in the ideal society, the only people in prison would be people like me. I meet the unfortunates in COP [the PRO's advice bureau] every night of the week and believe me, they are no match for the system. And prison can't cure them because they have no alternative'.[130]

The narrative of prisoners' powerlessness became even more pronounced in relation to prisoners with mental health issues. We can compare the comment about a prisoner fighting to 'maintain his sanity', referred to earlier, in an article from 1973, with the lack of agency expressed in a comparable article from early 1975: 'I can only say, God keep him sane'.[131] Indeed, from late 1973 onwards, prisoners' lack of agency and their mental health were inextricably intertwined in the PRO's discourse. The first signs of this can be seen as early as October 1973, the dying days of the PU, when the inquest was held into the suicide of Joseph Kavanagh. The PRO aimed to use it to assign blame for the death to the prison service and the Department of Justice. As a result, their reporting of the inquest represented Kavanagh being helplessly buffeted by institutional forces. In fact, a *Jail Journal* article which followed Kavanagh's story from his time as an inpatient in a psychiatric hospital to his death in Mountjoy mentions twenty-four intentional actions and inactions, only three of which could be construed as Kavanagh's own decisions, the rest were taken by doctors, Gardaí, prison officers, and others. The article was full of language that removed Kavanagh's agency ('[he was] obliged to discharge himself from the hospital') and invested it in the prison system ('the prison authorities ... [had] final responsibility for his welfare').[132] Of the three intentional actions/inactions that were attributed to Kavanagh, one was his original crime and the other two were to comply with prison discipline, emphasising his docility: 'He was quiet and reserved and made no fuss'.[133] Even Kavanagh's eventual suicide was stripped of any vestige of agency and represented as the inevitable outcome of the prison system's treatment.

By 1975, this tendency had become even more pronounced. When discussing the death of John Donnellan, for instance, the *Jail Journal* reported that the prison officers and other witnesses at the inquest convinced the court that 'the deceased was weak, unable to cope and so to find a way out he committed suicide'.[134] The PRO, however took a different stance and claimed that the court should have found it to be 'death by neglect of his jailers, while he was alone in a cell in an overcrowded and ill-equipped prison', thereby even removing the limited, desperate, agency of suicide from Donnellan's story.[135] The PRO's tactic, however, was quite successful. Offering a structural critique which was embodied by the narrative of individual people made blameless by their lack of agency caught the imagination of the press. The Irish newspapers published headlines like 'Prisons Exposed by Suicides', 'Momentum Added to Prison Reform Campaign', 'Psychiatric Care "Needed in Jails"', and even papers that were largely hostile to reform, like the *Irish Independent*, ran headlines like 'Suicides Blamed on Conditions: Death-Wish Prisons Rapped'.[136]

To illustrate this discursive shift, we can compare a newspaper article from 1971, which describes the life story of a twenty-nine-year-old man, Anthony O'Reilly, and an article about Karl Crawley from 1976.[137] There are clear parallels between the two men's stories, both had impoverished childhoods in troubled single parent families. Both had youths that were marked by institutionalisation and violence. Both had lived for a time in the UK. Both were engaged in regular, albeit comparatively petty, crime and had spent a significant portion of their lives in prison. Both were in their late twenties when the stories were written. The 1971 story, 'When Home Is Behind Bars ...', discusses O'Reilly's childhood, first imprisonments, and how his time in Reading Detention Centre in England nearly 'drove him to suicide', and indeed the article discussed how suicide attempts were common in the centre.[138] Although it discusses how O'Reilly was shaped by his difficult childhood, it emphasises, wherever possible, the positive influence that institutionalisation had on him; for instance, being coached in athletics by the Christian Brothers in the Artane Industrial School

The Prisoners' Rights Organisation | 89

and being taught to operate machinery in borstal. It also emphasises his decisions: 'I got this job in a factory', '[He] kept up athletics ... he got into a fight with his mother's husband ... he was "fed up" with life in England, so he borrowed money from a priest and arrived in this country'.[139] In doing so, it highlights O'Reilly's agency.

By comparison, a 1976 article about the court case, which centred on Karl Crawley, discusses many of the same aspects of his life, but it is structured by the PRO's narrative of the passive victim. For example, Crawley's case is framed by innocuous passive phrases like 'It is claimed on his [Crawley's] behalf', 'he was entitled to be protected' and 'the obligation that the authorities felt was their duty to prevent him from injuring himself'. While these clauses may be unobtrusive on their own, taken together, and with countless more like them, they form the picture of a person who cannot be trusted to, or simply cannot, speak or act for themselves. Even the occasions where Crawley's actions are alluded to, the incidents are either from his early childhood or they were immediately dismissed as symptoms of his mental illness: 'He was undoubtedly a sick man ... he could accidentally seriously harm himself'.[140] Even Crawley's 'protest against authority' was dismissed as 'his condition'.[141]

Conclusion

By the mid-1970s, a new discursive framework had emerged in which the prisoner is a passive subject, shaped by irresistible social forces on the outside and now powerlessly buffeted about by the authoritarian forces within the prison. Due in no small part to the constant pressure from the PRO, by 1976, this framework had come to dominate how the press in Ireland decoded information and activities within the prison system and then recoded them for the public. There was no area where this was more apparent than when discussing prisoners' mental health, self-harm, or suicide. However, in the next chapter we will see that this passive narrative contrasted sharply with the forms of transgressive agency available to prisoners.

3

'A Project against Authority'

A Microhistory of Karl Crawley's Disruptive Autonomy

Introduction

Working with the history of late twentieth century prisoners poses an interesting methodological problem. The surviving administrative minute books, officials' papers, and prisoner records, which are the backbone of so much excellent nineteenth century history, are closed to us by data protection and official secrets legislation.[1] Moreover, the published material is limited. The state is forbidden from commenting on individual prisoners lives and conditions except in rare circumstances. The prisoners themselves were forbidden to communicate directly with the press, and in chapter 1 we saw how seriously this rule was taken in the case of Noel Lynch and Daniel Redmond whose letter in the *Irish Press* on behalf of the Prisoners' Union (PU) landed them in the Curragh Military Detention Barracks for several years. Indeed, even tracking down the names of prisoner-activists, other than the very few who announced themselves to the public, can be impossible. The result of this is that the prisoners' narrative in this period is usually distorted by repeated decoding/recoding by the Prisoners' Rights Organisation (PRO), as the only organisation at the time that purported to speak for and in the voice of prisoners. These recoding events happened as the PRO processed the message and reframed it within their totalisation of the penal reform movement. In chapter 2 we saw that, after the collapse of the PU, the narrative of prisoners' experience that the PRO created was one of largely passive victimhood. In a sense, both the prison authorities and the PRO produced public representations of the prisoners as docile subjects who, on all but a very few occasions, lacked agency within the disciplinary machine of the prison. This chapter will use the case of Karl Crawley to challenge this representation of prisoners' inactions and demonstrate that the PRO's decoding/recoding of Crawley's activities effectively elided his own form of disruptive autonomy.

In the mid-1970s, Crawley, then a man in his mid-twenties with a long history of both incarceration and mental health issues, took a series of court cases against the Irish state, arguing that the conditions of his imprisonment amounted to torture. The PRO took up his case and pressed a similar passive victim narrative to the one they used in the cases of Kevin Kenna, John Donnellan, and others, as discussed in chapter 2. However, Crawley's case centred on questions about his long-term mental health and his historic treatment in various institutions. His application to the European Commission of Human Rights (ECHR) and the High Court generated nearly five hundred pages of psychiatric and medical reports, official records of Crawley's behaviour, descriptions of his daily routine, and legal debates.[2] As a result, the court documents offer a more comprehensive portrait of his life and treatment than any other ordinary prisoner in Ireland in this period. What clearly emerges through this documentation is the story not of a passive victim but of a troubled but determined person pursuing a decade-long 'project against authority'.[3]

The PRO's Campaign for Karl Crawley

As discussed in chapter 2, the cluster of incidents of self-harm and suicide in custody in mid-1975 sparked a wave of activism and gave the PRO a new focus on mental health in prisons. The campaign pushed Karl Crawley into the public eye – the PRO held a press conference with Bernadette Crawley, Karl Crawley's mother; picketed a court

92 | Prisoners' Bodies

when Crawley was on trial; and supported his legal battles.[4] As the campaign developed, newspapers began to report on Crawley's trials, his transfer to Meath Hospital after swallowing dangerous objects, and other incidents that he was involved in.[5] The following year, the press widely reported that Crawley, with the aid of the PRO, took a High Court case to be released from Mountjoy. During the case, the medical director of psychiatry at the Eastern Health Board, Dr. Brian McCaffery, gave evidence that Crawley 'is not able to resist his impulsive actions ... whenever he is confronted with what he would interpret as authority figures getting at him'.[6]

The narrative that the PRO created about Crawley's time in prison seems to have been instrumental in bringing his case to the public's attention and setting the tone of the media's reports. The PRO's representation of Crawley as a passive body can be seen in how his story was told in the PRO's *Jail Journal*. The *Journal*'s anonymous writer was very sympathetic to Crawley, but the case was framed in a patronising way. The *Journal* regularly made a point of referring to the court cases being taken 'on behalf of Karl Crawley'.[7] The few references to Crawley acting independently are couched in language that undermines his agency; for instance: 'Karl Crowley [*sic*] is a mentally disturbed young man who has made 17 suicide attempts and has succeeded in doing severe damage to his whole body. Yet he is arrested, brought before the courts and judged as if he were a citizen fully capable of knowing right from wrong'.[8] By contrast, the courts would later hear from Dr. McCaffery, the medical witness for Crawley's legal team, that he was fully capable of knowing right from wrong, a claim not disputed by the doctors at Mountjoy or Dundrum.[9] In spite of this evidence, the PRO persisted in representing Crawley as a passive victim and any apparent agency as a function of the 'mental disturbance' of 'a very sensitive man'.[10]

Although the newspaper coverage of Crawley's case peaked in 1975 and 1976, he went on to make two further applications to the High Court and made a submission to ECHR, alleging that his treatment in the Irish prison system amounted to 'inhuman or degrading treatment'.[11] Ultimately Crawley's application to the ECHR was rejected on the procedural grounds that he had not exhausted 'domestic remedies' before applying to the court.[12] This decision rested on two points. The first was that Crawley had not appealed Justice Finlay's High Court judgement to the Supreme Court. While Crawley's legal team argued that this was because by the time the judgment was made, Crawley had already been released from prison and that the short, but regular, sentences that marked out Crawley's time in prison made appeals to the highest courts impractical.[13] The second point on which the decision rested was that in his submission to the ECHR Crawley had introduced a new charge which had not been addressed by the domestic courts, namely that while incarcerated, Crawley had been excessively medicated, receiving thirty-five to forty pills a day, in order to keep him docile.[14]

These legal cases were important battles for the PRO, both in terms of public opinion and in challenging the state to reconsider its position. However, the passive narrative they constructed around them in the public press contrasted sharply with the agency expressed through Crawley's own personal, life-long battle against authority.

Karl Crawley's Early Life

Karl Alexander Crawley was born in April 1952, the eighth of twelve children, one of whom died aged just two years old from tuberculosis and one of whom was raised by his aunt.[15] Karl's parents married at sixteen and lived in Ballybough, a working-class area of north inner city Dublin. His father, Larry, was a haulier who lost his business to drink. He moved to England when Karl was an infant and divorced Karl's mother.[16] Karl later told a journalist 'Ma had been dealt a tough hand – and she played it'.[17] As a single mother of eleven living children in Ireland in the 1950s, Bernadette Crawley struggled to keep her head above water. She was a heavy drinker throughout Karl's youth and at one point the family had to squat in a shed.[18] To cope with the situation, Bernadette regularly placed her children in the care of orphanages. When interviewed by McCaffery, Karl did not remember ever living with his mother as a child. One of Karl's first memories was of his older brother, Mick, being unconscious for two days after a beating by a staff member at the Bird's Nest, an orphanage in the South Dublin town of Dun Laoghaire. The brothers were eventually taken out of the Bird's Nest when Karl, then six years old, contracted blood poisoning from severe bruising and cuts on his chest and legs, no explanation for this was offered but it was implied that it was the result of punishment for being 'wild'.[19] He later reflected that he had 'nothing to show for [his time in the Bird's Nest] except scar tissue'.[20] Having spent some time in hospital, he moved home to his mother for a few months. After a while, his mother found that she couldn't cope and Karl was sent to another orphanage, this time it was St Philomena's Home in Stillorgan, which Karl later described as 'ten times worse [than the Bird's Nest] ... the nuns used to batter you'.[21] The psychiatrist who assessed Karl before his High Court application in 1977 identified three events that happened in St Philomena's which he believed were central to Karl's development.

The first happened when Karl was eight or nine years old and one of his friends, Paddy Andrews, died. Karl believed that Paddy had been beaten to death by one of the nuns. He was terrified, believing that he had been 'ten times wilder' than Paddy and that if he stayed put he was going to face the same fate. He escaped over the wall and made his way to Stillorgan village, where he asked a man how to find the bus stop. The man recognised his uniform and brought him to his home for tea and quietly called for the Gardaí to pick him up. It was Karl's first encounter with the Gardaí. Karl was later told that Paddy had died of an untreated burst appendix, and, while he accepted the explanation, Gene Kerrigan, a journalist who interviewed Crawley in the 1980s, recalled that, years later, 'Karl would talk about how they had killed his pal Paddy Andrews'.[22] His psychiatrist concluded that this event had become the cornerstone of his belief that 'the battle with authority was, in fact, a matter of life and death'.[23]

The second event happened when he was ten years old. He had stolen a pound from the tailor's room of the school, and Karl, his brothers, and his friend were beaten in punishment. The nun administered the beating with a hurley, a metre-long stout stick made of ash used to play hurling. During the beating, the nun broke the arm of one of the younger members of the group. Crawley decided to avenge his young friend's injury and when he arrived in the basement for his beating, 'she [the nun] was like a fucking vampire with her teeth. I just went off my head and gave her a bang with a poker over the head. She fell to the ground groaning. I was in two minds whether to finish it off – so I just went upstairs to bed'.[24] The next day he expected to be killed but he actually only got, in his own words, 'a few clatters'. The psychiatrist concluded that this event became the cornerstone of another belief that would shape his entire life, namely, 'that if you hit back hard enough at Authority [sic] figures the chances are that they will not retaliate and, therefore, you will come out on top'.[25]

A little while after the poker incident, Karl was playing with some friends on a merry-go-round and someone threw a sewing machine bobbin at him. He ducked and the bobbin broke a window. Karl would not give the name of the person who threw the bobbin, so he got the blame for breaking the window. At the age of ten, he was expelled from St Philomena's. This, McCaffery concluded, in conjunction with the poker incident, reinforced the idea that 'authority is arbitrary in meting out punishment'.[26]

After what Karl described as 'nearly four years [and] four thousand beatings by this frustrated savage order of kindly women', St Philomena's sent Karl back to his mother.[27] After three weeks she tried to return him to the home but the nuns refused to take him back: 'They gave me 6/- at the door and sent me to St Vincent's in Glasnevin'.[28] Although it has since been obliquely implicated in the network of abuse outlined in the Ryan Report on institutional child abuse, St Vincent's was a well-respected school in the early 1960s serving both day pupils from the surrounding area and 'boarders', like Karl.[29] He remained at St Vincent's, where, Gene Kerrigan wrote, Karl was sexually abused by one of the Christian Brothers, for a year and a half.[30] Karl ran away from the orphanage, pausing only to 'slash hack, tear and piss' on one of the Brother's beds before he left.[31] Refusing to go back to the school, he had to sleep rough until he could find a job and his mother allowed him back into the family home, he was twelve years old and thought 'now was the time to face the world'.[32]

Karl's first job was sweeping a factory floor in a repurposed church. He lost it when the boss asked him to clean his car. Crawley, then twelve years old, wanted to impress him and do a good job so he used Vim, a scouring powder which, unbeknownst to Karl, stripped the paint off the Jaguar.[33] When he saw what had happened, the manager struck Karl in the face. Karl, thinking that the anger was understandable but that physical violence just 'wasn't on', kicked back, called him a 'baldy spine', and never went back.[34] When he was thirteen, he pretended to be sixteen and got a job working on an Esso petrol delivery truck. It was his longest lasting job, but after nine months he was laid off when the lorry drivers did a 'productivity deal' with the company.[35] Karl told MacCaffery, 'I loved that job, going up and down the country – I could not take another job after that'.[36] Over the next few years, he held a string of short-term jobs. His mother insisted that he supplement the income from these with what she called his 'free' – a certain amount that he had to steal each weekend or she would not allow him into the house. Karl's younger brother, Tommy, also recalled his mother sending him down to the supermarket every day with a 'shopping list' of groceries to steal.[37] Karl was athletic and he specialised in vaulting over shop counters and making off with the contents of the till, though his brother remembers that he 'wasn't a great robber ... if he done something he got caught ... he was just bad at it'.[38] It was at this time, aged twelve, that Karl received his first convictions, resulting in a two year suspended sentence for housebreaking in Ireland and a month in a police cell, being too young for prison, for an assault on the Isle of Man.[39]

It was in this period that Karl began using drugs recreationally. The drug scene in Ireland in the mid-1960s and early 1970s mainly consisted of stolen pharmaceuticals, particularly amphetamines and sleeping tablets.[40] Karl liked them both. He recalled that he would go to the pub with his mother before dinner, she would drink three pints and he would drop four Mandrax, hypnotic sleeping pills. In 1967, aged fifteen, he spent a week in Dr Steevens' Hospital, Dublin, after an overdose.[41]

'My Right to Resist'

In 1969, at seventeen years old, Karl was arrested for housebreaking and committed to St Patrick's for the first time. Between January of 1969 and December of 1977, he was committed to prison sixteen times and spent four out of every five months inside.[42] In that time, he accrued a fifteen page long 'curriculum vitae' (CV), the list of incidents that prisoners' are involved in during their incarceration. By 1978, he had been declared insane twelve times by the prison medical officer and transferred to the Central Mental Hospital (CMH) in Dundrum. He was first diagnosed as a psychopath nine months into his first sentence at St Patrick's, after an incident where he climbed onto the roof of the institution. He returned to St Patrick's three months later labelled 'a psychopath but not insane'.[43] This back and forth to 'the Drum' continued until 1976.[44] At one point, he was being sent so regularly that transportation from the Mountjoy campus to the CMH came to be known as the 'Crawley Bus'.[45] He was often transferred with different diagnoses, including schizophrenia, manic depression, psychopathy, and sociopathy, but his committal notes are clear that his main problem was his uncontrollability. For instance, the notes made on several of his committals refer to him as 'terribly aggressive, abusive, uncontrollable, threatening Officers and other prisoners ... assaulted an officer ... Had to be restrained ... manic depressive'.[46] During his longest spell in the Drum, four months in 1971, Crawley climbed onto the roof of the hospital twice, once with the intention to 'denude it of slates' and once to protest against his continued detention in the hospital and to demand his return to Mountjoy. Later, during that same stint at the hospital, he set fire to his own cell.[47] McCaffery later wrote that the CMH was not set up for sociopathic patients like Crawley and he could not take part in many of the therapies offered there. As a result, his treatment was largely medication-based and McCaffrey described it as keeping 'him in a chemical straight-jacket for months or whatever time it was, and once it was taken away he comes back [to Mountjoy] as the same Karl Crawley.' Crawley himself described how the drugs 'made me like a bloody animal'.[48]

While in prison and the CMH, Crawley also regularly swallowed dangerous objects, including batteries, bits of radiators and radios, broken bed springs, and cutlery. His CV, submitted to the ECHR, records thirteen incidents of swallowing objects between 1969 and 1977, although this is not a full picture and his barrister at the ECHR submitted that he had undergone more than nineteen surgical interventions at either the Mater or Meath Hospital to remove swallowed objects (see figure 3.1).[49] As early as 1973, his surgeons warned that his stomach was so scarred and damaged that it would be dangerous to attempt further operations. Nonetheless, he continued to swallow objects and

98 | Prisoners' Bodies

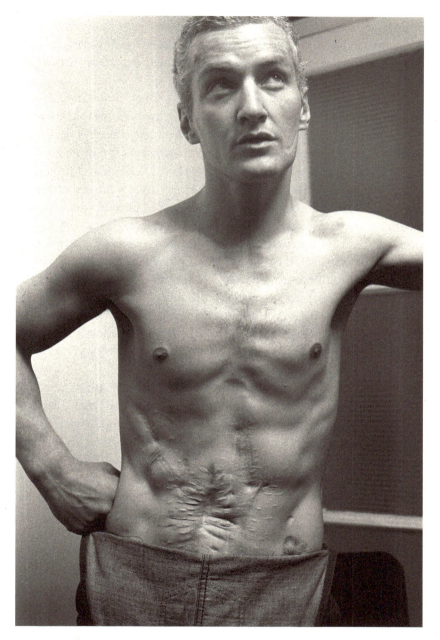

Figure 3.1 Karl Crawley showing some of the scars left by his numerous operations, Dublin, 1982.

emergency surgery was attempted, with two further warnings from surgeons recorded in 1974 and 1975.[50] At least seven of the operations happened after his surgeon stated, in November 1974, that further operations would be impossible.[51]

His CV recorded five escape attempts, although both Crawley and the prison authorities agreed the real number was closer to thirteen.[52] Some of these were elaborate plots, for instance, the time he made what officials referred to as 'an extraordinarily realistic model of a ... pistol' from a paperback book called *Yoga and Religion* and used it to hold three officers hostage and force them to unlock the cell of one of his four co-conspirators before a prison officer tackled him and put an end to the escape attempt.[53] On other occasions it was opportunistic, like the time he tried to escape in a stolen Garda car. Still other attempts demonstrated his desperation and 'an extraordinary fear of facing [more] treatment in Dundrum', including the time that he inserted pieces of wire and a biro refill into one of his scars above his left hip so that if he were committed to Dundrum again, he could cut out the wires and use them to pick the locks on the window shutters to escape the hospital. However, the scar became infected and the wires were discovered by the prison medical officer.[54]

Seán Reynolds, a prison officer who knew Karl in the 1970s, recalled, 'He had no fear for his own safety, he just didn't care'.[55] For instance, on six occasions he was recorded climbing onto the roof of the prison. On one occasion he fell thirty feet, breaking his elbow in an attempt to jump from one wing of the prison to the other, while on another occasion he climbed onto the roof of the prison on Christmas Day and spent twenty-eight hours throwing bricks and slates at anyone who moved below.[56] Crawley also set fire to his cell three times. Two of these occasions seem to have been aimed at causing general disruption, but in 1974, he attempted to burn away the Perspex panel covering his window, which was his only source of ventilation, in order to allow fresh air into his cell.[57] Finally, on five occasions he was treated after having cut or stabbed himself, including one occasion when he cut his wrists. When his wrists had been bandaged, he put carpet tacks inside the dressings to cause further damage. In spite of his risk-taking and intentional self-harm, however, his psychiatrists concluded that he had no intention of killing himself and that he had 'never made a real suicide attempt'.[58] Rather, this lifelong antagonism to institutions was what one psychiatrist called 'a project against authority' and what Karl himself referred to, in his unfinished memoir, as 'my life sentence and my right to resist'.[59] His was a campaign to disrupt the order of the prison and to negate the power of the prison authorities over him.

Crawley's legal actions were only the tip of the iceberg; they were the public face of a long and sometimes bloody campaign of ungovernability which was born from the traumatic events in St Philomena's and which he pursued through strategies of manipulation. Sometimes these manipulations were benign. For instance, on one occasion in the mid-1970s, when he had a reputation as a hard man in Mountjoy, he made a deal with a prison officer, called Soldier, that when the governor came in he would come up to Soldier and politely ask for a brush to tidy his cell. Soldier would answer, 'fuck off', and Karl would reply, 'thank you sir' and go back to his cell. The scheme made the officer look good in front of the governor as the tough man that had tamed the infamous Karl Crawley, and Karl got an ounce of tobacco for playing along. But the manipulations were not always so innocent; in 1977, his psychiatrist noted, 'After inflicting injury on a person, including himself, he does not feel any remorse or guilt. He is a bright intelligent young man who can and does manipulate his environment through his behaviour'.[60] Or, as he told Gene Kerrigan in an offhand way, 'Maybe you do the screw [prison officer]. Maybe you damage something', suggesting that for him there was little difference between smashing up furniture and beating prison officers as long as it furthered the manipulation.[61] Sometimes he went for objects, light fittings were a favourite because a governor had once told him they each cost £38 to fix, so he could calculate exactly how much damage he had done.[62] His CV is littered with notes like, 'Did extensive damage to effects and fittings', 'caused destruction of a large quantity of tableware, windows, tables, chairs and lights', and 'he overturned billiard table, swung cue at officers, and smashed light tubes'.[63] The CV also contains records of assaults or attempted assaults such as: 'He grabbed a scissors and attempted to attack an officer', 'assault [on a] Garda' and 'kicked another prisoner in the face'.[64]

'The Punishment Centre, Irish Style'

This 'project against authority' led to severe punishments, but he was willing to take them.[65] On one of the first occasions that he was reprimanded in St Patrick's, when he was just seventeen, the governor put him on a punishment diet (three days on bread and water; four days on bread, water, and porridge; and some more on bread, margarine, and porridge) and then intimidatingly said, 'I bet you never thought there was a place like this.' Karl recalled thinking, 'I can take a thousand times what you can dish out. You're looking at a throwback from a kinky fucking nun factory'.[66] Behind this hardmanship, however, Karl was troubled by the role he found himself in, later writing: 'I'm not the person they see me to be, even if I'm able for all this abuse, things shouldn't be the way they are'.[67]

As his time in prison progressed, his punishments became more extensive, although the exact extent of his privations were a matter of dispute in the courts. By the late 1970s, one of the cells in B Base was always referred to as the 'Crawley Cell'.[68] B Base was Mountjoy's segregation area, usually occupied by around ten prisoners in solitary cells who could not be kept with other prisoners because of their disruptive behaviour, determination to escape, or the danger posed to them by the ordinary prisoners. This final group included the Littlejohn brothers whose suspected betrayal of the IRA to British Security Forces made them deeply unpopular.[69]

When preparing the application to the ECHR, the authorities at Mountjoy recorded the contents and condition of the Crawley Cell and his daily routine. While the description is highly informative, it should be remembered that at that time Crawley had been largely cooperative with the authorities for months and had regained many privileges. The cell itself was twelve feet long, seven feet wide, and nine feet tall.[70] At the end facing the door there was a window three and half feet tall and two and a half feet wide, the glass in two of its six inch by three inch panes was broken and it was covered by a sheet of Perspex with rows of holes drilled in it for ventilation.[71] This is the only ventilation in the cell, as the two wall vents had been plastered over to stop Crawley from hiding things in them.[72] Throughout the mid-1970s Crawley complained that this lack of ventilation was

102 | Prisoners' Bodies

causing severe headaches. Inside the cell, there were two blocks of wood screwed to the floor with four planks nailed to them to form a bed, topped with a rubber mattress; a bookshelf; a plastic chamber pot; and a plastic ice-cream container for fresh water.[73] Throughout 1978, the prison authorities remarked on Crawley's increasing submission to prison discipline and by April of that year, the contents of the cell had grown to include a locker, a chair, a brush, two plastic basins, a set of plastic cutlery, a plastic cup and saucer, a plate and two bowls, a nail brush and soap tray, and two plastic containers for holding tea and water.[74] A radio speaker had been fitted inside the cell which could be controlled by prison officers outside. This precaution was to prevent Crawley from dismantling and eating parts of the radio as he had done in the past.[75] When he was out of his cell, Crawley usually had to wear 'figure of eight' handcuffs, whether he was watching television of exercising.[76] These are handcuffs in which the wrist shackles connect directly to each other without an intervening chain, the result is that the prisoner has an extremely limited range of movement. Crawley told his legal team that it was humiliating to have to wear these around the prison, especially while watching television in the communal area of B Base.[77]

Crawley also alleged that he had been made to wear heavy leg irons while exercising.[78] The government submitted to the ECHR that Crawley had been put in figure of eights because of his ability to climb walls and his multiple escape attempts but that since he had been cooperative for several months this restriction had been lifted in March 1978. They also denied that Crawley had ever been put in leg irons, 'nor have they been used in living memory of any prisoner'.[79] The government's submission also stated that in April 1978, he took part in normal prison work and recreation in a secure yard attached to B Base, although the memorandum from January of the same year stated that he was 'provided with no employment, educational or recreational activities' other than short periods of exercise, which he often refused due to the 'humiliation and degradation' of appearing in front of other prisoners in handcuffs, and short periods in the evening when he was allowed watch television while handcuffed and under the supervision of prison officer.[80] He did not take part in prison education, but the government submission suggested that this was by choice.[81] Karl's psychiatrist suggested that Karl was very bright and would like to partake in education but only if it were provided for his own good and not as part of the prison's disciplinary apparatus.[82]

One of the major bones of contention in the medical evidence given to the ECHR concerned the amount of medication Karl was receiving, some of which had to be forcibly injected.[83] The court was provided with a list of drugs he had received over the years, which included various combinations of painkillers, tranquillisers, antidepressants, antipsychotics, sleeping tablets, antibiotics, and antifungal drugs. The volume of the drugs listed is high but would not have been considered excessive given Crawley's probable increasing tolerance to the prescription.[84] Under examination from Patrick McEntee, Crawley's barrister, the medical officer at Mountjoy, Dr Samuel Davis, explained his use of drugs to the High Court in 1976:

> Davis: Well, we try to sedate him, we keep him at a low level.
> McEntee: Is that for his benefit or the institution's benefit or the benefit of both?
> Davis: For the benefit of everybody.[85]

This approach effectively left Crawley in a 'permanent high', and when he was released from Mountjoy in July 1976, not long after this evidence was given in the High Court, he moved directly into social circles where most people 'were hooked on something'.[86] On his first night out, his friend gave him an intravenous injection of the barbiturate Tuinal, and after that, he recalled, 'Life was a shower of Smarties [Dublin slang for pills after a popular brand of multicoloured, pill sized, chocolates]. Everything from hash to heroin. Tablets, mainlining [intravenous injecting], smoking'.[87]

Crawley believed that his addiction was compounded by the medication regime in the prison, which he claimed was extremely liberal. In his submission to the ECHR, he argued that this list of medications provided by the government was not the whole picture and that he had recently 'been reduced to the "official" level of eight tablets per day from the previous norm of 40–50'.[88] While coming down from the 'permanent high' that he had been in for months, Crawley complained of withdrawal symptoms and requested a drug commonly used in Mountjoy to relieve withdrawal symptoms called Rhiseptone, a tradename of a methadone based painkiller. The prison medical officer, Davis, told him to 'fuck off, you already have me in Strasbourg'.[89] While the government submitted that Crawley had not displayed any withdrawal symptoms, his solicitor, the PRO activist Pat McCartan, noted that he had displayed apparent symptoms during their interviews. Crawley's legal team tried to bring in a doctor from the Eastern Health Board to examine him but they were denied access until a High Court order could be obtained.[90] When McCartan and the doctor finally got to examine Crawley, they found him to be 'very high' and 'in a daze'. He later told McCartan that during the day he had been given twenty-three Distalgesic pain-killers and six Mogodan sleeping tablets by prison officials.[91] Crawley later told Gene Kerrigan that in Mountjoy 'he just had to ask the screws [prison officers] for a couple of Smarties'.[92] McCaffery related Crawley's description of the effects of one drug regimen during a particularly bad four-month period at the CMH in 1972, when he was nineteen years old: 'The drugs kept me in a dreamland and I did not get out of the cell only on visiting mornings. I started to go into a world of my own talking out loud and answering the fellow who was talking. They made me feel like a bloody animal'.[93] Regardless of the volume of drugs, McCaffery disputed the advisability of this kind of treatment regime, even as a way of keeping Crawley docile. He told the High Court that 'Karl is not psychotic and therefore in touch with reality, one can talk with him and get through', so he claimed these drugs would not be necessary in a proper therapeutic environment. Crawley asserted, though the Mountjoy medical officer denied it, that he had become addicted to drugs through this extended treatment.[94] Given the highly addictive nature of benzodiazepines, like Valium, Crawley's claim seems likely to be true, particularly in light of several incidents on his CV when he became violent after not receiving his medication, and on a number of other occasions he was recorded as demanding stronger medication to cope with headaches and the triggering of a traumatic memory of childhood sexual abuse during a cavity search.[95]

Crawley's experience of the world as a network of manipulations, as discussed earlier in the chapter, can be seen in his relationship with the PRO. As I have already discussed, Crawley was the PRO's cause célèbre in 1975, 1976, and 1977. His mother gave a press conference with the group; eight of their activists were arrested outside one of his court appearances; he had given power of attorney to one of its activists, Máirín De Búrca; the organisation had supported his legal battles, and his solicitor, Pat McCartan, had been a founding member of the PRO. However, in the middle of all this, Crawley wrote to McCartan, showing that he perceived their relationship as a manipulation, or what he referred to as 'a con', and in turn he tried to extort the PRO.[96] In the summer of 1976, the top story on the front cover of the *Jail Journal*, the PRO's monthly magazine, was entitled 'PRO & Karl Crawley v The State'. The article briefly laid out Crawley's case and used it to argue for the need for penal reform and for better psychiatric services. Crawley responded, incensed:

> Well Mr Pat McCartan you have really made me mad with
> you so when we meet again you better have some ancers as to
> what is your game [...] I want the person who put that joke in
> it [*Jail Journal*] about me and buy the way now my name is on
> aney employers lips you PRO lot thought you were conning
> me and it amused me to watch how yous played your game but
> yous played a game you knew nothing about and now have left
> yourself wide open for a High Court clame wich I have sent
> in so eather yous look after my family that is Tommy my kid
> brother mother and the baby Neil for rendering me useless, with
> your fast buck method of a story, of getting legal work and legal
> money and so I will have to go back to crime to look after my
> famely thanks to the PRO.[97]

A month later, Crawley was back on remand in Mountjoy. He had broken into the CMH to steal drugs and, in what he later described as a fit of nostalgia, decided to fix inside the grounds of the hospital, where he was arrested.[98] We cannot know whether, when writing the above letter, he was in earnest about 'getting legal work'.[99] It had been ten years since his last job (seasonal work as a kitchen porter on the Isle of Man) and it would be four more years before he found legal employment again. Nor can we know how sincere or feigned his anger was. It may

106 | Prisoners' Bodies

have been influenced by Davis, the medical officer in Mountjoy, who later said that he thought McCartan was only pursuing Crawley's case 'to make a name' for himself.[100] Whatever the motivation, the anger passed fairly quickly as McCartan was once again acting as his solicitor a few months later and the PRO were back campaigning on his behalf.

This was not the last time Crawley tried to use his legal battles in an attempt to extort money. In May 1978, while he was applying to the ECHR, Crawley met with the deputy governor of Mountjoy. During their interview, he suggested that he would withdraw the application if the Department of Justice 'bought his case', by which he meant that the department should buy the sole rights to his proposed book, *The Punishment Centre, Irish Style*.[101] The deputy governor refused.

Conclusion

In the 1980s, Karl Crawley's activities started to 'peter out'.[102] His prison terms became less regular and towards the end of the decade he got married, though the relationship did not last.[103] By the late 1980s he had become dependant on alcohol, as well as barbiturates and other drugs.[104] During a prison medical exam in the 1990s, he received a HIV diagnosis. Karl told his brother that he had not got the virus from using needles, but he told Gene Kerrigan that when he received the diagnosis, he looked back over his years of drug use and thought, 'When you get locked [drunk or high] you get careless'.[105] When he got out of prison, he was left homeless and became a long-term resident in a hostel for the homeless run by a charity called the Simon Community where he lived until his death, from a chest infection, in 1999, aged just forty-seven.

In 1982, when he was trying to 'go straight', Karl joked about writing another book.[106] This time it was an autobiography called *The Last of the Hard Men*. The title is, I believe, a reference to the 1976 Western *The Last Hard Men* in which an escaped prisoner of eleven years leads a violent, and ultimately mutually-destructive, mission of revenge against the man who arrested him. But Crawley went on to say, 'Shit, there's no such thing as a hard man. It's what happens to you that makes you what you are and, well, when it's put up to you, you can't back away from it. There's no glory in that. It makes you do vicious things, it gets vicious things done to you. But that's just the way it is. Where's the choice? ... Look, I didn't set out to be Karl Crawley'.[107]

Crawley's life was shaped by violence and the arbitrary exercise of authority, but he was not a docile subject of that authority. From the moment ten-year-old Karl lashed out with a poker at the nun who had brutalised his friends in St Philomena's Home, he fought to exercise any kind of power over his environment. Sometimes this meant making a bid for freedom, as with his thirteen escape attempts, or forcing the prison to move him someplace else, for instance, by swallowing batteries so that he would be moved to the Mater Hospital. At other times it meant creating chaotic situations in order to deny someone else their power over him, whether they were prison authorities or well-meaning reformers. While the narrative of passive victimhood may have proved to be a successful rhetorical strategy for the PRO when addressing the press and influencing public opinion, the details of Crawley's life demonstrate that it misrepresented a complex agency that he expressed in the most tightly controlled of spaces. He sought to exercise this agency alone against the institution because he believed that 'the individual scares the hell out of them'.[108]

The volume of available documentation on Crawley's life makes his story, as far as can be ascertained, unique among nonpolitical prisoners in this period. However, the medical evidence made it clear that his condition was not unique in Ireland, there were between six and ten people who needed similar care, and that his early life was typical of many men who exhibited 'anti-social behaviour' both inside and outside prison.[109] The narrative of the PRO battling the injustice inflicted on docile bodies in the prison system, as described in chapter 2, may not be as simple as they made it seem. The extreme nature of Crawley's disruptive autonomy may have been exceptional. Nonetheless, it clearly demonstrates that the public narrative propagated by the PRO, while in some sense successfully representing the experience of prisoners, also elided the limited agency that prisoners could exercise.

4

'The Beginning of the End'
Protest, Rioting, and Revenge, 1979–86

Introduction

After its final protest in 1977, the Prisoners' Union (PU) did not re-emerge as a public force, however, this did not mean prisoners stopped exercising their disruptive agency and protesting their conditions. In the late 1970s and early 1980s, prison protests continued but in less coordinated and, often, more violent forms. One of the primary reasons for this was the disintegration of social solidarity and community within prison that accompanied the wave of heroin that hit the streets of Dublin in 1979. This coincided with the collapse of many traditional working-class industries and a stark rise in unemployment from 6 per cent in the mid-1970s to nearly 17 per cent in the mid-1980s. Heroin had previously been considered the preserve of 'quasi-intellectuals' influenced by international ideas and travelling labourers who had been led astray in Britain. But in the early 1980s, it quickly became an unavoidable part of life in many Irish working-class communities.[1] In two years, the number of heroin users rose 600 per cent, and by 1981, eight out of every ten people between the ages of fourteen and twenty were using drugs in some Dublin estates.[2] In 1981, around 11 per cent of ordinary prisoners were categorised as regular drug users; this rose to 30 per cent in 1985.[3]

In 1981, the average daily prison population began a seemingly inexorable rise, increasing by 56 per cent between 1981 and 1985.[4] This represented a more punitive shift in sentencing culture which brought in more people who had been convicted of minor, often drug related, crimes on short sentences, transforming Irish prison culture by upending the prison population's demographics. The first major shift was in the age of prisoners. Throughout the 1970s, less than 60 per cent of people committed to prison were between twenty-one and forty years old.[5] In 1981, the number of people in this age bracket started to increase disproportionately to the rest of the population and by 1985 they made up over 72 per cent of the population.[6] This shift can be seen particularly starkly when we compare the ratio of twenty-one to twenty-five year olds, the youngest age bracket in adult prisons, to the number of people over forty. For every ten people over forty years old committed to prison in 1975 there were sixteen people aged twenty-one to twenty-five; by 1980, that proportion had risen to ten to eighteen, and by 1985, that had risen to ten to twenty.[7] The second shift was in average sentence length. Sentences of less than one year have always made up the majority of committals to prison. For most of the 1970s, they made up around 80 per cent of all committals; between 1981 and 1982, this percentage rose to 88 per cent; and by 1985, it was over 91 per cent.[8] This is indicative of the harsher approach taken to what was perceived to be drug motivated petty crime. The third shift was a sharp rise in the proportion of people with no prior convictions being sentenced to prison. From 1955 to 1979, the average proportion of people committed to prison who had no prior convictions was less than 34 per cent. In the early 1980s, this began to rise, peaking in 1985 at nearly 61 per cent.[9] This sharp rise represents a generation of young people who had not fallen foul of the law before but who, in their twenties, had become involved with heroin and, in turn, criminality. These three trends illustrate the problem faced by the Irish prison system, and indeed the prison population, between 1980 and 1985. The prisons took in a wave of young prisoners in their twenties and thirties, on their first offence, serving short sentences. This was a transitory population with no experience of prison discipline, or the social conventions observed by prisoners, and it posed a serious threat to the social order of the prisons and the prison system as an institution.

Joe Costello, then chairman of the Prisoners' Rights Organisation (PRO), described this period as the 'beginning of the end' of the organisation.[10] Up until that point, the majority of the prison population had been made up of, what were termed, 'ordinary decent criminals', that is to say not involved in drug dealing or use, most of whom had first encountered the law early in life through the industrial school system, had come up through St Patrick's Institution, and had graduated to the adult prison system. They understood the discipline and organisation of the prison and had some sense of solidarity which enabled them to combine into the various iterations of the PU. However, the 1980s brought this structure to an abrupt end. The PRO activists believed that the new generation of prisoners, in contrast to their predecessors, 'lived for drugs'.[11] The result was that the PRO became increasingly disconnected from the prison population. Their contacts inside prisons represented an ever-decreasing part of the prison population, which had different concerns to incarcerated drug users. The result was that prisoners increasingly began to organise their own protests with demands that were specific and local and did not reflect the broader structural reforms demanded by the PU or the PRO. However, the decade of activism by the PU and PRO ensured that in spite of this localism the prisoners' demands continued to be understood, in the public sphere, within what Stuart Hall would call the 'totalization' of general penal reform.

This chapter discusses the tensions between the Prison Officers' Association (POA), the prisoners, and the Department of Justice, which shaped many of the prisoners' protests in this period. It then considers two prisoners' protests, one in Mountjoy in 1979 and one in Arbour Hill in 1986, through which we can see the changing understanding of prison protest. The final section examines the two campaigns in 1979–80 and 1984–85 of the Prisoners' Revenge Group through which former prisoners, dissatisfied with the political lobbying and peaceful protests of the PRO, sought to advance the prisoners demands through violence against prison staff outside prisons.

The Prison Officers' Association

In this section, I examine how a growing militancy among the POA, from 1977 onwards, led to heightened tensions between prison officers and both the Department of Justice and the prisoners themselves.

For the first forty years, since its foundation in 1947, the POA was locked in a perpetual conflict with the Department of Justice, which employed all prison staff at the time. In the late 1960s, the tensions intensified as prison officers' conditions worsened. By 1972, they were routinely obliged to work seventy hour, seven day weeks rather than their contracted forty hour, five day weeks; staff shortages meant that there was often nobody to cover breaks, so officers had to work entire days without eating; and new officers received no training, leaving them unprepared for their role.[12] The prison officers' long-running dispute reached a new level in 1973 when the POA threatened to strike unless the number of officers was increased and working conditions were improved, including a reduction in working hours. This would have been the first prison officer strike in the history of the state.[13] After talks with the Department of Justice in 1973, the POA shelved its planned industrial action, working conditions were improved slightly, and a hiring campaign was set in motion to expand the service. However, the improvements were not enough for the officers and the hiring campaign did not bring in sufficient new recruits to reduce levels of mandatory overtime significantly. As a result, the POA remained on the verge of industrial action over these issues for the rest of the 1970s, periodically coming to the brink of strike before being brought back by talks and small concessions from the Department of Justice. However, on the whole, tensions between the POA and the department remained high.

The POA's disputes with the Department of Justice were not the only source of tensions for the prison officers in the mid-1970s. There was also an intergenerational war within the POA. The younger officers brought in by the 1972 hiring campaign had become increasingly frustrated at the slow progress that the POA had made both in relation to the officer's working conditions and the reform of the prison system.[14] In 1974, Arthur Broomfield, a young officer and the former chairman of the Portlaoise branch of the POA, claimed that he had been unfairly dismissed in a 'purge' of prison officer activists under the pretence that they were who could be considered 'security risks'.[15] He criticised both the POA and the Department of Justice for ignoring the terrible conditions for officers and prisoners in the prisons.[16] Broomfield claimed that he and others had been dismissed for defending 'the rights of his fellow worker' and called on officers to show greater solidarity with prisoner-activists, who, 'like their prison officer counterparts have suffered too much at the hands' of the prison system.[17] He pursued this claim of unfair dismissal in the courts until it was finally rejected by the High Court in 1981.[18] In 1977, the younger officers fought back. Seamus Mac Uardain, who had been the general secretary of the POA since the mid-1960s, was forced to resign by the younger prison officers.[19] Mac Uardain was replaced by Stephen Delaney, who adopted a more militant stance. Tensions between the POA and the Department of Justice intensified through the late 1970s. Full strikes were only narrowly avoided every year between 1977 and 1985, and the POA regularly engaged in industrial action short of a strike. This included picketing the canteen in Limerick Prison to protest its outsourcing to an external company, temporarily closing the workshops at Mountjoy to protest cuts to rehabilitation funding, and numerous work-to-rules protesting pay and conditions. The POA's work-to-rule actions in particular led to fierce animosity between officers and prisoners, who were often left locked in their cells with extremely limited recreation during the disputes. In 1983, the *Irish Press* described it as one of the 'bitterest industrial disputes in recent years', a damning epithet in an era of particularly bitter disputes.[20] In 1985, a new general secretary of the POA, Denis McGrath, was elected and immediately attempted to deescalate the tension with the Department of Justice, telling the association's annual conference: 'I think it is time for both sides to get together and face reality'.[21] While this marked the beginning of a new approach for the POA, it was, by no means, the end of their dispute with the department, which culminated in a bitter strike in 1988.

Throughout the late 1970s and 1980s the Department of Justice's underdevelopment of the prison service and the POA's industrial actions both threatened and realised heightened tensions within Irish prisons. The combination of increasingly overcrowded prison conditions and the infliction of effective solitary confinement on prisoners by the POA's protests turned prisons into what one chief prison officer called 'a time-bomb'.[22]

Prisoner Protest after the PU: Mountjoy, 1979

This 'time-bomb' exploded repeatedly, in the form of prisoner protests and riots, between 1979 and 1985 – in Mountjoy (1979), Arbour Hill (1980), St Patrick's and Mountjoy (1983), Mountjoy (1984), and Cork, Arbour Hill, Mountjoy, and the newly opened Fort Mitchell Prison on Spike Island (1985). This section will focus in particular on a disturbance that occurred in Mountjoy in 1979 which was representative of this broader trend.

In November 1979, tensions in Mountjoy seemed to have subsided from the crux of union activity in 1977 but were still running high. A hiring campaign in the spring of 1979 had increased the number of prison officers and relieved some of the need for excessive overtime, although it failed to reach the target for the net increase in prison staff, and 'substantial overtime was still necessary'.[23] The level of officer training had also increased, in particular a ten week course for new recruits was introduced, including five weeks of classroom work, and the Department of Justice acquired a new dedicated training headquarters.[24] All of these developments were in line with the long-standing demands of both the POA and the PRO, and their implementation served to ease tensions within the prisons. Indeed, the Visiting Committees' report that year remarked that the 'morale of prison staff during the year was for the most part very high'.[25] Although this may betray a degree of bias in the Visiting Committees; in June the POA, supported by the prison governors, voted for industrial action for the first time in the history of the state. The association's demands included the creation of a psychiatric custodial centre in Mountjoy, a pay rise, improvements in prisoner living and staff working conditions, the establishment of an independent inquiry to recommend reforms of the prison system, and the establishment of an independent advisory service that would take the prison system out of the sole control of the Department of Justice.[26] The action was called off after about a week when the Department of Justice agreed to an independent arbitration, relieving some of the tension on the side of the prison staff.[27]

Prisoner morale in Mountjoy was not particularly low at the time, due in part to Pope John Paul II's visit to Ireland. In September, the men in Mountjoy made a leather-bound Bible and carved a Celtic cross, inscribed with 'To Pope John Paul from the Inmates of Mountjoy Prison, Dublin, Ireland', which was to be presented to the pope on their behalf and which caused 'great excitement' in the prison, according to the chaplain.[28] Moreover, around one hundred prisoners on short-term sentences were released in an 'amnesty' to celebrate the visit. This may have improved the morale in some parts of the prison by relieving the problems caused by overcrowding, but, as Joe Costello of the PRO pointed out, it may also have been resented by long-term prisoners who desperately needed 'a break'.[29]

Due to this lower than usual level of tension, when the riot came, as a POA spokesman said, there was 'no warning', which left the prison officers on duty in a very 'vulnerable position'.[30] It began when the 105 prisoners on A Wing were moving from their workshops to collect their supper. The prisoners rushed the twelve officers on duty, forcing them out of the wing. They then barricaded the doors and proceeded to destroy the furniture, take doors off their hinges, and set a small mattress fire. Around two hundred riot-gear-clad Gardaí were called in from nearby barracks and the Dublin Fire Brigade arrived with extra hoses.[31] The Gardaí and prison officers sprayed the prisoners from either end of the wing with the Fire Brigade's hoses. As they advanced through the barricades into the wing and up the gantries in a 'pitched battle', one of the prison officers fell through a hole the prisoners had cut in the upper landing as a 'booby-trap' and two others were chased onto a rooftop from which they fell.[32] The riot only lasted about two hours, but sixty-two people were injured, including thirty-six prisoners and twenty-six prison officers. Twenty-three prisoners and three officers were hospitalised.[33]

The government denied that the riot had been caused by overcrowding and claimed that the prisoners had not given a reason for the riot or 'made any demands'.[34] A POA spokesman told the press that it was a well-planned operation that aimed 'to disrupt the system and ... a number of them [the ringleaders] had the intention of breaking out.[35] The prisons' Visiting Committee similarly blamed the riot on 'a group of "evilly disposed" prisoners who aimed to create anti-prison

Figure 4.1 Rooftop protest over prison conditions at Mountjoy Prison, Dublin, 1984.

propaganda' and who 'coerced other prisoners into joining them'.[36] Moreover, the committee claimed that it had interviewed ten people from the wing the morning before the riot and none of them had complained about anything.[37] The PRO on the other hand claimed that official reports did not 'tally with the real situation'.[38] They claimed that the riot had been sparked by the strip searching of prisoners and by the regular assaulting of prisoners in the basement punishment cells.[39] The organisation held a press conference with former prisoners who described the overcrowding in Mountjoy: 'Many prisoners had to share a cell with one or two others and a large cell nicknamed the 'caravan' accommodated 15 itinerants [a euphemism for members of the Traveller community]'.[40] They also pointed out that although the country's Visiting Committees had written around three hundred reports since their formation, they had only ever included twenty-eight complaints by prisoners and had never upheld any of them.[41] Indeed, some of the prisoners who made the complaints were, apparently, disciplined for making false allegations.[42]

Although short-lived, the riot was a catalyst for changes in the prison system. Despite the denial by the minister for justice that there was an overcrowding problem, four days after the riot he announced the building of three new prisons – one for women and one for juveniles in Clondalkin, County Dublin, and one for juveniles in Cork. These facilities would increase the number of custodial beds for women and juveniles and would enable the department to close St Patrick's and the women's prison on the Mountjoy campus, presumably facilitating the expansion of the Mountjoy men's prison. This plan met with a mixed reaction. The opposition Labour Party accused the minister of looking at the overcrowding problem 'from the wrong end', and both the PRO and the local community in Clondalkin objected fiercely to the creation of the new prisons.[43] Fine Gael, the main opposition party, joked that 'prison construction was becoming an Irish growth industry' but welcomed aspects of the plan.[44] This solution, however, was a long-term one. The minister expected that the prisons would not be built for three years and, in reality, the two Clondalkin prisons, Wheatfield and Cloverhill, were not actually opened until 1989 and 1999, respectively, and the Cork detention centre was never built. In the meantime, overcrowding became a growing issue, and by spring of 1980, the minister for justice had begun to discuss doubling-up, the accommodation of two or more prisoners in single occupancy cells, as an undesirable inevitability in the prison system.[45]

The riot also wrought a change in the POA's relations with the Department of Justice. The association, which had been relatively pacified since the department had agreed to arbitration the previous June, suddenly began to threaten industrial action again. The POA's spokesman, Stephen Delaney, warned the department that, unless it took immediate steps to protect prison officers, the officers would take it on themselves 'to solve the problem'.[46] When asked what steps would be taken, Delaney reminded journalists that officers' overtime was voluntary and that without it there could be no evening recreation time for prisoners.[47] This was simultaneously a threat aimed at the Department of Justice but also at the prisoners themselves. The department needed the POA's support to move forward with their plans to 'improve the educational, medical and general conditions of prisoners', and although the association claimed to back these plans, they could have made them very difficult to implement by embarking on a fresh industrial dispute.[48] The POA's threat reminded prisoners that prison officers could, in essence, impose twenty-three hour solitary confinement on the entire prison population.

The 1979 riot in Mountjoy was, in many ways, a template for the non-PU related prison disturbances in Ireland in the period. It began with underlying tensions, many of which we have already discussed in the introduction and chapter 1. These tensions eventually arrived at a flashpoint, which might otherwise seem innocuous but which set off the unrest. The prisoners' primary concerns were local and specific, but they were understood by prisoners, the prison system, and the press to be part of a much larger totalization of prisoners' protests – the creation of which, by the PU and PRO, we discussed in chapter 3. We can see this in the Visiting Committee's understanding that the riot leaders were attempting to create 'anti-prison propaganda' and the PRO's press conference which connected the riot to the nationwide and perennial problem of overcrowding.[49] From 1972 to 1985, almost every unaligned disturbance in the Irish prison system followed this pattern with a grim inevitability. However, some prisoners had become disillusioned with the possibility of protest inside prison. One such prisoner was Eddie Cahill, who had smuggled out the 'comms' for the PU in the early 1970s and who spent more than two decades in institutions, from Letterfrack to Mountjoy, between the late 1960s and the mid-1990s. However, by the late 1970s, he, like several other prisoners, had become frustrated with the violent reprisals by prison officers against protesters inside the prisons and with the 'soft' approach of the PRO:

There was nothing you could do. You had to do it yourself, and the only way you could do it in the prison was through protest. Then you find out that all you were getting was your head crashed in, beaten up, charged with causing disturbances, so the only way then to fight them was to fight them on the outside …

I used to think, with Joe Costello and the Prisoners' Rights, that he was always going on about education, education, education, and getting books in [to the prison], and I'd be going 'that's a waste of fuckin' time, burn the fuckin' town down.' You know? That was the difference between him and me at the time, that's why he would never let me be a member of his organisation, he kept saying 'Jesus get rid of him.' But I realised then that he was right.[50]

At the end of the decade other ex-prisoners who shared this frustration decided to take more direct action.

Prisoners' Revenge Squad, 1979–86

Riots were not the only form of protest mounted by prisoners and ex-prisoners in the late 1970s and early 1980s. Some former prisoners felt increasingly disillusioned with the PRO's 'political lobbying and penal reform' and suspected that it was growing apart from the prisoners' movement.[51] While this led some to disengage from the organisation, others took matters into their own hands and formed the Prisoners' Revenge Squad (PRS), later referred to as the Prisoners' Revenge Group (PRG).

Attacking prison officers had become a commonplace tactic in Northern Ireland after the 1976 decision to withdraw 'special category status' from paramilitary prisoners. The Provisional IRA (PIRA) considered prison workers to be 'legitimate targets' as members of the security forces, and between 1976 and 1979, a governor, assistant governor, two prison clerks, and fourteen prison officers were killed by the PIRA. These attacks were part of the PIRA's general aim to make the Northern Irish security state untenable. However, there was also an element of revenge for the harsh treatment received by republican paramilitary prisoners. For instance, when the PIRA applied the same tactic in the Republic of Ireland, a bomb planted at a Portlaoise prison officer's home in 1977 came with the note: 'Torturers beware – informers next'.[52] As we will see in this section, this idea of prison officers as the legitimate targets of violent revenge clearly had an impact on the ordinary prisoners' movement.

The first attack occurred in November 1979, on the night of the riot in Mountjoy described earlier in this chapter. Four men in balaclavas broke into a house in Finglas and beat a retired chief prison officer,

Protest, Rioting, and Revenge | 119

Michael Weldon, and his wife with crowbars. When he was released from the hospital, Weldon told the press that the only thing the attackers had said during the attack was 'you are a screw'.[53] He went on to speculate that he may have been targeted specifically because of his son, who was also a prison officer: 'I am no longer a prison officer, but as my son is also in the service, it could have something to do with the riot in Mountjoy'.[54] The *Evening Press* and others interpreted this to mean that Weldon's son may have been involved in the suppression of that night's riot in Mountjoy.[55] However, this would have implied instantaneous communication between the prisoners inside and their comrades on the outside, which seems very unlikely. The press did not raise the prospect at the time, but an alternative reading might be that the attackers believed that Weldon's son was involved in the punishment beatings which the PRO claimed were the cause of the riot.[56] Whatever the motivation behind it, the attack prompted fears of a 'wave' of revenge attacks, as the Gardaí connected it with a recent incident in which a gang followed a garda home and smashed his windows.[57]

Between spring and autumn 1980, the group undertook a campaign of arson and graffiti. The targets of the campaign seemed disconnected, some were loosely related to government functions but others seem to have been chosen out of an underlying bigotry. They included the government stationary warehouse, six public busses, University College Dublin's city-centre campus, and three schools, one for children with disabilities and a Jewish primary and secondary school.[58] Each target was painted with the slogan 'close the Curragh' and was set alight. Years later, one member of the group reflected, 'The Curragh did close ... We're not saying the attacks were the only reason but we were effective'.[59] However, the group's campaign petered out in early 1981, over a year before the Curragh ceased to function as a prison.

While the campaign was ongoing, the PRS, as it named itself in its few public communiques, began physically assaulting prison officers. In mid-July 1980, two prison officers were beaten with an iron bar outside a pub near Mountjoy. Then, on a Sunday at the end of August, the homes of two prison officers and the governor of Loughan House were attacked in one night. Their house windows were smashed; the attackers tried to break down the governor's door; and one of the officer's

120 | Prisoners' Bodies

car windows were smashed, the seats slashed, and a note was left that read: 'We know you're not a bad screw. If you were, your house would be burned down'.[60] A week later, three prison officers were badly beaten over the course of a weekend by attackers who just said 'you are a screw'.[61] After these attacks, a representative of the PRS called the *Irish Press* and threatened further attacks on prison officers if there was 'a repetition of the harassment they [prison officers] have engaged in against some prisoners'.[62] The following weekend, two more officers were attacked as they left pubs on Parkgate and Dorset Streets.[63]

After the second attack, in which staff member's windows were smashed, the POA blamed the PRO. A POA representative told the press that, two weeks previously, at a PRO picket, a prison officer had been threatened: 'Weldon was the first, he will not be the last'.[64] The PRO were quick to deny any involvement in these attacks and, when interviewed for this book, Joe Costello, the then chairman of the PRO, remembered: 'There was no sympathy at all, I mean, we saw that as outrageous and we condemned that from the very beginning'.[65] Indeed, the PRO was so intent on distancing itself from the accusation of involvement that Margaret Gaj, then treasurer of the PRO, sought a High Court injunction against the secretary of the POA, Stephen Delaney, and the editor of the *Irish Press*, Tim Pat Coogan. The injunction would have forbidden Delaney and the *Irish Press* from repeating claims that the PRO was responsible for the attacks, but the High Court refused to grant the injunction.[66]

Pat McCartan, who had been a leading member of the PRO in the 1970s but had disengaged with it in the late 1970s, offered a more nuanced explanation for the discrepancy between the PRO and POA accounts: 'You may well have had a number of individuals that were involved in both groups, but ... I would have been very surprised if there was any ... organisational contact between the two'.[67] The idea that members of the PRS were on the peripheries of the PRO, attending their protests but playing no role in the planning or day-to-day running of the organisation, makes sense given the small, tightknit, organisational core of the PRO and the relatively large number of people who came to the organisation's pickets. This would explain why prison officers might have been threatened by someone on a PRO picket while the PRO's committee knew nothing about it.

Protest, Rioting, and Revenge | 121

In the aftermath of the attack on the Weldons in 1979, the POA's secretary announced, 'Unless certain measures are taken by the Minister and his Department we will take the necessary measures ourselves'.[68] Believing that the attack had been coordinated with the riot in Mountjoy, the POA threatened to institute an effective work-to-rule by withdrawing overtime. This was a common threat in their industrial disputes of the late 1970s and would have resulted in an end to recreation and prisoners being locked in their cells for twenty-three hours each day.[69] The department managed to assuage the POA's fears and a protest was avoided, but after a tense few months, the threat became a reality during the spate of attacks in autumn 1980.[70] The POA's protest was due to last a week but was called off on its third day in anticipation of a meeting with the minister and amid fears that this kind of retaliatory action would heighten tensions in the prison and could potentially, as the PRO warned, result in a riot.[71]

After this initial flurry of attacks, the PRS campaign trailed off over several months, probably as more and more PRS members were returned to prison on unrelated charges.[72] An officer was stabbed in the face with a broken bottle in October.[73] In March, two more officers were run over by a car and beaten with 'clubs' in the carpark of St Patrick's Institution.[74] In July, six prison officers' cars had their windows smashed in the carpark of St Patrick's Institution.[75] In August, petrol bombs were thrown at the home of an elderly couple, whose adult sons were both prison officers in Mountjoy, while they slept, but due to the attackers poor aim, the bombs burned out in the front garden and caused no serious damage.[76] After this the group went quiet for a few years.

In March 1983, Brian Stack, a chief prison officer in Portlaoise, was shot as he left a boxing match in Dublin's South inner city. Stack remained in hospital until his death in September 1984. After three decades of campaigning by the Stack family, the PIRA took responsibility for this attack in 2013. However, in the immediate aftermath of the shooting, it was not clear who the perpetrators were and some suspected the PRS. In April 1984, a list of 120 prison officers, their details, and many of their recreational activities, along with newspaper clippings about court cases dating back to the 1970s, were discovered in

122 | Prisoners' Bodies

a tangle of ivy in Bushy Park, South Dublin.[77] In the light of the Stack shooting, the POA and the Gardaí interpreted it as a 'hit list' – a view which seemed to be confirmed by later developments.[78]

In August 1984, an assistant chief prison officer, Patrick Hayes, was driving home from work through the secluded Strawberry Beds area of West Dublin when a car ran him off the road into a field. When Hayes got out of the crashed vehicle, three men followed him and beat him with iron bars.[79] After the assault, a man called in to Raidió Teilifís Éireann (RTÉ), the Irish national broadcaster, to claim responsibility for the attack on behalf of the, now slightly renamed, Prisoners' Revenge Group (PRG). Not long after that, two men knocked on the door of another officer. When the door was answered by a babysitter, who informed the men that the officer was out at mass, they told her to tell the officer that 'he was next'.[80] As they had in 1979 and 1980, the POA reacted by threatening to introduce an overtime ban, effectively locking prisoners in their cells for twenty-three hours a day, unless the minister for justice reacted swiftly to protect them.

On the day before Christmas Eve 1984, a petrol bomb was thrown through the window of a house belonging to the daughter of a Fianna Fáil TD while she and her husband slept upstairs. The PRG claimed responsibility for the attack but said the bomb had been intended as a punishment attack on a prison officer, who had been the previous resident of the house and who had been involved in 'an incident' in Mountjoy three weeks previously.[81]

In January 1985, the PRG made a statement to the press that they were targeting officers who they believed took part in the 'beating of prisoners and those who refused to report such incidents', clearly echoing the justification issued during the group's initial spree in 1980.[82] However, in 1985, the group also stated that they were expanding their campaign:

Up to now we have held back from really serious attacks because of families but they [prison officers] have shown that they don't care about our families so we are not going to care about theirs.

Our members have voted to carry out attacks against "screws" and their families.[83]

Protest, Rioting, and Revenge | 123

In an interview with RTÉ on the popular current affairs programme Today at Five, a PRG representative told journalist Colm Keane that there were twenty-two members, all of whom were former prisoners. He claimed that their members had been responsible for the 1979 attack on Weldon, as well as several petrol bombings, although they denied the accusation that they had been involved in the shooting of Brian Stack.[84] He told the journalist that, as ex-prisoners, they had 'learnt brutality ... from the masters' and went on to explain: 'People call us vicious thugs but we are the product of the prison system. That's what they produce in prisons, vicious animals. They're responsible'.[85] There was an extensive Garda investigation into this report, and in January 1985, the Special Branch announced that they had identified six members of the PRG. However, this may have been posturing, or they may simply not have had the evidence to support their suspicions in court, because there were no major prosecutions for any of the PRG attacks until an alleged member of the group named James Rock was brought before, and acquitted by, the Circuit Court for the assault on Hayes in the Strawberry Beds.[86]

The PRG worked with prisoners inside Mountjoy to identify prison officers to target. In August 1985, another hit list was discovered, this time it was a tape-recording discovered in Mountjoy, which included the names of six or seven officers, their addresses, hobbies, movements, and information about their families.[87] This discovery does not seem to have caused too much of a disruption in the PRG's targeting process, however. A few weeks later, in September 1985, they petrol bombed a senior prison officers' home in Whitehall, North Dublin, while he and his family slept inside.[88] The family managed to escape across a flat roofed extension at the back of the house, but the house itself was gutted by fire.[89] A contemporary of the PRG suggested that this attack was the work of a lone actor rather than an official PRG action, but nonetheless, the press saw it as the work of the PRG.[90] The same weekend, two prison officers were beaten with chains outside a nightclub in Dun Laoghaire.[91] The campaign seems to have trailed off again after this, and the last attack the PRG planned was in March 1986, when it issued a death threat and planned to shoot a prison officer in an ambush, but the attempt was foiled when a Garda patrol happened upon the gunman's hiding place.[92]

One of the reasons for this trailing off may have been that the PRG members returned to prison or became occupied with other activities. In October 1985, the Gardaí warned that the PRG had branched out into more traditional forms of organised crime, using 'heavies' to wage a 'campaign of intimidation against small grocers'; for instance, by burning down a potato storehouse in the north inner city to establish a monopoly on grocery shops in the area.[93] In April 1986, the Gardaí raided an abandoned house on Buckingham Street, near the PRO's headquarters, and found a cache of arms that they believed had been used by an organised criminal gang related to the PRG in a number of recent armed robberies.[94]

Prisoners' Bodies and Antibodies: The 1986 Arbour Hill Riot

In March 1986, thirty-eight men barricaded themselves into the east wing of Arbour Hill Prison in Dublin. They climbed onto the rooftop and shouted demands for improved medical, work, and educational facilities.[95] Some of the group managed to run along the top of the prison wall and climb onto the Garrison Church, outside the walls of the prison. The Gardaí tried to disperse the group with a water cannon and the prisoners retaliated by throwing roof slates at them. In the confusion, five jumped to the ground and the three who did not break their legs escaped to freedom.[96] Superficially, it looked like any other prison riot from the 1970s and early 1980s: barricades, rooftop demands for improved conditions, and a handful of attempted escapes. Moreover, it was the latest in a series of related protests at Arbour Hill which had begun in January of that year. In retrospect, it is tempting to see these protests as simply a continuation of the previous year's 'strife', when Mountjoy, Arbour Hill, and Fort Mitchell all experienced major riots in quick succession.[97] However, the Arbour Hill protests were a fatal moment of rupture in the prisoners' body politic, which the PRO and PU had worked so hard to create.

The first case of HIV in the prison system had been identified in November 1985, when Peter 'Ben' Hogg tested positive for HIV antibodies and was diagnosed with what was then called ARC (AIDS Related Complex).[98] Hogg was bluntly told, 'You could be dead in five years' time' and hurriedly released from Mountjoy.[99] Since becoming a heroin user at fifteen, Hogg had never spent more than five months out of prison at a time, and while he was inside, he had shared needles with other prisoners.[100] This prompted calls for the mass testing of prisoners and even the PRO demanded that Mountjoy be 'quarantined'.[101] Over the next six months, three hundred prisoners in Mountjoy volunteered to be tested for HIV, many in the hope of securing an early release like Hogg, and around one in six tested positive.[102] A deputation of prison workers were sent to Brixton Prison in London to find out how the high rate of HIV infection was being handled there, and based on their recommendation, and because of 'unease' in the general prison population, the government decided on a policy of segregation. In January 1986, forty-five men and women with HTLV-3 antibodies, as HIV antibodies were called at the time, were segregated in Arbour Hill.[103] Prisoners who tested positive were sometimes given no information about the virus or their prognosis, just a slip of brown paper with their diagnosis and a black plastic bag to put their belongings in before being transferred to Arbour Hill.[104]

In contrast to most aspects of ordinary prisoners' lives in this period, the failure of the policy of segregation has been well examined by Janet Weston and Virginia Berridge in 'AIDS Inside and Out' as well as the attendant podcast *Positive in Prison*.[105] Arbour Hill was completely unprepared for the needs of its new prisoners. Until the transfer, it had been known as the 'middle-class prison' and had dealt with low risk prisoners, like people convicted of sexual offences.[106] John Lonergan, former governor of Mountjoy, described the change, 'You know, Micky Mouse could run it [Arbour Hill in the early 1980s]. Sex offenders are generally very easy going people, a lot of elderly people, a lot of clergy. They could look after themselves so the staff got spoiled. They had to deal with no aggression, no difficulties, no nothing. Now you can imagine busloads from Mountjoy, they'd be hyper some of them, arriving at Arbour Hill. The staff were terrified of them, they'd no skills in dealing with them, and, sure, it was a disaster'.[107]

Within three days of their arrival, three prisoners had cut their wrists to protest the refusal by Arbour Hill's medical officer to prescribe enough drugs, a fourth man had tried to hang himself, and a two more men had been found unconscious after a drug overdose.[108] Initially, the prison officers refused to allow the prisoners out of their cells except to collect their meals and to empty their chamber pots; however, after they were threatened with suspension, the officers agreed to allow the prisoners their usual recreation time.[109] Even then, the prisoners were only given single-use paper bedclothes, plates, and cups.[110] The teacher at Arbour Hill criticised the creation of the segregation unit, calling it a 'Leper Colony', a sentiment echoed by prisoners during the riot in March.[111] An allegation that was certainly borne out in the press coverage of the unit, which emphasised the 'spacesuit' type PVC protective clothing worn by prison officers, the officers' refusal to handle the bodies of dead prisoners who they suspected of having HIV, the hospitalisation of two firemen after coming in contact with prisoners' blood, and the fact that the ambulance used to transport HIV positive prisoners to hospital was immediately taken out of service after the journey.[112] Beyond the isolation, Arbour Hill was not set up to cater for the needs of this new population. Costello, on behalf of the PRO, told the press: 'The people are working on a part time basis. The prisoners need constant counselling. At night there are no medical staff on hand'.[113] Moreover, the fact that little was known about the treatment of HIV meant that the prisoners felt that they were being treated like 'guinea pigs'.[114] During the riot, one prisoner claimed that the 'mystery drugs' that the prison was giving him had caused him to have a series of blackouts, while another prisoner was sent into a five day coma and had to be transferred to hospital.[115]

In previous protests, the prisoners' grievances had often been local but, because of the work of the PU and the PRO in the 1970s and 1980s, they were also seen, both inside and outside the prison, as part of a broader totalization. When prisoners burned the newly opened prison on Spike Island in 1985, for instance, they were protesting the local lack of facilities in Spike. However, the riot drew energy from the numerous riots and escape attempts by prisoners in the preceding months. As such, the Spike prisoners were not only seen as decrying the lack of facilities in their prison; rather, they were understood to be part of a broader protest over the general overcrowding and expansion of the prison system which had led to their transfer to Spike in the first place. The protestors at Arbour Hill in 1986, by contrast, were not seen to be acting on behalf of all prisoners. Nor, for that matter, were they thought to be acting locally in the interests of the prisoners of

Arbour Hill specifically. Rather they were protesting on behalf of all prisoners who had tested positive for HIV antibodies. They had been excluded from the prisoners body in every way: the prison system had segregated them and they were 'despised by the main prison population'.[116] Although HIV did little more than amplify the preexisting problems in the prison system – the lack of access to medical and psychiatric care; the deteriorative effects of prolonged isolation; and the chronic overcrowding, understaffing, and underfunding of the prison service – in the public discourse, the 'AIDS scare' was treated as a new problem which seemed to be unrelated to the long-standing problems in the prison system and which applied to a new and distinct body of prisoners.

Conclusion

Throughout the 1970s, there was an understandable animosity between prisoners and prison officers. This was ensured by the coercive and violent nature of the prison system. However, as we have seen in earlier chapters, there were also moments of common cause, a shared animosity towards the Department of Justice, and shared aims for the reform of the prison system. From 1979, this began to disintegrate. The attack on the Weldons and the subsequent attacks on prison officers and their property, as well as the increasing violence of prisoners' protests, contributed to this. So too did the prison officers' collective punishment of prisoners through the withdrawal of recreation time, the constant threat of further industrial action, and, allegedly, systematic beatings of prisoners in punishment cells. Moreover, the common aims which drove the PU activity dissipated. Even the militant organisation of former prisoners, which began by burning buildings to demand the closure of the Curragh, quickly transformed into the PRS, with 'little time for ... political lobbying or penal reform' and no more detailed programme than revenging itself on prison officers and a vague hope that this would lessen the violence experienced by prisoners.[117] Indeed, if Garda reports are to be believed, it eventually abandoned even this motivation and became a for-profit criminal organisation. The popular understanding of prisoners' protests as relatively unified and speaking to system-wide problems had been

128 | Prisoners' Bodies

destabilised by the heroin epidemic and the division between drug users and 'ordinary decent criminals'. But the final death knell for the prisoners' discourse of common cause came in the form of the 'AIDS scare', which divided the prisoners' body, socially and physically, into those who had tested positive and those who had not.

The late 1970s and 1980s were the 'beginning of the end', not just for the PRO, as Joe Costello observed, but for the organised prisoners' movement more generally. The demographic transformation of prison culture wrought by the heroin epidemic and the government's response, the dissolution of organised prisoners' groups inside prisons, the fracturing of the more militant former prisoners from the PRO, all of these led to disorganisation among prisoners, and, as we will see in the next chapter, to the PRO becoming distanced from prisoners' everyday concerns.

5

'It Is Doubtful If There Is a Single Prisoner or Ex-prisoner Here'

The PRO's Sociological Turn, 1977–86

Introduction

Chapter 2 began with two Prisoners' Rights Organization (PRO) activists, disguised as press photographers, sneaking into the United Nations (UN) Congress on the Prevention of Crime and the Treatment of Offenders in 1975 to unfurl a banner and give a speech about prison conditions in Ireland, before they were ejected by security guards. In 1980, the PRO returned to the congress, but this time as invited speakers. Being invited, however, did not make the PRO particularly conciliatory. Before the congress, Joe Costello, the PRO's delegate, met with a group of other penal reform organisations including the Howard League (UK) and the National Council for Crime and Delinquency (US) to discuss the 'almost total absence' of representation of penal reform organisations from the global south. Costello's address to the congress, which was reproduced in the *Jail Journal*, was similarly critical and castigated the 'inadequacy of prisoner representation' at the congress: 'It is doubtful if there is a single prisoner or ex-prisoner here. There are plenty of state delegations here to speak about the problems to the state of criminals and prisoners but there are no prisoners to present the experiences and problems of the individual in society prior to arrest and imprisonment, and also his experience, problems and perception of prison'.[1] Significantly, however, this lack of prisoners or ex-prisoners included the PRO delegate. Five years earlier, in 1975, one of the two PRO activists who infiltrated the congress, to proclaim, 'We make this protest on behalf of all Irish social prisoners who cannot make it for themselves', had been a long-term prisoner released just two years previously.[2] In 1980, however, the PRO delegate was a schoolteacher with political ambitions.[3] In the intervening five years, the PRO had undergone drastic changes – many founding activists had left, the organisation's tactics had changed, it was building alliances with other social and political groups, and it had become, in some sense, respectable.

This chapter examines the PRO's shift towards respectability. It begins with a discussion of the changing personnel at the executive committee and the tensions within it. It then examines the organisation's sociological turn and the formation of the influential MacBride commission; the PRO's use of its newfound respectability to win its decade-long campaign to close the Curragh; and finally, it dissects the PRO's failure to slow prison expansion in the mid-1980s.

The Old Guard: McCartan, de Búrca, and Walsh

Pat McCartan, Máirín de Búrca, and Brendan Walsh were all central figures in the PRO from its inception in 1973 until 1977. However, they each had markedly different life experiences when they became interested in penal reform activism. Pat McCartan grew up in County Wexford and came to Dublin to read law at University College Dublin (UCD), at a time when less than 3 per cent of the population had a third level education.[4] At university, he became involved with the Law Students Union for Action (LSUA), an organisation of left-wing law students, and later Official Sinn Féin, the left-wing republican party from which Provisional Sinn Féin split in 1970. He became a founding member of the PRO when he was just twenty years old.

Máirín de Búrca grew up in Newbridge, County Kildare, and left school in her early teens. She joined Sinn Féin at the age of sixteen, in 1954, and from the mid-1960s, she became the party's general secretary, siding with the Officials during the 1970 party split and renouncing all political violence.[5] In the late 1960s, she also became involved in a number of key civil rights campaigns, including the Dublin Housing Action Committee and the Irish Women's Liberation Movement, as part of which she organised the famous 'contraceptive train' which illegally imported contraceptives from Northern Ireland.[6] She later sued the Irish state to ensure that women were equally represented on juries. She became a founding member of the PRO after she was released from Mountjoy, where she had been held on a charge relating to her activism.

Brendan Walsh's background was also different. He grew up in Drimnagh, a working-class suburb of Dublin. His older brother Liam, a welder by trade, was a leading member of the militant Trotskyite republican organisation, Saor Éire, who was killed in 1970 when a bomb he was carrying accidentally exploded during a raid on McKee Army Barracks in Dublin.[7] The Gardaí believed that Brendan had followed his brother into Saor Éire.[8] In 1972–73, at the age of thirty, Walsh spent time in Mountjoy, accused of assaulting a special branch Garda. He was tried in the Special Criminal Court along with four other people on charges related to membership of Saor Éire, including a bank robbery and firearms offences.[9] Indeed, he was in Mountjoy during the early days of the Prisoners' Union (PU) and had used his court appearance to protest the prisons' conditions and to highlight a hunger strike by prisoners there.[10]

In 1973, McCartan, as a member of the LSUA, invited Walsh and de Búrca to UCD to speak about their experiences in prison. The success of this event, which was attended by seven to eight hundred people, led to the formation of the Ad Hoc Committee on Prison Reform, which quickly became the PRO.[11] Walsh became the chairman of the organisation and both McCartan and de Búrca took up places on the executive.[12] As a solicitor, McCartan represented the families of deceased prisoners at inquests as well as Karl Crawley, other people the PRO advocated for, and any members of the PRO who wound up in court. De Búrca acted as the organisation's press secretary for much of the 1970s, wrote most of their press releases, and built up the PRO's profile and relationship with the press. All three took part in the organisation's demonstrations. Walsh and McCartan went to Geneva to protest the UN Congress on the Prevention of Crime and the Treatment of Offenders. All three picketed a senior civil servant's house and were named in a High Court injunction, for which McCartan received a stern warning from the head of his law office.[13] All three also took part in the picket on the trial of Karl Crawley, which resulted in the arrest and conviction of Walsh and de Búrca. McCartan narrowly avoided the same fate because he was called away for work just before the Gardaí arrived.[14] For a time, McCartan's law offices were even the corresponding address of the PRO's *Jail Journal*.[15]

In July 1977, less than a week after the PU's final protest was suppressed in Mountjoy, Walsh split with the PRO to form his own organisation with four other former prisoners who were not, according to Joe Costello, regular members of the PRO.[16] They called the new organisation the Prisoners' Committee. When the organisation was launched, Walsh admitted to the *Irish Times* that the PRO's and the committee's aims were 'very similar'.[17] The split was not about the aims, he told the press, but about the nature of the organisation itself: 'We will not allow the Prisoners' Committee to become predominantly identified with any political organisation. And the executive committee will always have a majority of ex-prisoners on it'.[18]

When asked about the split in an interview for this book, McCartan gave a different explanation. He suggested that the root of the split was a 'personal grievance' between himself, Brendan Walsh, and an unnamed former prisoner for whom he had acted as a solicitor. In that context, the reference to the alignment of the PRO with a political organisation, McCartan said, was Walsh 'having a go at me primarily and my political involvement with Official Sinn Féin, at the time or Sinn Féin the Worker's Party, which obviously was the same party that Máirín de Búrca was involved with, so it was an easy thing to pick – two of the more active members in the PRO also happened to be members of the same political party'.[19] However, both de Búrca and McCartan denied that Official Sinn Féin was exercising any control over the PRO through them. Indeed, they both claimed that they came in for criticism within the party for spending so much effort on ordinary prisoners because there was no 'political milage in the cause'.[20] Indeed, apart from a broadly left-wing political slant, there is no discernible continuity between the PRO's activities and those of Official

Sinn Féin. This is particularly apparent in the PRO's consistent refusal to represent the interests of political prisoners, some of whom were aligned with the Officials. This came to a head at the end of September, when the unnamed former prisoner used the PRO's annual general meeting (AGM) to air his grievance with McCartan. McCartan appealed to the chairman that the issue had nothing to do with the activities of the PRO, but the prevailing attitude at the time was that former prisoners should be allowed to raise any issue at PRO meetings. This made McCartan's position in the executive committee untenable and so he resigned from the committee and left the organisation. The PRO's AGM, however, went on to pass a resolution welcoming the formation of the Prisoners' Committee and planning a joint demonstration in early October.[21] It was around this time that de Búrca also left the PRO. The Prisoners' Committee's attacks on her political involvement, and the PRO's resolution to welcome the formation of that committee, may have influenced this decision. Although, when interviewed, she did not recall any specific event that precipitated her resignation: 'I think I had too much to do ... and the meetings were always miles away'.[22] This is entirely plausible, of course. De Búrca was extremely busy with other campaigns at the time and she had already committed an enormous amount of her time to the PRO in the mid-1970s.

The Prisoners' Committee may have been driven by personal disputes, it may even, have been 'only designed to do damage', as McCartan put it, and it was certainly short-lived, disappearing from the public discourse after just four months.[23] However, one of its critiques of the PRO does highlight an important shift that was taking place within the organisation in 1977 and which accelerated after these three central personalities – de Búrca, McCartan, and Walsh – departed. In their final press release, the Prisoners' Committee wrote:

> Four months ago ... ex-prisoners of the PRO, frustrated and disillusioned by the virtual inactivity of that organisation, came together, and formed the Prisoners' Committee which they felt reflected their needs more accurately.
>
> While we recognise and welcome the dialogue at academic seminars on penology – such as that held by the PRO over the weekend – to have this divorced from the day-to-day running

and organising of a prisoners' association makes it merely an exercise in semantics.[24]

From 1977 onwards, this academic, sociological, turn became central to the PRO's approach. The organisation increasingly eschewed the street-level activism of the mid-1970s in favour of more surveys, inquiries, and lobbying aimed at directly influencing public policy.

Respectability: Surveys and the MacBride Commission

As we discussed in chapter 2, in the early and mid-1970s, most of the PRO's energy was dedicated to highlighting the individual stories of particular prisoners as a way of highlighting broader issues within the prison system. This was reflected in the content of the *Jail Journal*. Between the first issue, in 1973, and the tenth issue, in 1976, an average of 54 per cent of the articles in each issue engaged with individual's stories. These included the experiences of people with alcohol dependance in prison, the kinds of mental health treatment received by Karl Crawley, and the details of several men's suicides in detention. However, between 1977 and 1980, the average number of articles that engaged with individual stories fell to just 17 per cent, and in several issues there was no engagement with individual's stories at all. This was not just a stylistic shift; rather, it marked a shift in the PRO's approach to campaigning. The organisation took a sociological turn, moving away from street-level organisation towards a more research-driven agenda. When asked about why the organisation changed direction so abruptly, McCartan ascribed it to a change in the organisation's leadership: 'Joe [Costello], I know, was very anxious to do research and to pursue a campaign that was backed up by fact. That was one of the positions that he held strong to, and I think that perhaps it [the change in approach] is as much to do with his chairmanship as anything'.[25] Joe Costello was a secondary school teacher from rural county Sligo who had been part of the PRO's executive committee from its formation in 1973.[26] He was the editor of the *Jail Journal*, and in 1975, he became the organisation's public relations officer.[27] He was appointed as the acting chairman immediately after the turbulent 1977 AGM in which McCartan came into conflict with the then chairman and members of the newly formed Prisoners' Committee and subsequently resigned. In all likelihood, the chairmanship fell to Costello because he was the most active member who was not affiliated with a political organisation – a key consideration in light of the Prisoner's Committee's accusations that the organisation had become an 'adjunct' of Sinn Féin – The Workers' Party.[28] He was later officially elected as the chairman of the PRO, a position which he held for the rest of the organisation's existence. One of the first new issues to arise under Costello's chairmanship was the government's plans to repurpose Loughan House.

In the late 1960s and 1970s, the sporadic and incomplete nature of penal reform created a dangerous loophole in the laws governing the imprisonment of juveniles. The Criminal Justice Act (1960) had created St Patrick's Institution for juveniles between the ages of seventeen and twenty-one. Older people were to be handled by the adult prison system and younger people by the country's industrial schools and reformatories. However, under the Children's Act (1908), children under the age of seventeen could also be legally imprisoned in adult prisons, an anomaly which became increasingly significant from the late 1960s as the industrial schools and reformatories began to close, leaving fewer places for children to serve carceral sentences. The result was that between 1966 and 1977 nearly five hundred children, under the age of seventeen, were committed to the adult prisons in Mountjoy and Limerick.[29]

By 1977, the media had fixed on the idea that there was 'increasing juvenile delinquency' around the country.[30] In June, a Catholic Auxiliary Bishop gave an interview to the *Independent* about Ireland's young people in which he stated matter-of-factly that there was 'also, of course, the need for some place where young delinquents under sixteen and out of everyone's control can be sent for rehabilitation'.[31] The same month, a judge, sentencing two boys who had set fire to a house to two years of probation warned, 'The day is fast coming when places will be set up for juvenile delinquents. They will just have to be put away'.[32] In July, a new Fianna Fáil government took office and quickly promised that 'a top priority will be to provide suitable accommodation for young offenders'.[33] By the end of the year, Gerry Collins, the new minister for justice, had decided to move juvenile prisoners (aged seventeen to twenty-one) out of the open prison at Loughan House,

County Cavan, and to convert it into a closed prison for children, aged twelve to sixteen.[34]

This became the first challenge for the new leadership of the PRO and the trial-run for their new approach. In early 1978, the PRO conducted a detailed survey of '12–16 year-old male offenders'.[35] The survey focused on the Seán McDermot Street–Summerhill neighbourhood of dilapidated Georgian and Victorian tenements in Dublin's north inner city. Rather than using specific stories to highlight broader injustices within the penal system, the PRO used the surveys to produce a statistical conglomerate of these boys' lives. They found that the children came from large families and their parents were absent, unemployed, or worked in unstable and 'unskilled' jobs; over 90 per cent had fathers or brothers who had been in prison; on average they had left school at thirteen, none had gone to secondary school, and two-thirds were unable to read or write; on average they had each appeared in court fifty-two times and been convicted of offences six times; over half the offences were related to car thefts and only 4 per cent were for offences against the person, most of the offences could be put down to, in the PRO's opinion, 'youthful energy, devilment and high jinks'.[36] Ninety-two per cent of respondents expected to end up in prison someday.[37] Indeed, in a report on a survey that the PRO undertook in 1979, with very similar results, the author noted that 'the results confirmed many theories in relation to the ex-prisoner and his/her life'.[38]

The strategy that the PRO derived from these findings was markedly different from their previous approach. In the short term, they argued for diverting the expected cost of converting and running Loughan House into 'voluntary and professional organisations' that could provide noncustodial alternatives to the detention centre. However, their report made clear that this would be a stop-gap measure. Instead, the PRO argued that the solution was to address three issues – families, education, and employment. Large family sizes were 'helping to perpetuate the slums', so they proposed that 'family planning and contraception should be made available as a priority by the state'.[39] A pupil-teacher ratio of over fifty children for every teacher in disadvantaged areas contributed to the high drop out and low literacy rates, so the PRO proposed deploying large numbers of teachers to these areas.[40] Finally, to address the lack of job opportunities, the

PRO proposed government incentives to establish an industry in the area and to lower the age requirement for apprenticeship and trade training courses with AnCO, the national industrial training council.[41] What is notable here is that none of these 'obvious' solutions proposed by this PRO document addressed prison conditions, sentencing standards, or inequalities in the criminal justice system. Indeed, none of the solutions they proposed were within the remit of the Department of Justice; rather, they fell under the remits of the Departments of Health, Education, and Economic Planning and Development. The understanding that a significant amount of crime was the result of structural inequalities in society had always played a part in the PRO's outlook, and in both a press release in 1973 and an open letter in 1975, they explained by focusing on reforming prison conditions they were merely addressing the most immediate problems and the long-term solution would need to address social structures.[42] From 1977, this need became a central part of its message.

This shift towards a more structurally focused form of activism can initially be seen in minor changes in their activism. In the early years, the PRO had given a Christmas present to some of 'the more needy prisoners' of some of the organisation's surplus funds.[43] In December 1977, however, they instead decided to use the money they customarily gave to prisoners to buy a collection of 'dictionaries, craft, legal, fictional and general educational books' to donate to the Mountjoy Prison library. The prison, however, refused to take the books and the organisation used the event to highlight the low levels of literacy among prisoners, the 'virtually non-existent' educational facilities in the adult prisons, and the library offerings which they claimed were limited to 'Mills and Boone romances' in the women's prison and 'comics and cheap paperback fiction' for the men and juveniles.[44] The minister for justice dismissed the attempted donation as 'a propagandist exercise'.[45] Indeed, in that respect, as a consciousness-raising action, it was quite successful at prompting several questions to be asked in the Dáil and numerous articles about prison libraries in national newspapers.

The following year, the PRO conducted a second survey, this time based on a larger sample group of 202 former prisoners.[46] The questionnaire consisted of sixty questions and subquestions and again demonstrates the PRO's sociological turn. Over a third of the questions did not relate to the respondent's criminal or penal history at all, covering similar topics to their earlier survey of juveniles like their parents' occupation, reading ability, and the kind of area they grew up in. Over a quarter of the questions dealt with how the respondents first became entangled with the criminal justice system, specifically asking about respondents' first offences and court appearances. Other questions asked about parents' and siblings' prison records, the time since respondents' left prison, their employment record since incarceration, and whether their labour inside prison prepared them for work on the outside (only one, out of 195 respondents, said yes). Still other questions collected information on the number and type of sentences respondents had served and the relevant offences. In fact, only seven of the questionnaire's sixty questions actually asked about the respondent's experience as a prisoner, marking a further shift away from the PRO's 1973–76 focus on prisoners' experiences.[47] Indeed, early in the PRO's report the author wrote: 'It soon became evident that society had failed the majority of those interviewed long before their involvement with crime. They grew up with poverty at their doorsteps, doorsteps in need of repair and far too overcrowded ... the lack of recreational facilities in the city centre soon meant that private spaces – cars, warehouses, houses, shops – became public playgrounds and this inevitably meant – if they had not been caught for missing school – their first serious brushes with the law'.[48] What is clear from both the design of the survey and the contents of the report is that the PRO's focus was no longer trying to represent the prisoner as the subject of specific injustices within the prison system; rather, they were attempting to construct people as the subjects of injustices within society at large which were both the cause and result of entanglement with the prison system.

The PRO's new, more holistic, approach to reform brought new energy to the organisation's demand for a full public inquiry into the prison system. This demand may have been introduced to the PRO's agenda by McCartan. He had been a leading member of the radical Law Students Union for Action at UCD, which agitated in the early 1970s for a public inquiry into the prison system which would include evidence from 'medical- and social-services personnel but above all from the prisoners themselves'.[49] As early as the autumn of 1973, the PRO began calling for public inquiries into the prison system, some of these were about specific events, for instance, the suppression of prisoners protests or the circumstances surrounding prisoners deaths, however, some were for a general inquiry.

The frequency and intensity of these calls increased as the decade wore on, and in late 1975 and early 1976, the PRO began collecting signatures for a petition calling for a full public inquiry. Joe Costello and two other activists presented this petition to the Dáil in October 1977 by which time they had amassed 10,223 individual signatures and eighteen endorsements from organisations as diverse as the Midleton Urban District Council, Cherish: An Association of Unmarried Mothers, and the Gaelic Athletic Association. The petition stated that the penal system had been 'devised in a pre-industrial society by a foreign nation' and that it was 'now too rigid to ever be capable of adapting to modern developments in criminology, penology and social science'.[50] It demanded a full public inquiry into the prison system, after which they could begin to 'build again'.[51] The minister for justice refused to accept the petition when a march of one hundred PRO supporters brought it to the Dáil.[52] Instead, the opposition Socialist Labour Party TD, Noël Browne, accepted it, saying that he would 'seek to hand [it] over' to the minister.[53] The government initially ignored the petition, but when Browne asked, in the Dáil, whether the government would establish a public inquiry, the minister for justice replied flatly, 'The answer is "no"'.[54] He went on to say that while he himself had called for an inquiry while he was in opposition, now that he was in power, he thought that it was unnecessary. In response, the PRO decided to organise its own inquiry. It established an 'international tribunal' which would hear submissions from both organisations and individuals, including former prisoners, and produce a report on their findings.[55] The final part of this section examines why the PRO chose to create a commission which was so self-consciously independent.

There were twelve people on the commission, none of whom were publicly associated with the PRO, although one member, Matt Merrigan, had been briefly involved with the Ad Hoc Committee for Prison Reform which preceded the PRO. Instead, the members were, for the most part, drawn from the ranks of the centre-left of Ireland's middle-class establishment. The two chairmen were Seán MacBride, a senior counsel and former government minister in Ireland, recipient of Lenin and Nobel Peace Prizes, and founder of Amnesty International; and Louk Hulsman, a Dutch professor of criminology who worked with the Council of Europe and who had been an active member of the Dutch Resistance during the Second World War.[56] The ten ordinary members included two academics (sociology and criminal law), a Jesuit priest and former army officer who lectured in sociology at Ireland's National Seminary, a senator (Independent at the time, but she later joined the then centre-right Fine Gael party) and TD (Fine Gael), a solicitor and two barristers, and the general secretary of the Amalgamated Transport and General Workers' Union. One marker of the respectability of the commission is that one of the members went on to be a minister of state, another became a minister in three governments, and two of them even became presidents of Ireland (Mary McAleese, 1997–2011, and Michael D. Higgins, 2011–2025).

In the introduction to its report, the MacBride commission, as it became known, included a section specifically dealing with its relationship with the PRO. The report noted that there 'has been apathy, or even downright hostility on the part of the public and the political establishment in general to some organisations involved in helping prisoners' and the PRO has been at the forefront of advocating for prisoners and as a result has borne the brunt of the hostility.[57] Although the commission commended the work of the PRO over the years, in spite of the public and political hostility, it firmly asserted its independence: 'The members of the Commission were originally approached by the P.R.O. and asked to undertake this work. We did so on the understanding that our work was entirely independent of any group, and since the formation of the Commission, we have not had any meetings with or assistance from the P.R.O. Therefore, the findings of this commission must be regarded as being totally independent of any organisation'.[58]

From Joe Costello's ascent to the chairmanship of the PRO in 1977, the organisation courted respectability. Its tactics shifted towards sociological evidence gathering and the presentation of that evidence with the appearance of objectivity and rigour. Increasingly, their work was focused on creating what Ian Taylor, Paul Walton, and Jock Young called in their key work *The New Criminology* (1973), a 'politically informed social psychology of ... ongoing social dynamics'.[59] The PRO increasingly began to develop a vicarious respectability by building relationships with prominent legitimate voices in the public and policy spheres.

This is perhaps best represented by comparing the organisation's activities in 1975 and 1980. In 1975, PRO activists courted controversy by picketing the home of a senior civil servant and then breaking a High Court injunction to picket it a second time; they engaged in illegal activity by putting fliers on the jury benches during the trial of Karl Crawley, and received a year's prison sentence for it; and they challenged international authority by sneaking into, and being ejected from, the UN Congress on the Prevention of Crime and the Treatment of Offenders, even questioning the legitimacy of the congress because no prisoners or prisoners' representatives had been invited to speak at it. That year, in a draft statement, the PRO seemed acutely aware of the disadvantage of their position in respectability politics: 'We do not have the ear of the mass media, the Minister has, We do not have the support of the law, the Minister has, We have no financial reserves, the Minister has, the people we represent are poor, and uninfluential'.[60]

By contrast, in 1980, they sought to influence public opinion by publishing and promoting the report of the MacBride commission, they denounced illegal activity in the cause of prisoners' rights as counterproductive, and they were invited back to officially address the UN Congress on the Prevention of Crime and the Treatment of Offenders. By 1981, the PRO's respectability was such that Joe Costello could run for one of the National University of Ireland seats in the Seanad, the Irish Senate, making his involvement with the PRO a central plank of his campaign. Although his bid was unsuccessful, he 'polled a respectable total' of votes for a first attempt, and the poll was topped by Gemma Hussey, who had been a member of the PRO-sponsored MacBride commission.[61]

'The Toilet Assumption:' The MacBride Commission Report (1980)

The MacBride Report was not framed as a radical document. In its opening sentences, it castigates the 'moral degeneracy of the age' and sets aside 'questions of Christian morality' as the best justification for examining the penal system in favour of practical budgetary consider-ations.[62] This conventionalism is clearly a product of the largely bour-geois makeup of the committee – four lawyers, four academics, three politicians, and a trade unionist. However, it was also an important feature of the attempt to frame the report as a 'serious contribution to the solution of ... a grave problem' that the government could legit-imately consider.[63] We can see this particularly clearly in chapter 4 of the report which discusses alternatives to incarceration. The first half of the chapter is dedicated to a partial literature review. However, the review does not draw together evidence about the efficacy of prisons; rather, it is focused on producing an apparent consensus about the idea that 'prison ... militates against rehabilitation'.[64] This section pulls together a collection of publications from the United States, Can-ada, Sweden, and Britain. Many of these were official reports or fact sheets and included, among other things, a statement by the director of the Federal Bureau of Prisons in the US that 'we must phase out the penitentiary as the mainstay of our correctional system' and the Canadian special parliamentary subcommittee's report which asserted that 'incarceration has failed in its two essential purposes – correcting the offender and providing permanent protection to society'.[65] Hav-ing manufactured this apparent consensus, the report, with seeming impartiality, concludes, 'The Commission agrees with the view that prison is probably the least suitable environment for the proper rein-tegration of the offender'.[66] It also concludes that prisons enable the state to move social problems away from public view rather than ad-dressing their root causes or long-term effects – which the report col-ourfully, and less than sensitively, calls 'the toilet assumption'.[67]

The final chapter includes seventeen pages of recommendations which sought to rebuild the justice system from its foundations up. These recommendations can be divided between setting policy aims, structural alterations, changes to the treatment of people in prison (with subdivisions for juveniles and women), a statement about pris-oners' rights, the process of rehabilitation, the prevention of crime, and the abolition of three institutions. The four most far-reaching re-forms dealt with policy aims. The report recommended that the state officially specify that the aim of any sentence should be that the sen-tenced person is integrated into society during or after it. It argued that prison should only ever be a sanction of 'last resort,' and even then only in cases where a person needs to be detained to ensure the public safety. Following on from this, it claimed that the aim of the criminal justice system should be to reduce the number of people in prison. Finally, the most ambitious of the recommendations was that the state should aim to reduce the circumstances that lead to crime, particularly naming unsatisfactory housing, schools, and social amenities.[68] The subsequent list of targeted reforms aligned with these general policy aims. The commission recommended that a 'treatment of offenders board' should be established to run the prison system. The board would be independent of the Department of Justice, and the vast majority of its members would be people from civil society with expertise in relevant areas like social work or education. Only the prison security division of this board would be run by members of the Gardaí and Department of Justice.[69] The report goes on discuss how the prison population might be reduced. This included regular reviews of all carceral sentences to determine when prisoners were ready for reintegration. It also recommended a series of alternatives to imprisonment including Community Service Orders, supervised hostels and day centres, and schools with specially trained teachers.[70] The prisoners' rights outlined in the report largely dealt with the prisoners' agency and engagement with civil society. This included asserting prisoners' right to vote and form unions and to have minority religions recognised by the prison system through the provision of certain diets and prayer mats. The report went on to list nine ways to address the causes of crime. Some of these addressed economic inequality, including recommending 'positive discrimination for jobs in favour of inner-city children' and new youth work programmes. More of the recommendations focused on reforming the Gardaí, like educational standards and community-engagement training for Gardaí, the establishment of a Police Authority to run the Gardaí independent of the Department of Justice, and the establishment of an independent tribunal to receive and assess complaints against the Gardaí. Finally, the report recommended the closure of St Patrick's Institution and the Curragh Military Detention Barracks and the abolition of the death penalty.

The MacBride Report was produced by a committee of respectable representatives of the Irish middle class, it was framed in the most conventional of terms, and it was presented as an apparent consensus in international penological thinking and best practice. In spite of this, the report offered an extensive programme of social reform which not only reimagined the purpose and functioning of the prison system, but also sought to transform the social conditions that gave rise to crime in the first place.

Partial Success: The Death Penalty (1981) and the Curragh (1981–83) Campaigns

An important part of the PRO's new approach was building alliances with influential figures and organisations. In 1981, the PRO banded to-gether with the Irish Council for Civil Liberties (ICCL), of which Joe Costello was also a prominent member, and Amnesty International to run a unified campaign to abolish the death penalty in Ireland. The campaign argued that 'the taking of human life, whether it be by mur-der, assassination or hanging strikes at the heart of two of the most fundamental human rights – the right to life and the right not to be subjected to cruel, inhuman or degrading punishment'.[71] The Irish state had not executed anyone since 1954, and the Criminal Justice Act (1964) had abolished the death penalty as a punishment for all civilian crimes except treason and 'capital murder' in 1963 (capital murder re-ferred to the murder of a garda, political assassination, or murder in the course of political subversion). The question of abolishing the death penalty arose again when three men were sentenced to be hanged for the murder of Garda Henry Byrne during a republican bank raid in 1980 (one of these sentences was later overturned and the other two were commuted to forty year sentences by the president, just weeks before their execution).[72] A few months after the anti–death penalty campaign's launch another man, this time an escaped IRA prisoner from Belfast, was sentenced to death for murdering a detective garda. The result was an extensive public debate about the ethics and efficacy of the death penalty. One timely feature of the campaign was that it built on the arguments of the pro-life movement. The Irish pro-life movement had been growing in power and influence throughout the end of the 1970s, and a few months after the campaign against the death penalty was launched, the Pro-Life Amendment Campaign began to campaign for a constitutional change that would ban abortion – this would become the eight amendment to the constitution in 1983. Although the ICCL, and many within the PRO and Amnesty, opposed the eighth amendment, Joe Costello called on the pro-life campaign to support the anti–death penalty campaign, saying, 'I think the pro-life lobby should be foremost in the campaign to abolish capital punishment'.[73] Although the pro-life movement, unsurprisingly, did not lend its considerable weight to the new campaign, it did help to heighten the public profile of the death penalty campaign, and over the next two years, public debates about abortion were regularly redirected into debates about the death penalty.

The anti–death penalty campaign ran throughout 1981. It began with a letter writing campaign asking various organisations to endorse the demand – just as the PRO had done at the outset of their campaign against Loughan House. In February, a month after it began, the campaign organised a public meeting of high-profile figures who denounced the death penalty, including Catholic, Methodist, and Jewish religious leaders; Noël Browne, of the Socialist Labour Party; and the Labour Party spokesman, Ruairi Quinn.[74] A month after that meeting, Fine Gael, the largest opposition party, supported, by a narrow margin, a motion to abolish the death penalty at its Ard Fheis (annual party conference).[75] In May, Noël Browne introduced a private member's bill into the Dáil that would have abolished the death penalty, but the government refused to allow a debate about it.[76] The following month, a general election put Fine Gael into a minority coalition government with the Labour Party. The new government quickly drew up the Criminal Justice Bill (1981), which abolished the death penalty, replacing it with a forty year jail term; however, the bill was controversial within Fine Gael and threatened to destabilise the government, with a spokesman for the Labour Party warning that the issue could 'rock the coalition to its very foundations'.[77] As it happened, the bill was passed in the Seanad after much debate, but the government fell, over an unrelated issue, before there was time to pass the bill in the Dáil. After which, the momentum of the Amnesty-ICCL-PRO campaign dissipated and each organisation turned its focus to other issues.

Although the campaign was unsuccessful, and the death penalty was not abolished in Ireland until 1990, it can be seen as an indicator

Figure 5.1 Prisoners' Rights Organisation protest to end civilian detention in the Curragh Military Detention Barracks, Newbridge, co. Kildare, 1978. When this march arrived at the Curragh Camp, the photographer, Derek Speirs, was arrested and his film temporarily confiscated.

of the PRO's successful move towards respectability. The combination with Amnesty and the ICCL and the ability to mobilise prominent cultural and political leaders and to convince a government to bring a bill before the Oireachtas which, in spite of its controversiality, only failed to become law because of the wider political and economic turmoil of the early 1980s, all mark an enormous step forward for the PRO, given that it was only five years since one Fine Gael minster for justice referred to the PRO as being 'either subversives or the dupes of subversives'.[78]

The PRO took the lessons-learned and connections-made during the death penalty campaign and applied them to the organisation's long-running campaign to close the Curragh. Originally opened in 1972 as emergency accommodation for prisoners after a riot destroyed a significant portion of Mountjoy, the Curragh Military Detention Barracks quickly became a high security prison for 'troublemakers'.[79] Throughout the early and mid-1970s, it maintained a population of around thirty prisoners, many of whom were involved with dissident republican groups who could not be housed with the provisional IRA prisoners in Portlaoise, as well as Prisoners Union leaders who were seen as threats to the good order of other prisons. In the early years, the PRO based its campaign against the Curragh on the anecdotes of men who had spent time there. This was partially because it suited the organisation's approach at the time but also because, until 1978, the reports of the Curragh Visiting Committee had never been published and there was no official source of information about the Curragh. When Costello, on behalf of the PRO, got permission to inspect the unpublished reports, he had to travel to the Curragh Camp where he was allowed to view the reports but not to take notes. When the PRO challenged this restriction, the High Court ordered the government to publish the reports.[80] The reports were highly critical of the Curragh, calling the prison 'unsatisfactory' and arguing that it was not suitable for prisoners on long sentences or with mental health issues.[81] The PRO's campaign against the Curragh was reinvigorated. It argued that the original prisoners had mainly finished their sentences and that the Curragh was 'being converted into a dumping ground jettisoned by the civilian prison authorities'.[82] In particular they highlighted the disproportionally high percentage of prisoners with mental health difficulties:

1. Over 50% receiving drugs regularly.
2. Over 33% attending the visiting psychiatrist regularly.
3. 20% with records of sex offenders.[83]

The PRO organised a series of public demonstrations in support of closing the Curragh over the next few years, as well as presenting its findings to the MacBride commission in 1979. The commission's report concluded: 'The prison at the Curragh Military Camp provides probably the most bizarre aspect of our entire prison system ... The Commission of Enquiry into the Irish Penal System has no hesitation in recommending that the continued detention of civilian prisoners in the Curragh Military Detention Centre should be discontinued at the first possible opportunity'.[84]

A year after the report's publication in 1981, Seán MacBride officially launched the PRO's renewed campaign to close the Curragh.[85] The PRO partnered with two TDs, the Democratic Socialist Party's Jim Kemmy and the Labour Party's Michael D. Higgins, later president of Ireland, and committed to appealing to independent TDs and senators as well as making 'strong representations to the Catholic hierarchy'.[86] The PRO also appealed to Amnesty International, with whom they had also worked on the death penalty campaign, to designate the prisoners in the Curragh as 'prisoners of conscience', because Amnesty refuses to make representations on behalf of ordinary prisoners.[87] Nine days after the launch of the campaign, a deputation of members of the Oireachtas, including Higgins and Kemmy as well as long-term fellow travellers of the PRO Noël Browne TD and Senator Brendan Ryan, met with Minister for Justice Jim Mitchell.[88] During the meeting, Mitchell promised to close the Curragh within six months. The PRO, although concerned about the delay, issued a statement which concluded, 'It will be nice to celebrate the 10th anniversary of the opening of the Curragh, exactly six months from now, by closing it'.[89] However, just as the collapse of the Fine Gael–Labour minority government had dashed the PRO's hopes of ending the death penalty, it also disrupted Mitchell's plan to close the Curragh.

Unlike the anti–death penalty campaign, the collapse of the coalition government did not stop the PRO's 'close the Curragh' campaign. When forming the 1982 minority government, the leader of Fianna Fáil, Charlie Haughey, had to make a pact with a number of independent TDs including the first-term socialist TD Tony Gregory. In his previous role as a Dublin city councillor, Gregory had nominated Costello for his unsuccessful 1981 bid for a seat in the Seanad and had generally been a fellow traveller of the PRO.[90] In the Dáil, Gregory continued to push for the PRO's campaign and made the closure of the Curragh a condition of his deal to support Haughey's government.[91] In November 1982, the minister for defence announced that the Curragh would be closed to civilian prisoners by the end of the year, at which the PRO expressed 'absolute delight'.[92] However, by the time this statement was made, the government had already lost a motion of confidence and four days later they lost a general election to a Fine Gael–Labour coalition government. Although the Department of Justice reaffirmed the plan to close the Curragh by the end of January 1983, late February found the PRO again protesting outside Leinster House carrying signs demanding that the new Taoiseach (Irish head of government), Garret Fitzgerald, follow through on his election promises and close the Curragh.[93] The issue was raised in the Seanad by then senators, and later presidents of Ireland, Mary Robinson and Michael D. Higgins (Higgins had lost his Dáil seat in 1982 but won a Senate seat for the National University constituency the following year).[94] Around this time, a new secure unit was opened in Mountjoy, which was intended to receive the prisoners from the Curragh; however, by the beginning of March, it had already been occupied by other prisoners, and the minister refused, in the Dáil, to set a date by which the Curragh prisoners would be transferred.[95]

In March, a man, Anthony Cahill, died of a suspected heroin overdose in his cell in the Curragh, although the prison authorities initially claimed that he had died of natural causes.[96] He had spent five years in the prison, had endured months of solitary confinement which were only ended by a court order, had alleged that he was regularly beaten by prison officers, and the week before his death he had been refused compassionate parole to attend his mothers' funeral.[97] As they had done in the 1970s, the PRO tried to use the case to highlight broader problems in the Curragh. However, even after the death, and the mounting public and PRO pressure, when Minister for Justice Michael Noonan was asked if he would give a commitment to transfer the civilian prisoners out of the Curragh in light of Cahill's death, he responded that 'military custody for some civilian prisoners was a necessity'.[98] It was not until May 1983 that the decision was finally made to transfer the civilian prisoners from the Curragh and to allow the Prisons Act (1972) to lapse, removing the legal mechanism under which civilians could be transferred to military custody. It had taken ten years, but the PRO's campaign to close the only military prison for civilian prisoners in Western Europe had succeeded.

150 | Prisoners' Bodies

Conclusion: The 'Crime Wave', Prison Expansion, and the Decline of the PRO

In the mid-1980s, the PRO's newfound respectability was dealt a hard blow by the changes that were taking place both inside and outside Irish prisons. In the last chapter, we discussed the emergence of the heroin epidemic and the resultant dissolution of the prisoners' organisation, which Costello characterised as the 'beginning of the end' for the PRO.[99] Outside the prison, the little sympathy and respect that the PRO and the PU had managed to win for ordinary prisoners in the 1970s and early 1980s was quickly fading away. The number of crimes recorded by the Gardaí had risen rapidly between 1970 (61,032) and 1983 (204,340). However, it was not until the 1982–85 period, as the rise in crime statistics slowed and began to decline, that the idea of a 'crime wave' really took off in the public discourse. A frequency analysis of the four leading national newspapers, the *Irish Times*, *Irish Press*, *Irish Independent*, and the *Sunday Independent*, shows that there were an average of 14 references to a crime wave in the Republic of Ireland each year between 1970 and 1981; however, between 1981 and 1982, the number of references rose by a factor of two and a half, and from 1982 to 1985, the average number of references was over 81, peaking at 136 in 1985, when the number of actual reported crimes of all types had already been declining for two years. This abrupt increase in the references to a 'crime wave' was more than a simple shift in language. It was not that the press of the 1970s were not aware of or concerned about the rising crime rates, rather that the rise of the 'crime wave' as a signifier denoted a shift in the frame of reference through which crime was understood, a shift that would have serious implications for the newfound respectability of the PRO.

In the 1970s, crime was usually discussed in terms of serious offences, like the armed robbery of banks, post offices, and delivery vans. These offences often seemed to be relatively thought through and coordinated, the perpetrators could be expected to be semi-organised gangs or at least 'career criminals'. The idea of a 'crime wave', however, is related to a very different type of offence. In 1977–78, during the debate about the government's plan to open Loughan House as a prison for children under seventeen years old, the press began to report on disorganised petty crime by working-class youths in Dublin, Limerick, and Cork, even though this did not correlate with a significant increase in the crime rate. In fact, the number of reported crimes fractionally decreased from 1977 to 1978, while the number of references to a 'crime wave' jumped from ten (1976) to twenty-seven (1977) and thirty-seven (1978) before falling back to nine (1979) once Loughan House was open and the controversy had died away. Similarly, the 'crime wave' period of 1982–85 was dominated by coverage of disorganised antisocial crimes driven by either desperation and addiction, or, as the PRO put it in their 1978 survey report, 'youthful energy, devilment and high jinks'.[100] These included drug offences, mugging, petty theft, vandalism, and joyriding. The 'crime wave' narrative reimagined the problem of crime not as a set of career criminals planning and perpetrating serious crimes but as a profusion of chaotic youths who threatened to tear the social fabric apart through the volume, rather than the seriousness, of their crimes. The other side of this refiguration of crime and criminals was a reimagining of the victims of crime. Rather than the employees of banks and post offices, whose jobs predictably put them in harm's way, the victim of the 1982–85 period was represented as an everyman figure. News reports bemoaned the mugging of shoppers and the burgling of the elderly and asked whether anyone could avoid being the victim of crime.[101] The result was the concerted demonisation of the particular type of ordinary prisoner whom the PRO had worked so hard to humanise in the public eye. The very signifiers which the PRO had emphasised as reasons that prisoners should not be demonised – their deprived youth, lack of education and opportunity, and even the pettiness of their early crimes – became the signifiers of a nihilistic underclass and the existential threat that it supposedly posed to Irish society.

For the PRO, this discursive shift undermined a decade of campaigning and forced it into a defensive position. In 1984, Richie Ryan, then a member of the European Parliament and a former Fine Gael minister for the public service and minister for finance, addressed a party meeting in Foxrock, a wealthy Dublin suburb. He told the meeting that 'the first and fundamental reason for imprisonment is deserved punishment ... [and] the public at large, particularly victims of crime, are outraged by prisoners' demands for greater comforts and privileges'.[102] He went on to attack the PRO in particular, which he implied did not represent 'the law-abiding people of Dublin'.[103] Nearly a month later, Joe Costello responded with a letter in the *Irish Times*:

> Perhaps Mr Ryan would explain what he means by 'presumptuous hypocritical pronouncements from the self-created Prisoners' Rights Organisation.' I challenge him to detail a single hypocritical pronouncement that I have ever made as spokesman for the PRO. What can he possibly mean by self-created? If he knows something miraculous about the birth of the PRO perhaps he would reveal it ...
>
> His Victorian attitudes towards the treatment of prisoners reveal him to be quite out of line with his colleagues in the European Parliament. His knowledge of the present situation in Irish prisons is faulty and his vicious attack on the Prisoners' Rights Organisation which has campaigned since 1973 for much-needed changes in our prison system is simply scurrilous.[104]

This exchange was typical of many of the PRO's interactions in this period, which often lapsed back into the tropes that had been used to invalidate the PRO in the early 1970s. For instance, Costello also clashed with the Department of Justice, when it referred to the PRO's 'subversive innuendo-style of presentation', and with the deputy Garda commissioner, J.P. McMahon, when he described the PRO as 'extremists seeking to destabilise democracy' after the organisation published a series of allegations of Garda violence.[105] The PRO's defensiveness deepened as the Prisoners' Revenge Squad began its 1984–86 campaign, during which PRO committee members 'expressed dismay at the damage the revenge group could inflict on the cause'.[106] Unlike in the 1970s, not all of the criticism came from the political establishment, and tensions grew between the PRO and some elements of the working-class communities, where they had traditionally found the most support. In 1984, a speaker for Concerned Parents Against Drugs, a community organisation which sought to expel drug dealers from working-class communities, implied that there were drug dealers on the PRO's executive committee. The PRO quickly wrote a defensive letter stating that although the organisation 'fights for the rights of prisoners no matter what they are serving sentences for', they denied that there were 'any drug pushers' on the committee.[107]

In 1984, the government announced the formation of the Committee of Inquiry into the Penal System, chaired by T.K. Whitaker, a former senator, governor of the Central Bank, senior civil servant, and a paragon of respectability. Not long after his appointment to the chair, the commission of inquiry, Una O'Higgins O'Malley, sent him a copy of the report of the MacBride commission, of which she had been a member. Whitaker replied: 'I have ... carefully read the report of the Commission on Crime and Punishment of which you were a member. I have arranged that copies will be in the hands of all our members. Indeed when I read what you have written + the reports prepared by the Council for Social Welfare + the joint Churches group I wonder why another body was set up'.[108] This reassurance was echoed a year later with the publication of the Whitaker Report, which recommended that the government adopt almost all of the penal reforms for which the PRO had been campaigning for over a decade. These ranged from the reduction of the prison population so that only the most serious crimes resulted in imprisonment; the development of social and community services to address the causes of crime and to create alternative forms of sentencing; and the improvement of psychiatric, medical, and education facilities for prisoners. This report came as the PRO had begun to lose support and respectability, its activities were becoming less frequent, and its activists were drifting away into other areas. Joe Costello, who had become the driving force of the organisation in the late 1970s, described the impact of the report and the sense that the PRO had effectively achieved its aim: 'I began to move from there to the more political side of things. From there on in I wasn't able to devote my time to it [the PRO], and I was doing most of the work at the time ... I think that was, you know, that was very much a watershed, the fact that the powers-that-be had more or less accepted [the PRO's principles]'.[109]

6

'What We Thought We Had Achieved'
Whitaker, Reform, and the Legacy of the Prisoners' Rights Movement

Introduction

In 1983–84, tensions in the prison system were reaching a crux. Overcrowding had become such a serious problem that people with convictions had to 'queue up', waiting in the community for a place to become available in prison so they could be committed, while others were being sent home for three or four weeks 'holiday' after completing part of their sentence, on condition that they would return to complete the rest of it.[1] Most of the state's prisons were operating at, or above, capacity – the average daily population of Mountjoy in 1984 was 486, while there were only 460 individual cells and fourteen shared cells; similarly, Portlaoise had an average population of 202 but had 178 individual and fifteen shared cells; while Cork had an average population of 183, but only 79 individual and ten shared cells.[2] This overcrowding meant that the prison authorities restricted the amount of time prisoners could spend outside their cells.[3] Meanwhile, pressure for reform was mounting from outside the prison service.

The Prisoners' Rights Organisation's (PRO) independent inquiry into the prison system, chaired by Seán MacBride, published its report in 1980, sparking a chain reaction of similar inquiries. In 1981, the ecumenical Irish Council of Churches' Board of Community Affairs published its report on the prison system, and in 1983, the Council for Social Welfare, a committee of the Catholic Bishops' Conference, published another.[4] However, while the MacBride Committee had struggled to get important information from the Department of Justice, the religious organisations, with their cultural weight and political influence, were given far greater cooperation, even including access to the prisons themselves.[5] Significantly, these reports endorsed many of the concerns and recommendations that MacBride had raised, and indeed that the PRO had been campaigning for since the early 1970s – for instance, that the prison estate was too old and had not been modernised, that most of the women in prison had committed petty offences and did not need to be in prison, and that there was no coherent justification for imprisonment in the state. The findings of the inquiries were widely reported and further added to the pressure on the government. Indeed, we can use the reportage by the *Irish Independent*, a conservative newspaper which had been antagonistic to the prisoners' movement since its outset, as a barometer of this growing pressure. In 1980, the *Independent* did not dedicate a single report to the publication of the MacBride commission, indeed it was only mentioned a week after its publication in the last third of a report about the expense of the construction of the new women's prison in Clondalkin.[6] A year later, the *Independent*'s editor deemed that the Irish Council of Churches' report merited a response. However, the paper, still antagonistic to penal reform, only gave it a short article and endorsed the Fianna Fáil minister for justice's refutation of the report with the headline: 'Prison Welfare Very Well Run, Says Collins'.[7] By the time the bishop's report was published in 1983, the article was significantly longer and more sympathetic, as we can see from the headline, 'prisons Cannot Solve Crime – Bishops'.[8] The pressure was further amplified by the deaths of three people in detention over the course of just six weeks in February and March 1983, prompting renewed demands for an official inquiry.[9] Finally, throughout the early months of 1983, tensions between the Prison Officer's Association (POA) and the government had been particularly fraught.[10] The ever-growing prison population necessitated large amounts of overtime for prison officers, and the government, concerned about the growing expense of this, had proposed capping the amount of overtime. In response, the POA threatened industrial action which would keep prisoners in their cells for twenty-three hours a day.[11] The tensions escalated further when the Department of Justice mobilised the army and Gardaí, which they planned to use as strike-breaking labour in the prisons.[12] Industrial action was averted the night before the cuts were due to be implemented when, after four hours of talks, the department agreed to defer the proposed cuts and to establish an independent inquiry into the prison system.[13]

The Establishment of the Whitaker Inquiry

In spite of the apparent urgency of this last-minute agreement, it took nearly a year to establish the Committee of Inquiry into the Prison System. T.K. Whitaker was appointed as the committee's chairman, a pillar of respectability in the Irish establishment. At the time of the appointment, he was the chancellor of the National University of Ireland (1976–96), but he had previously been the governor of the Central Bank (1969–76) and a Taoiseach-appointed senator (1977–82).[14] Indeed, it was this respectability alone that qualified him for the appointment; when responding to the Taoiseach's invitation to lead the inquiry, he initially suggested that Supreme Court Judges Séamus Henchy or Brian Walsh, who also sat on the European Court of Human Rights, would be better placed and more authoritative chairmen and accepted the position on the understanding that his only qualifications were 'ignorance' and 'open-mindedness'.[15] Nonetheless, Whitaker's open-minded respectability carried such weight that when Mr Justice Séamus Henchy was invited to join the committee as an ordinary member, he wrote to Whitaker: 'When asked to sit on the Committee I inquired who the Chairman was and, on being told it was you, I accepted the invitation without inquiring further about the personnel. I knew that, with you in charge, the results would be fruitful and sensible'.[16] Most of the other eight appointees were similarly respectable and had extensive experience in relevant fields, like Fr Peter McVerry, a Jesuit priest and well-known campaigner on behalf of homeless people; and Dr John G. Cooney, a consultant psychiatrist and founding director of the National Council on Alcoholism. Breege O'Donoghue's inclusion was less relevant to the everyday life of prisoners but, as a personnel manager in the Primark Group and a former chairperson of the Irish branch of the Institute of Personnel Management, her expertise would have been relevant to the long-running industrial dispute between the POA and the Department of Justice. However, the role of Declan Doyle, a marketing director at Irish Cement Ltd., was less readily explicable.

The committee was given a broad remit, which ranged from assessing the law relating to imprisonment to the conditions in the prison estate, and included the prison regimes themselves, staffing issues, and employment conditions for people working in the system. Although these terms of reference had been floating around the Department of Justice since the idea of an inquiry was first internally floated in August 1982, nonetheless, there was a good deal of resistance to the breadth of these terms. The Department of Finance in particular argued that the inquiry's terms should be limited to an examination of the law around imprisonment, the possibility of reducing sentence lengths, and methods of reducing the number of people committed to prison. They warned that if the committee's terms were too expansive, their recommendations would inevitably be too expensive:

> It is considered that there is a grave risk of costly recommendations arising under this. Members of the proposed committee could be expected to visit prisons. The impact of prison conditions on people not familiar with them can be very strong and can generate a feeling that everything possible, irrespective of expense, should be done to ameliorate them and this could extend to accommodation in so far as this relates to regimes ... [these draft terms are] opposed by the Department of Finance because of the risk of costly recommendations which might be made by an over-impressionable Committee.[17]

Although they were changed slightly to ease the Department of Finance's concerns, the committee was still given 'deliberately wide' terms of reference.[18] However, altering the terms was not the only way that the administration sought to shape the outcome of the inquiry.

Recognising that the inquiry was, first and foremost, a concession to an industrial dispute with the prison officers, the terms of reference issued to Whitaker included a reminder about the relations between management and staff: 'This is a most important area. The minister would like it to be examined and to have the analysis and recommendations made public. He hopes that the committee would be satisfied with the approach of management and will "reprimand" staff for their militancy. Discipline in the Prison service is very poor and the Minister hopes that the Committee would have something to say about it'.[19] It is, perhaps, a mark of Whitaker's even-handedness that the final report did not bow to this departmental pressure to 'reprimand' the POA. Rather, it was confidently asserted in the report's introduction that it was not the task of the committee to 'attempt to apportion blame' in the industrial dispute and went on to suggest changes that would need to be made on all sides to create a fully functioning prison system.

Ultimately, the committee was asked to assess 'the whole way of life of the prison' system, and as such, it was given access to all of the state's prisons, as well as sixteen hostels, training, and treatment centres used by former prisoners.[20] It also received detailed information from the Department of Justice and advertised in the newspapers for submissions from the public and civil society organisations. The committee received 101 public, and several more confidential, submissions. Most of the submissions came from organisations that one might expect to be represented in such an inquiry, including the Department of Justice, three Visiting Committees, several public service unions, and the Gardaí. Some of the submissions were more unexpected, including that of the Transcendental Meditation Department of the Irish branch of the Maharishi International University. One of the most notable features of the process was the consideration given to people with experience in prison.

Extensive submissions were made by prisoners and former prisoners, or their representatives. This included deputations of 'subversive' prisoners from both Limerick and Portlaoise Prisons. More significantly, it also included a group of ordinary prisoners from Cork Prison, and, although I have been unable to confirm it, I believe that about 30 per cent of the individual submissions came from people who had direct experience of prison. Finally, the PRO made an extensive submission to the commission. We will not, here, discuss the contents of their submissions; rather, I want to draw attention to the end of one of the red threads that has run through this book. That is the acceptance of the legitimacy of the prisoners' voice when discussing prison conditions and penal reform. As we have seen throughout the last six chapters, the legitimacy of prisoners' voices grew throughout the 1970s and early 1980s. However, of the five reports on the prison system made between 1973 and 1985 – produced by the Prison Study Group, the MacBride commission, the Council of Churches, the Bishops' Council for Social Welfare, and the Whitaker Inquiry – Whitaker was the first to speak to current prisoners. Each of the other commissions had made varying levels of effort to speak to people with experience of prisons, and although they had spoken to ex-prisoners, they were restricted from speaking to current prisoners by the Department of Justice. The department's notes on the brief justified its breadth by saying that 'the inquiry should be comprehensive as regards the "penal system." An inquiry which might appear superficial could not be defended'.[21] As such, the establishment of the Whitaker Inquiry with its 'deliberately wide' remit to look at the 'whole life of the prisons', including the experiences of prisoners, was also a recognition by the department of the legitimacy of prisoners voices.[22] Conversely, it was also a tacit acknowledgement that an inquiry which excluded prisoners' voices would be unacceptable, and indefensible, within the public discourse.

The Reception of the Whitaker Report

At the time of the publication of the Whitaker report in August 1985, the prison system was 'in peril of collapse'.[23] In the public sphere, the conservative newspapers bemoaned the spiralling costs of the prison system, the left-leaning newspapers derided the prisoners' inhuman living conditions, and all papers complained about the apparent ineffectiveness of prison as a deterrent to the 'crime wave'.[24] Within this milieu, there was a consensus that the prison system needed to change and, due in no small part to the PRO's long campaign, it was accepted by most interested parties that this must entail a reduction in the prison population and the development of noncarceral alternatives.

When the Whitaker Report was published, it met with 'unanimous approval' from normally divided groups.[25] The prison governors welcomed it, while the PRO and POA found themselves agreeing about the need to fully implement the recommendations of the report.[26] The *Irish Independent, Irish Press,* and *Irish Times,* so often at loggerheads over issues of social and economic reform, all emphatically welcomed the publication while the report was praised across the political spectrum from Fianna Fáil to the Workers Party, on the opposition right and left.[27] It was also welcomed by the government coalition parties Fine Gael and Labour. This shared purpose was short-lived, however. Michael Noonan, the Fine Gael minister for justice, was slow to commit to specific actions based on its conclusions and very quickly old battle-lines began to reemerge as various groups disagreed about the details, interpretation, or limitations of the report.[28] The POA warned that the government must not appoint 'political hacks' to the new independent board that would administer the prison system.[29] The PRO argued that there needed to be greater representation for prisoners within the running of the prison system.[30] The prison governors complained that there was not sufficient detail about how ex-prisoners should be supported after being released.[31] Mary McAleese, then the Reid Professor of Criminal Law at Trinity College Dublin (TCD), a former member of the MacBride commission, and later the president of Ireland (1997–2011), suggested that the report did not offer a coherent strategy to deal with the influx of drug users into the prison system.[32] Perhaps the most critical, and least expected, of all was the *Response to the Report of the Committee of Inquiry into the Penal System,* which was produced collaboratively by the Catholic Bishops' Council for Social Welfare and the Irish Council of Churches' Commission for Justice and Peace, both of which had previously produced damning reports on the prison system. Although the *Response* welcomed the reforming principles laid out in the Whitaker Report, it, among other things, questioned the report's budget estimations, queried the statistical methodology used to identify the one-third of prisoners who would be released under the new regime, and cast doubt on whether there would still be enough space to house even the reduced estimate of the prison population once the reports' recommended improvements were made to prison buildings.[33] Whitaker, who had deliberately stayed out of the public limelight since the publication of the report, broke his silence only to correct what he saw as factual inaccuracies in McAleese's criticism, responding to the criticism, in July 1986, in a private letter to the minister for justice, then Alan Dukes, who had recently replaced his fellow Fine Gael member Noonan. He explained that it had been the role of the committee to establish the principles of reform, not to set out a detailed blueprint which, Whitaker felt, would have been a 'usurpation of the responsibilities of the administration ... This fundamental point seems to have escaped the authors of the so-called "response," who confused themselves on other matters as well'.[34] For the most part, as Whitaker's letter to the minister suggests, the criticisms of the report were procedural issues for the administration to work out. The reforming principles of the report, however, received widespread approbation from across the spectra of criminal justice and political positions.

The Implementation of the Whitaker Report

While these debates about the details of implementing the report were ongoing, there were already hints that the report might not have been that welcome within the coalition government. Contrary to the custom of the civil service, when the Committee of Inquiry concluded its work neither Whitaker, as chairman, nor any of the ordinary members, received a letter thanking them for their efforts and the department did not organise the 'farewell dinner' that usually followed the completion of such an inquiry.[35] While this may seem like a point of relatively obscure protocol, it raised a red flag for the committee members, warning them of the hostility of the department to their recommendations. Nine months after the publication of the report, when a cabinet reshuffle replaced Michael Noonan with Alan Dukes as minister for justice, Whitaker wrote to the new minister to complain about this snub. Dukes's reply included a copy of the speech he delivered, a week after receiving Whitaker's letter, at the annual conference of the POA which endorsed and called for the full implementation of the inquiry's recommendations. In the speech, the minister briefly expressed his gratitude to the committee and continued: 'I know some

162 | Prisoners' Bodies

people have expressed disappointment at the alleged lack of progress since the Report was published. Some have expressed fears that – to use the relevant cliché – it will be left to "gather dust on a shelf". What these expressions of concern fail to take into account is that it is inevitable, given the far-reaching and wide-ranging nature of the Committee's conclusions, that some time must elapse before decisions can be taken on many aspects of the report'.[36] The committee quickly saw this vague and noncommittal comment for what it was. In private letters to Whitaker, the prominent antihomelessness campaigner Fr Peter McVerry commented, 'I'm afraid my cynicism is not in any way allayed by reading Alan's address'.[37] Meanwhile, the Supreme Court Justice Séamus Henchy was still more direct: 'Knowing the Department of Justice as I do, I have not much hope that they will implement this particular recommendation', meaning one of the report's foundational recommendations to establish an independent prison board.[38] Their suspicions seem to have been well founded. In October 1985, Tomás Mac Giolla, a Worker's Party TD, asked the minister whether he accepted the report's recommendations and whether he intended to make a statement on the matter, to which the Minister responded vaguely: 'I am not in a position to make any statement ... I do not expect that decisions will be finalised for some time yet'.[39] When, seven months later, Mac Giolla asked what measures had been taken to implement the report, the minister flatly referred him back to the vague response he made in October.[40] In September 1986, over a year after the publication of the report, when he was pushed about the report's key recommendation to create an independent prisons board to run the prison system, Dukes confirmed that there were still 'no proposals to remove Justice officials from close control' of the prison system.[41] In this section, I will consider how, in the intervening thirty-six years since the release of the report, many of the reports key recommendations have been entirely ignored, and those that have been implemented happened several decades after the report and even then only half-heartedly.

One of the first recommendations to be enacted was the appointment of women as prison officers, point 2.71 in the report, which occurred for the first time just five months after the publication of the report.[42] However, this rapidity was exceptional. Points 2.49 and 2.51, for instance, made some of the reports' most significant recommendations: to establish an independent prisons board which would handle the day-to-day running of the prison service and the appointment of an inspector of prisons who would be of equal rank to the director general of the prisons board. It took eleven years and five changes of government before these two recommendations were acted on. In 1996, Nora Owen, then Fine Gael minister for justice in the Rainbow Coalition government, announced the establishment of an independent prisons board, which would take the day-to-day running of the prison system out of the hands of the Department of Justice. Owen also established an expert group, under the chairmanship of Dan McAuley, whose report in 1997 led to the eventual establishment of the Irish Prison Service (IPS), the independent body which has run the prison system since 1999.[43] The McAuley Report also led to the appointment of an inspector of prisons of equal standing to the director general of the IPS.[44] The powers of the inspectorate were further strengthened by the passing of the new Prison Rules (2007).[45]

Another recommendation that has gradually been enacted was 2.22, which advised that all prisoners should have access to a wash basin and toilet facilities at all times. Progress on this front has been extremely gradual. When the Whitaker Report was published, almost all prisoners, with the exception of those on Spike Island, had no access to in-cell sanitation and so they had to 'slop out' each morning, meaning that prisoners would, before breakfast, carry their full chamber pots out of their cells to a shared toilet where they would queue up to empty them. By 2011, the number of prisoners who had to slop out had been reduced to around 30 per cent and Ireland was coming under pressure from the international community. In 2011, the UN Committee Against Torture produced a report on the Irish prison system which was 'deeply concerned' by the continuation of the practice which it concluded 'amounts to inhuman and degrading treatment'.[46] Since then, the number of prisoners who have to 'slop out' has been reduced to forty-two, as of April 2021, which constituted about 1 per cent of the average daily prison population. This is a significant decrease in a decade; however, the recent pandemic certainly highlights that, as well as the psychological harm done by being forced to publicly

164 | Prisoners' Bodies

dispose of one's waste, it can also pose a physical danger to everyone in the prison system.

Other recommendations were partially enacted. For instance, in 2.40 and 2.41, the report recommended establishing a separate institution for juvenile women, closing St Patrick's Institution and replacing it with a new institution for juvenile men. St Patrick's continued to be used to detain juveniles for nearly three more decades until it was finally closed in 2013, after a 2011 report by the UN Committee Against Torture condemned the practice of imprisoning under-eighteens with over-eighteens, and another in 2012 by the Inspector of Prisons which found a culture of human rights abuses in the institution.[47] However, rather than following the recommendations of the Whitaker Report, the department gradually abolished the juvenile category, which had applied to those aged between sixteen and twenty-one. Instead, it created a hard line between those under and over eighteen years old. So, since the closure of St Patrick's, those aged under eighteen have been sentenced to the Oberstown Detention School and those aged between eighteen and twenty-one, who would formerly have been considered juveniles, have been incorporated into the adult prison system. Similarly, young women aged over eighteen have continued to be imprisoned with adults, while those under eighteen have been moved to Oberstown.[48]

Other aspects of these recommendations, however, have been completely ignored. 2.40, for instance, also argued for the establishment of an open centre where most women could be incarcerated and the establishment of a small, closed centre for the remaining group of women who needed to be held in a higher security regime.[49] This recommendation was ignored. Women continue to be held in medium security closed centres in Limerick and on the Mountjoy campus. The most significant changes in the women's regime happened when the women being held in the women's section of St Patrick's were moved to the newly built Dóchas Centre in 1999, but while this meant a significant improvement in living standards, it is a far cry from the open centre envisaged in the report. Similarly, partially implemented recommendations include raising the age of criminal responsibility from seven years old to fifteen (3.6); the age of responsibility was eventually increased, in 2001, but only to twelve years old.

Indeed, many of the recommendations were flatly ignored by successive governments. For instance, the Vagrancy Act (1847), which made begging and homelessness punishable with imprisonment, was only replaced after the act was found to be unconstitutional in 2008;[50] the proposed increase in remission, from one-quarter to one-third of the length of the prisoner's sentence, never occurred; and the recommended decrease in 'lockup', the time that prisoners are locked in their cells every day, from sixteen hours a day to twelve has still not occurred. As the Irish Penal Reform Trust (IPRT) regularly notes in its annual Progress in the Penal System Reports, information about out-of-cell time is not regularly published and so it is difficult to assess; however, the average is still eight hours, meaning that prisoners continue to be locked up for sixteen hours a day.[51] However, this deteriorated during the Covid-19 pandemic, during which average out-of-cell time was decreased in eight of the country's prison's, in some cases to as little as four and a half or five hours a day.[52]

Perhaps the most important, and certainly the most radical, of the report's recommendations was never implemented: this recommendation was that prison should be reserved only for the most serious crimes which included offences against the person or extremely serious offences against property (2.10–2.14). This would have made imprisonment a 'punishment of last resort and suitable only for those offenders who are a continuing threat to society'.[53] Adopting this recommendation would have entailed an almost revolutionary transformation of the Irish justice system. The report estimated the implementation of its recommendations would have meant an immediate reduction in the average prison population of about 30 per cent. This would have relieved the need for prison officers' overtime and made way for a significant increase in prisoners' out-of-cell time. The reduction in prisoners costs and overtime would have released a significant proportion of the available prison systems budget, which, in turn, could have been reallocated to the provision of alternatives to incarceration. The report recommended the implementation or expansion of a range of different sanctions from probation and fines to community service orders and partial 'restraints on liberty' such as residence in approved hostels. For instance, in a public letter responding to McAleese's criticism of the report, Whitaker clarified that most drug users, who primarily

166 | Prisoners' Bodies

came into conflict with the law for possession of an illegal substance or petty nonviolent property crimes, had no place in prison under the principles of the report. Rather, they would receive addiction treatment and/or mental health supports to address the issues underlying their original offence.[54]

In the intervening decades, some mechanisms have been put in place to divert those convicted of low-level offences away from the prison system. Community service orders, for instance, which were legislated for in 1983 but were not actually applied by the courts until 1985, have become a limited part of the criminal justice system, with the numbers issued rising from 1,204 in 1986 to 2,291 in 2019. However, although this is a 90 per cent increase, it has not kept pace with the increase in prison committals in the same period, which rose by nearly 150 per cent. So, while the orders have been used to divert some people away from the prison system, they have only ever formed a small, and declining, proportion of the total sanctions. Another step, albeit a faltering one, was the establishment of the Dublin Drugs Treatment Court in 2001, which takes a holistic rehabilitative, and largely noncarceral, approach to people who use drugs. The court, however, has had consistently low referral numbers, limited success, and is only accessible to Dublin-based people.[55] While the courts' supporters claim that it has had significant successes that are not captured in the course-completion statistics, its detractors claim that it denies due process to participants and it diverts money that could be more effectively used in medical and probation programmes.[56] Indeed, in its first nine years of operation, it only received an average of forty-two referrals a year, almost half of which were deemed unsuitable for the programme, and of the eligible participants, only 14 per cent actually completed the programme. However, of those that did complete the programme, 85 per cent did not return to their former patterns of offending, suggesting, albeit from a small sample size, an impressively low recidivism rate.[57] These programmes barely scratch the surface of the reforms that Whitaker recommended. In spite of the increased use of non-carceral sentences, the average daily population of the prison system grew by 13 per cent between 1985 and 1990, while the total number of indictable offences actually fell by 5 per cent. Between 1990 and 2012, the prison population continued to rise, reaching 232 per cent of the population when the Whitaker Report was published, and while it has remained relatively stable since then, even declining by a few per cent, the proportion of committals for nonviolent offences, which Whitaker recommended should not lead to incarceration, has remained at about a third of the total.

The report, however, was not solely focused on dealing with convicted people; it also dealt with the prevention of crime. Early on in the report, Whitaker notes that 'not all crime can be attributed to social deprivation' and that to some extent crime is an inevitable result of 'human nature'.[58] However, it concludes that most crime can be traced back to some level of 'physical, emotional, or cultural deprivation'.[59] As such, the report spends a good deal of time arguing, not for criminal and penal reform, but for social reform that would create a more equitable, caring, and supportive society – shifting the state's focus away from punitivism. Here, the report is less radical than in its assessment of the justice system. It notes that around one-third of all offences are committed by young people, meaning those under twenty-one. As such, it emphasises the need to develop youth support services, fully endorsing the recommendations of Declan Costello's National Youth Policy Committee Report (1984). Both of these reports put the emphasis firmly on the role of the family. For instance, Whitaker recommended, 'The state's primary concern should be for the welfare of family, child and juvenile rather than for punishment of the negligent, the wayward or the criminal'.[60] While Costello wrote, 'A National Youth Policy aimed at assisting young people must recognise the primary position of the family which through its role in the rearing of young people is central to the adequate development of personality and the building of a community.[61]

The emphasis that the report puts on the family, here, is indicative of a broader trend in 1980s Ireland which presented the family as the primary unit of social enforcement. Indeed, it was on this principle that many of the most successful arguments were made in the 1983 abortion referendum, which enshrined a prohibition of abortion in the constitution; the 1986 divorce referendum, which rejected the legalisation of divorce; and the long-running campaign against the decriminalisation of homosexual activities, which eventually failed in 1993. Moreover, the report openly describes the authors' anxieties about the deterioration of traditional social units, the increased urbanisation of the population and the 'lowering of behavioural standards'.[62] As such, both reports firmly stress the need for the government to deploy social policies that would strengthen the family 'to fulfil this vital role'.[63] Both the Whitaker and Costello reports were welcomed by religious groups – not least the Catholic Bishop's Conference and the Commission for Justice and Peace which, although critical of the detail of the report, warmly welcomed its principles.

The Legacy of the Prisoners' Rights Movement

The assurance that Whitaker gave to O'Higgins O'Malley, mentioned in chapter 5, that 'copies [of the MacBride Report] will be in the hands of all our members' had not been an empty promise. [64] The early discussion papers, circulated to members of the committee, made reference to each of these reports in ways that suggest the reports had been required reading.[65] In light of this, it is unsurprising that the PRO was pleased with the Whitaker Report. Not only did Whitaker endorse most of the key findings of the MacBride Report, which the PRO had commissioned, but it also endorsed most of the demands that the PRO had been making since its formation in 1973. Indeed, if we compare manifestoes of the Prisoners' Union (PU) and the PRO with the recommendations of the Whitaker Report, we can see a remarkable overlap. Of the eleven demands in the manifesto of the Portlaoise PU, eight were endorsed in whole or part by the Whitaker Report. Of the PRO's six demands in the 1973 manifesto, four were similarly endorsed. What is more, this included one of the most far-reaching reforms, the demand for the establishment of an independent Prison Board which would take the administration of the prison system out of the purview of the Department of Justice. Moreover, almost all of the organisations' demands which emerged later were included in the report in some form. For instance, the call for the psychiatric screening of all new prisoners, which emerged after the series of suicides in custody in 1974 and 1975, was incorporated into one of the report's fundamental recommendations. This was the recommendation that every potential prisoner should receive a social and psychological assessment which would be used to help determine the nature of their sanction, whether it ought to be imprisonment or a noncarceral alternative.[66] Similarly, the related call for an improvement in the provision of psychiatric, and medical, services across the prison services was formalised in the Whitaker Report as the recommendation to establish the position of an independent medical director who would coordinate medical and psychiatric services across the prison service. To drive this point home Whitaker specified that the director should be 'a highly qualified psychiatrist with experience in forensic psychiatry'.[67]

It is important to clarify, however, that the Whitaker Report did not accept all of the PRO's demands. One central demand of the PU and of the PRO, in its early years, which the report did not endorse was the right of prisoners to unionise, for their union to be recognised, and for its representatives to be included on various administrative committees, like the proposed Prisons Board. However, since the collapse of the PU in the late 1970s and the subsequent changes in the prisons' demographics and cultures, as we discussed in chapter 4, this point was no longer as relevant as it had been in the early 1970s.

One of the report's recommendations, more than any other, stood out for the members of the PRO: 'that prison should be defined not in retributions, not in punishment, but in terms of loss of liberty. The censure of imprisonment was the loss of liberty and that was what we thought we had achieved in 1984/85 with the Whitaker Committee of Inquiry'.[68] This was one of the central principles of the PRO's position, particularly in the later years, and, when the Whitaker Report discussed the justification of imprisonment, it was the first thing that the report addressed. The report proposed four explanations for imprisonment: 'punishment', 'deterrence', 'reformation/rehabilitation of offenders', and 'prevention'.[69] When discussing punishment as a justification for imprisonment, the committee was at pains to point out that 'offenders are sent to prison *as* punishment and not *for* punishment. It is a warning we wish to repeat because of the insidious danger that attitudes and practice may erode this distinction, which is vital to a fair, non-vindictive and humane administration of justice. The idea of vengeance, as distinct from legitimate and limited punishment, should be totally excluded'.[70] In other words, the report was recommending that imprisonment itself, meaning the loss of liberty, ought to be the punishment, rather than prison being a place where other punishments are meted out. The main corollary of this principle was that a person's living standards should not necessarily drop when they were committed to prison, they should have access to decent food, exercise, healthcare, education, and other public services equivalent to those available to people at liberty. As such, the PRO members felt that all of their substantive demands would necessarily follow, once this fundamental principle had been accepted by the Department of Justice. In the belief that these reforms were almost inevitable, subsequent to the publication of the report, the PRO began to drift further and further out of everyday public discourse.

In the three years prior to the Whitaker Report's publication, the leading four national newspapers collectively published, on average, over a hundred articles a year that mentioned the PRO. In the three years after the publication, this number fell by two-thirds to just thirty-four articles a year. Indeed, many of these were not about prisoners' rights at all. Rather, they dealt with other campaigns which included activists who were best known for their involvement with the PRO. For instance, fourteen of the twenty-six articles that mentioned the PRO in 1987 did so only in passing and were really about Joe Costello's protest in 1985 against a Garda crackdown on traditional street trading which had been rendered illegal under the Casual Trading Act (1980). This shift clearly represents Costello's shift away from prisoners' rights campaigning and towards more traditional political activism, but it also represents the ambiguous existence of the PRO throughout the late 1980s. The PRO was never formally wound up and, over the next eight years, the press regularly referred to Joe Costello as the leader of the PRO. However, these references were simply contextual identifiers, phrases used to remind the reader who Costello was and to contextualise the story. In some cases, these were stories about Costello commenting on prison matters, but in his capacity as a senator rather than as the head of the now defunct PRO.[71] However, the vast majority of the stories that used these references did not have any bearing on prisoners' rights at all.

Ultimately the PRO dropped out of the public eye entirely in 1994. In 1993, Joe Costello was elected to the Dáil and, although one of his first acts as a TD was to call for the establishment of a Prisons Board, he had ceased to identify himself with the PRO.[72] This may have been because he was warned that there was no political gain to be made in representing prisoners, but it might also be that he felt that the mantel of penal reform activism had been taken on by the IPRT, which was form in 1994. One of the IPRT's founding members was Pat McCartan, who had also been a founding member of the PRO, but had, since leaving the organisation, gone on to be elected to the Dáil as a TD for the Workers' Party and later Democratic Left. While he was a TD, he entered into a correspondence with a prisoner, which ultimately led to his meeting Tom O'Malley, a lecturer in law at University College Galway; Paul O'Mahony, a psychologist and criminologist who had recently left his job at the Department of Justice; and James Kavanagh, a retired auxiliary bishop of Dublin. Together, the four established the IPRT, which has since gone on to be Ireland's longest lasting and most vocal penal reform organisation and has led successful campaigns for widespread reform within the Irish prison system, not least for ending the detention of children within the prison system.

Conclusion

The prisoners' rights movement rose and fell in less than thirteen years, from the first proto-PU protest in November 1972 to the publication of the Whitaker Report in August 1985. Over the years, it successfully campaigned for concrete reforms in the prison system, from the expansion of the prison education and medical services and the closure of the Curragh camp to civilian prisoners to the establishment of the Committee of Inquiry into the Prison System. The movement also achieved a less tangible, but no less real, shift in the discourse around prisoners. Transforming the representation of prisoners from that of a violent, animalistic hoard into a group of individuals, who, although flawed, were deserving of human rights and dignity.

The Whitaker Report was a watershed moment in Irish prison history not because it revolutionised the system but because it was the moment that prisoners' rights and penal reform were fixed into the mainstream discourse. Whitaker took the agendas of the PU and the PRO, which had often been attacked as fringe or even subversive, and expressed them in the voice of the 'reasonable', 'respectable', bourgeois establishment. What is more, these agendas met with widespread ac-

172 | Prisoners' Bodies

ceptance across the political spectrum, from Fianna Fáil to the Workers' Party, and throughout the prison hierarchy, from governors all the way down to prisoners. This was a moment whose foundations had been laid by the prisoners' rights movement through years of hard campaigning. The PRO and the PU set the agenda for penal reform, drawing the prison system's flaws into the open and outlining how the system could be changed, and they kept those agendas close to the top of the news for over a decade. They popularised and campaigned for the establishment of an inquiry into the prison system, which became the Whitaker Inquiry. Finally, they instrumentalised the prisoners' bodies within the discourse in order to build a new discursive frame in which they could be seen as independent actors and human beings with rights – thereby laying the foundations for the positive reception of the Whitaker Report.

Although the names of the PU and the PRO have been forgotten by many, and their history has been overshadowed by the contemporaneous campaigns of republican prisoners, the prisoners' rights movement has cast a long shadow across the modern penal system. From the establishment of the IPS as an independent prisons board to administer the penal system in the late 1990s and the closure of St Patrick's in the 2010s to the ongoing campaign to end slopping-out, almost every major penal reform in Ireland in the last thirty-six years has been shaped by the agenda of the prisoners' rights movement.

Epilogue
Communicating Bodies

Constructing Articulate Bodies

I began this book with its central claim, that prisoners bodies, stripped of their ordinary civil and political agency, become 'a site of communication', and in the intervening chapters, I have explored this claim in depth. In chapter I, we saw how Daniel Redmond and others established the Portlaoise Prisoners' Union (PU), combining into a coherent and mutinous body which projected ordinary prisoners into the public discourse as an active presence. The union members used their bodies to disrupt the functioning of the prison; through sit-ins, through roof-top protests where they imposed a human presence on the dehumanised landscape of the prison, and through hunger strikes and self-harm to reject the prison's power to punish or isolate them. As the union developed, strengthened, and spread to Mountjoy and the Curragh, their discursive presence began to change. Increasingly, the ordinaries were seen as agents rather than as objects. The press began to drop the undermining epithets, like 'self-styled prisoners' union', and the heavily freighted quotation marks around the words 'prisoners' union', which had been a constant feature of earlier reporting of unions in British and US prisons.[1] The claims by the minister for justice and Prison

Officer's Association (POA) representatives, that the union was either a 'subversive' or 'mafia-like' organisation, began to be treated with increasing scepticism.[2] Some newspapers, like the centre-left *Irish Press*, legitimised the prisoners voice not only by expressing sympathy for their demands but by publishing the union's communiques.[3] Meanwhile, other newspapers that were antagonistic to the prisoners, like the conservative *Irish Independent*, began to refer to the 'allegations and counter-allegations' flying back and forth between the Department of Justice and the PU, and even went so far as to offer arguments refuting the prisoners claims.[4] Even though the *Independent* was siding against the prisoners, this new approach still acknowledged that ordinary prisoners could, potentially, have valid complaints about the prison system – inadvertently validating the prisoners' voice and their agency within the public discourse. This agency was not achieved by the PU alone, however.

In chapter 2, we examined how the Prisoners' Rights Organisation (PRO) initially amplified the PU's voice within the public discourse and then worked to establish the discursive role of ordinary prisoners as powerless 'unfortunates', as the PRO's press officer Michael Fardy referred to them, buffeted by the vagaries of poverty, chaotic family lives, and a cruel and inhuman penal system.[5] Throughout the early and mid-1970s, the PRO repeatedly highlighted the tragic stories of individual prisoners – from the suicides of named prisoners like John Donnellan to the countless stories of unnamed prisoners who told their stories in the *Jail Journal* and who detailed the abuse they suffered in the industrial school system or the negative impact that imprisonment itself has on people's mental health.[6] The repetition of these stories constructed prisoners as articulate bodies. The PRO ensured not only that prisoners' actions articulated their own stories, but that they contributed to the articulation of broader arguments about the nature of imprisonment and penal reform. Thus, the death of John Donnellan was used to tell the story of his ill treatment at the hands of a wealthy neighbour – but also spoke to the absence of psychiatric screening in the prison system and the failure of the system to safeguard the people over which it wielded almost absolute power.[7] From 1977, as argued in chapter 5, the PRO began to shift its tactics by side-lining individual prisoners' stories in favour of a more sociological approach. Although the PRO continued its street-level organisation and kept working with released prisoners, it increasingly focused on large-scale data gathering exercises including conducting surveys and organising the MacBride Inquiry. This change enabled the organisation to achieve a degree of respectability so that, by the early 1980s, they were able to work with elected officials and powerful pressure groups to shape and advocate for new legislation and to successfully resolve two of the key demands the PRO had been advocating for since its establishment – the closure of the Curragh and the establishment of an official commission of inquiry into the prison system, which, in turn, endorsed most of the PRO's other demands for penal reform. However, as the PRO began to represent the prisoners' collective body as a subject to be examined, rather than as a collective of named agents, many ex-prisoners became frustrated with the organisation's 'political lobbying' and decided to take matters into their own hands.[8] In chapter 4, I examined the emergence of smaller, more militant, prisoners' bodies, like the Prisoners' Revenge Squad. I also explored how the activities of the PU in the early and mid-1970s, which constructed the prisoners as an articulate body, enabled the less organised protests of the late 1970s and 1980s to be understood within the same framework of demands. This continued in spite of the disintegration of a coherent prisoners' body politic, caused by the shifting demographics in prison, the influx of heroin users who had little experience of prison, and the divisive fear of those identified as having HIV antibodies.

As well as these collective bodies, this book has also sought to emphasise the articulation of individual prisoners' bodies. Many of these have been prisoners, and ex-prisoners who organised activist groups, like Danny Redmond and Noel Lynch, but chapter 3 constructed a microhistory of Karl Crawley. Crawley's conflict with the prison system was motivated by a deeply personal rejection of authority, a rejection which was medicalised and pathologized by the prison authorities and medical officers. While his experience was not universal, and the extremity of his protests may have been exceptional, it was also, in some sense, representative of many others of his generation. Reflecting on his prison career in 1982, he told journalist Gene Kerrigan: 'I didn't set out to be Karl Crawley'.[9] He meant that his life and experience had

176 | Prisoners' Bodies

been shaped by uncontrollable forces of poverty, abuse, mental health issues, drug use, and institutionalisation. These were influences which, his psychiatrist noted, were 'typical' of many men like him within the prison system.[10] As such, Crawley's experience, although individual, represents many of those who instrumentalised their bodies, outside the framework of collective organisation, as weapons of protest against the prison system, but whose stories have been lost to the institutional silence of that system.

This book has been a history of constructions. Individual or collective bodies discursively assembled to express and be expressed, to represent and be represented. In their time, they each articulated some intersection between the personal and political, because all life in prison is such an intersection. Every moment, whether one is sitting quietly in a cell or throwing slates off a roof, can be interpreted as a manifestation of both everyday lived experience and a submission to, or rejection of, the disciplinary apparatus of the state. However, early in the book, I asked the reader to keep in mind the absent bodies whose stories have been omitted from this book, whether that is because their communications have not been recorded, because their stories have not been made public, or because I have been unable, for various reasons, to include them in this book.

A Haunting Absence: Kevin and Paul Kenna

While writing this book, I have been haunted by two bodies – those of Kevin and Paul Kenna. Their stories have not featured to any great extent in the text and yet they have lingered with me throughout. I have often tried to write them into chapters, but every time I run into an epistemic wall. I know intimate details about their lives, but I lack much of the basic and superficial information. Most notably, it remains unclear whether Kevin and Paul Kenna were brothers. Paul certainly had a brother called Kevin and their relative ages make sense for siblings, but the activists I have spoken to who remember both men have been unable to recall if they were related. Their stories remain unwritably vague as microhistories, and so unremittingly personal that they resist interpretation, even within the wide frame of prisoners' protest.

As I approach the end of this book I realise that their voices are not clamouring to be a specific part of the narrative, rather they represent my increasingly troubled relationship with the lacunae within this book – the prisoners who did not, or could not, communicate.

In 1975, when he was eighteen years old, Kevin Kenna refused an order to scrub a floor in St Patrick's Institution to protest his remission being delayed by a month. As punishment, he was locked in his cell.[11] Later that day, he set fire to his cell. He told a journalist, 'I was going mental in there and wanted to kill myself'.[12] The prison officers rushed him across the road to the Mater Hospital where he was treated for serious burns to his arms and chest. It was three days before a priest, who had visited Kevin in hospital, decided to inform his family about the boy's injuries.[13] Kevin had been sentenced to six months in St Patrick's and his father told the press that the months had wrought a terrible change on his son: 'He was a normal level headed boy before he went to prison but now his nerves seem to be shattered'.[14]

I have encountered many deeply troubling stories while researching this book, but Kevin's has stayed with me the longest. This may be because it was the first difficult story I uncovered during this project, but it was also because the story was, quite literally, close to home. Kevin had grown up in Fatima Mansions, a deprived and neglected flat complex in Dublin's south inner city.[15] Although the mansions have long since been demolished, their sister blocks in Dolphin's House and St Theresa's Gardens still stood around the corner from the house where I lived when I started this research. Over the last six years, I have often caught glimpses of young men walking along the banks of the Grand Canal, standing on street corners in Rialto, or turning into the shadowed laneways of the Liberties and, in that trance-like reverie that comes to a long-distance runner on a winter's night, I have wondered if I saw some revenant of the young 'level headed' Kevin Kenna – or his 'shattered' older self.

Five years after Kevin ended up in hospital, Paul Kenna and a friend, both seventeen, set fire to a school in Cabra, on Dublin's North Side – a school that still stands a couple of blocks from the house where I now sit finishing this book.[16] In 1984, Paul was arrested after robbing the takings of a pub in Kerry during the Rose of Tralee Festival, but a

178 | Prisoners' Bodies

week later he escaped from Cork prison and returned to his home in Dublin.[17] To deal with the fear of being recaptured, he began using heroin. Two years later, he was arrested for robbing a young woman's purse in a McDonalds.[18] By that time, he was dependant on heroin and was, although he may not have known it, carrying HIV. While he was in Mountjoy, going through withdrawal, his girlfriend gave birth to a son. She too used heroin – and also had a husband on a nine year sentence in Mountjoy.[19] When Paul, who was then just twenty-one years old, found out that his baby had been born with syphilis, hepatitis B, and HIV, he hanged himself from the window bars of his cell. He had been scheduled to be transferred to Cork prison the next day to finish his sentence for the 1984 pub robbery.[20] Cork was hours away from his family's home in Dublin and it probably seemed likely that, given his sentence length and his son's health and prognosis, he might never get to see the child. Not long after his death, Paul's brother Kevin was interviewed on RTÉ's popular *Today Tonight* programme, where he described how his brother was 'worried that somebody else might think that [he had AIDS], and also that prison warders ... they might not want to go near him, might not want to help him, and people who weren't drug addicts and were spending time in Mountjoy, they might not want to share a cell with him.[21]

Paul Kenna's death, early on a January morning in 1986, could be tied to key issues in the prison system. It speaks to the discrimination against intravenous drug users and the stigma of HIV positivity, to the failure of the medical screening process to identify and treat a person in withdrawal, the failure of the psychiatric service to identify a man in need of immediate care, the lack of compassion within the prison system which proposed to move Kenna hundreds of kilometres away from his family and his dying baby. Similarly, Kevin Kenna's attempted self-immolation may be framed as a consequence of overcrowding in St Patrick's, of the failure of the prison system to protect juveniles, or to offer them the education and training that would give them hope for the future. However, throughout this project I have found that both stories resist such complex and coherent interpretations. Like so many others, these are inarticulate bodies, not because they did not have anything to say, but because what they did say expressed such profound and personal hopelessness that it defies articulation. Their actions were not words but screams at, rather than about, the cruel arbitrariness of life and the inhumane nature of imprisonment. So, having spent the preceding chapters interpreting the actions of individual and collective bodies, and carefully reconstructing the communications of people who had been institutionally stripped of their voice, I thought it was important to end the book not with a word, but with a scream.

Notes

INTRODUCTION

1 Kantorwicz, *The King's Two Bodies*, 7.
2 Miller, *A History of Force Feeding*, 167.
3 Ruesch and Bateson, *Communication*, 6.
4 Ruesch and Bateson, 275.
5 Hall, 'Encoding Decoding', 163.
6 Ruesch and Bateson, *Communication*, 281, 282.
7 Ruesch and Bateson, 42.
8 Ruesch and Bateson, 274.
9 *Rules for the Government of Prisons*, Section 26.
10 *Rules for the Government of Prisons*, Section 68.
11 *Criminal Justice Administration Act.* Act number 58 of 1914. London: Eyre and Spottiswode, 1914, Section 10; *General Prisons (Ireland) Act.* Act number 49 of 1877. Dublin: Irish Statute Book, Section 12; *Prisons (Ireland) Act.* Act Number 68 of 1856. Dublin Irish Statute Book, Section 28; *Prisons (Ireland) Act.* Act Number 74 of 1826. Dublin Irish Statute Book, Section 6.
12 *State (McDonagh) v Frawley* (1978) IR 131, 135.
13 *State (McDonagh) v Frawley* (1978) IR 135.
14 Foucault, *Discipline and Punish*, 136.
15 *Rules for the Government of Prisons*, Section 68.
16 Sheridan, *The Liberty Suit*, 5–6.
17 *Prevention of Crime Act*, Act Number 59 of 1908, London: His Majesty's Stationary Office, 1908, Part 1, Section 1, Article B; *Criminal Justice Administration Act*, Act number 58 of 1914, London: Eyre and Spottiswode, 1914, Section 10, Article C.

18 *State (Boyle) v Governor of The Military Detention Barracks, Curragh* (1980) 3 JIC 2810.

19 Foucault, *Discipline and Punish*, 138.

20 *State (Boyle) v Governor of The Military Detention Barracks, Curragh* (1980) 3 JIC 2810.

21 Quoted in *State (Murphy) v Kielt* (1984) 1R 458, 464.

22 *Rules for the Government of Prisons*. S.I. No. 320 of 1947, Dublin: Stationary Office, 1947, Section 65.

23 Anon, 'Review: The Liberty Suit', 10. 'Culchies', in Dublin slang, refers to Irish people from outside Dublin. It has connotations of a rural innocence or ignorance but can also be applied to people from smaller towns and cities. 'Jackeen', in Irish slang, is used to refer, disparagingly, to people from Dublin. It connotes a Dublin-centric insularity and often a dandy or effete personality. 'Lick-ups' refer to people who behave obsequiously towards the prison staff to curry favour, while 'hards', short for 'hard cases', refers to people who adopt a more defiant attitude to authority, although it can also refer to people serving longer sentences for serious crimes.

24 Ball, *Education Policy and Social Class*, 45.

25 Hall, 'Encoding and Decoding Television Discourse', 16.

26 Hall, 17.

27 Hall, 16.

28 Wall and Grannell, 'From "Opium Smoking Orgies."'

29 Hall, 'Encoding and Decoding Television Discourse', 11.

30 Ruesch and Bateson, *Communication*, 44.

31 Hall, 'Encoding and Decoding Television Discourse', 15.

32 Hall, 'Encoding Decoding', 169.

33 Hall, 'Encoding and Decoding Television Discourse', 18

34 Gramsci, *Selections from The Prison Notebooks*.

35 Ball, *Education Policy and Social Class*, 45.

36 Department of Justice, *Annual Report 1973*, 19.

37 Cooney, 'Committee on Finance – Vote 20'.

38 Department of Justice, *Annual Report 1973*, 17.

39 Anon, 'Prison "Mafia Bosses"', 3.

40 Joe Costello, interview with author, 13 August 2020.

41 Richardson, 'Letter to Concerned Parents'.

42 Nicky Kelly was a member of the Irish Republic Socialist Party who, along with three other men, had been arrested in 1976 for the Sallins Train Robbery and was violently forced to make a confession by the Gardaí. He spent four years in prison in the early 1980s, even after a court had ruled that his co-accused's confessions had been made under duress. The Free Nicky Kelly campaign became a cause célèbre for republic sympathizers, as well as anyone interested in police and criminal justice reform.

43 Murphy, *Political Imprisonment and the Irish*, 1–2.

44 See, for example, Beresford, *Ten Dead Men*; Sweeney, 'Irish Hunger Strikes'; Kenney, 'I Felt a Kind of Pleasure'.

45 McConville, *Irish Political Prisoners, 1848–1922*; McConville, *Irish Political Prisoners, 1920–62*; McConville, *Irish Political Prisoners, 1860–2000*.

46 Klienrichert, *Republican Internment*; Reinisch, 'The Fight for Political Status'.

47 O'Mahony, *Frongoch*; McDiarmid, 'Comradeship'.

48 Naughton, *Markievicz*; O'Hearn, 'Bobby Sands'; Fitzpatrick, *Harry Boland's Irish Revolution*.

49 Beresford, *Ten Dead Men*; Sweeney, 'Irish Hunger Strikes'; Miller, *A History of Force Feeding*.

50 Murphy, *Political Imprisonment and the Irish*.

51 Wall, 'Embarrassing the State', 389.

52 Notably: Carroll-Burke, *Colonial Discipline*; Cox and Marland, 'Broken Minds and Beaten Bodies'; Rogan, *Prison Policy in Ireland*.

53 Cox and Byrne, 'Straightening Crooked Souls'; Weston and Berridge, 'AIDS Inside and Out'; Wall, 'Embarrassing the State'.

54 Behan, *Citizen Convicts*.

55 Behan, 'We Are All Convicted Criminals?'; Behan, 'The Prisoners' Rights Organisation'; Behan, 'Putting Penal Reform on the Map'.

56 Smith, 'Karl Alexander Crawley v Ireland, Appendix 10', 18.

57 Weston and Berridge, 'AIDS Inside and Out'; Weston, *Positive in Prison*.

58 See, for example, Moore, 'The Politics and Ethics of Naming', 337; Parle, *States of Mind*, 25–6; Wright and Saucier, 'Madness in the Archives', 78.

59 Christine Buckley interviewed in Lentin, *Dear Daughter*.

60 Anon, 'Sub-Citizens', 4.

61 O'Donnell, O'Sullivan, and Healy, *Crime and Punishment*, 150–3.

62 O'Donnell, O'Sullivan, and Healy, 312–31.

63 De Burca, 'Press Release, 22 November 1973'; Anon, 'The Women's Prison'.

64 Carroll-Burke, *Colonial Discipline*, 103–4.

65 MacBride, *Crime and Punishment*, 28.

66 Martin, *Prisoner Population and Trends*, 3.

67 Martin, 3.

68 Rogan, *Prison Policy in Ireland*, 95.

69 Walsh, 'Prisons Bill, 1956'.

70 Rogan, *Prison Policy in Ireland*, 82.

71 *Criminal Justice Act*. S.I. No. 27 of 1960. Dublin: Stationary Office, 1960, Sections 12 and 13.

72 Butler, *Building the Irish Courthouse*, 507–8, 454, 490.

73 Even in those three years the decline is minimal (averaging 12 per cent per annum). Department of Justice, *Annual Report 1963*; Heylin, *Evaluating Prisons,*

Prisoners, and Others, 116; Department of Justice, *Annual Report 1967*; Department of Justice, *Annual Report 1968*; Department of Justice, *Annual Report 1971*; Department of Justice, *Annual Report 1972*; Department of Justice, *Annual Report 1973*.

74 The annual report on prisons indicates that the percentage of committals for periods of 6 months or over was 24 per cent of a total of 1,679 in 1963 and 21 per cent of 1,692 in 1962. Neither of these percentages work out as whole numbers (397.923 in 1963 and 355.32 in 1962), the difference between them is 42.603 prisoners. As a result, it is not currently possible to say whether in increase was forty-two or forty-three prisoners. Department of Justice, *Annual Report 1963*.

75 Department of Justice, *Annual Report 1972*.

76 Rogan, *Prison Policy in Ireland*, 112, 134.

77 O'Donnell, O'Sullivan, and Healy, *Crime and Punishment*, 152–3.

78 O'Donnell, O'Sullivan, and Healy, 278–331.

79 Department of Justice, 'Memorandum to the Government, 30 January 1974'.

80 Department of Justice, *Annual Report 1973*, 9; Department of Justice, *Annual 1975*, 4; Department of Justice, *Annual Report 1978*, 7.

81 MacBride, *Crime and Punishment*, 38. This number excludes the salaries of full-time teachers paid for by the Department of Education, of which there were forty-eight in 1979.

82 While these were new institutions, the buildings themselves already had long histories. Arbour Hill and Fort Mitchell had both previously been prisons and Cork had been a military detention barracks.

83 Joint Working Party, *Punishment & Imprisonment*, 36.

84 Joint Working Party, *Punishment & Imprisonment*, 36.

85 Dunne, *Prisons and Places of Detention*, 6.

86 Joint Working Party, *Punishment & Imprisonment*, 36.

87 Allen, 'Criminal Justice', 226.

88 Bailey, *The Rise and Fall*, 1.

89 Allen, 'Criminal Justice', 226.

90 Garland, *Punishment and Welfare*, 3.

91 Rogan, 'Rehabilitation, Research and Reform', 20.

92 Fitzgerald, *Prisoners in Revolt*, 305.

93 Rogan, *Prison Policy in Ireland*, 176.

94 Rogan, 93.

95 Dwyer, *Haughey's Forty's Years of Controversy*, 33.

96 Kilcommins et al., *Crime, Punishment*, 68–70.

97 Department of Justice, *Annual Report 1967*; Department of Justice, *Annual Report 1968*.

98 Geiran, 'The Development of Social Work', 92.

99 Department of Justice, *Annual Report 1978*, 29–31; Rogan, *Prison Policy in Ireland*, 107.

100 Rogan, *Prison Policy in Ireland*, 133; Collins, 'Oral Answers'.

101 O'Malley, 'Committee on Finance – Prisons Bill, 1972'; Patrick Cooney, 'Prisons Bill, 1974'.

102 Cooney, 'Committee on Finance – Vote 20'.

103 Jim Mitchell, 'Criminal Justice Bill, 1981'.

104 Ben Briscoe, 'Private Members' Business'.

105 Byrne, Hogan, and McDermott, *Prisoners' Rights*, 7–9.

106 The Advisory Forum on Human Rights, *Prisoners in the Republic of Ireland*, 8.

107 Joint Working Party, *Punishment & Imprisonment*, 37.

108 *Rules for the Government of Prisons*, S.I. No. 320 of 1947, Dublin: Stationary Office, 1947, Section 54, Articles 1 and 2.

109 Prison Study Group, *Examination of the Irish Penal System*, 49, 56, 61.

110 Prison Study Group, 44–5, 58. The rural nature of the work in Portlaoise was particularly unsuitable given the urban background of the majority of the prisoners there.

111 Weston and Berridge, 'AIDS Inside and Out', 247–67, 249.

112 Seddon, *Punishment and Madness*, 36.

113 Prison Study Group, *Examination of the Irish Penal System*, 51–2.

114 Prison Study Group, 50–1, 57, 62.

115 RTÉ, *Central Mental Hospital Dundrum*; Prison Study Group, *Examination of the Irish Penal System*, 54–5.

116 Prison Study Group, *Examination of the Irish Penal System*, 54–5.

117 Walker, 'Irish Republican Prisoners', 195.

118 O'Donnell, O'Sullivan, and Healy, *Crime and Punishment*, 152–3.

119 McConville, *Irish Political Prisoners*, 509; Anon, 'Department Denies "Chaos at Joy"'.

120 Anon, 'Provo Calls Off Hunger Strike', 4; Anon, 'Provos End 36-Hours Prison Fast', 3; Martin Daly, 'Another Striker Takes Food', 1.

121 Behan, 'We Are All Convicted Criminals?', 507.

122 McCaughren, *Escape by Helicopter*.

123 Dunne, 'Nineteen Portlaoise Escapees', 1; McCaughren, *Escape by Helicopter*.

124 Anon, 'Bomb Killed Escaper', 1.

125 Anon, 'Portlaoise Worse Than Long Kesh', 4.

126 Anon, 'Obduracy on Both Sides', 8.

127 *Prisons Act*. S.I. No. 7 of 1972. Dublin: Stationary Office, 1972.

128 O'Malley, 'Committee on Finance'.

129 *Prisons Act*. S.I. No. 7 of 1972. Dublin: Stationary Office, 1972, Section 2, Article 2.

130 Anon, 'Prisons Act, 1972 Statements'.

131 Anon, 'Challenge on Curragh by Prisoners' Group', 3.

132 Mary Rogan, *Prison Policy in Ireland*, 150; Kilcommins et al., *Crime, Punishment*, 71.

133 Seán Reynolds, interview with author, 8 January 2019.

134 Cummins, *The Rise and Fall*, 202–3.

135 Colley, *Ain't Scared of Your Jail*, 7.

136 *Soledad Brother* first went on sale in Ireland in 1971 for £2.50. Parker, 'Prison Prophet', 12; Colley, 'War without Terms', 286.

137 Jackson, *Soledad Brother*, 27.

138 Bosworth, *Encyclopedia of Prisons and Correctional Facilities*, 764.

139 Parker, 'School for Revolution', 11.

140 Barkley, 'The Attica Liberation Faction Manifesto', 35.

141 Useem and Kimball, *States of Siege*, 55.

142 Anon, 'Agree of We Kill', 5; Anon, 'Injunction for US Prisoners', 1; Anon, 'Free Prison Hostages Bid Fails', 5; Anon, 'Prison Rioters: No Surrender', 3.

143 Anon, '37 Killed as Police Quell Prison Revolt', 1.

144 Anon, 'Attica Hostages Shot not Knifed', 1; Anon, 'Jail Riot Riddle of Shot Hostages', 1; Anon, 'Riot Jail Deaths Riddle', 6; Anon, 'Hostages Died from Gun Shot Wounds', 3.

145 Lewis, 'The Corruption of Officially Condoned Violence', 7.

146 Kraft, 'Attica', 9.

147 Anon, 'Tribute Paid to Fermoy's Patriot Soldier', 1, 16.

CHAPTER ONE

1 Arnold, 'Reconstruction or progress?'.

2 Rowley, 'Drink – A Mass Killer Stalking the Roads', 22.

3 Anon, 'Solicitor Cleared of Obstructing Sergt'.

4 Anon, 'Listowel's Golden Harvest Festival'.

5 Rowley, 'Drink – A Mass Killer Stalking the Roads', 22.

6 Anon, 'Remanded in Robbery with Violence Case', 1.

7 Anon, 'Girls Beaten in Raids on Bookmakers', 14.

8 Anon, 'Parting Kiss for Her £143,000', 9.

9 Anon, 'Man Freed, 2 Bailed in Raid Case', 6; '£8,648 Raid: Three Convicted', 7.

10 Anon, 'Three charged with £8,864 robbery raid', 4; Anon, 'Robber Protests at 7-Year Sentence', 9.

11 Anon, '£8,648 Raid: Three Convicted', 7.

12 Anon, 'Man Wanted Case Put to Rights Court', 7; Anon, 'Wants His Case to Go to Human Rights Court', 4.

13 Elements of this section have been drawn from: Wall, 'Embarrassing the State'.

14 Anon, 'Prison Back to Normal in Portlaoise', 1.

15 O'Donnell, 'Portlaoise Prisoners' Union', 10; Anon, 'Committee on Prison Reform Dossier for Minister', 3.
16 Anon, 'Prisoners Allege Brutal Treatment', 11.
17 'Prisoners Allege Brutal Treatment', 11.
18 Anon, 'Portlaoise Cases for Amnesty', 3.
19 Anon, 'Portlaoise Prison Officer Found Not Guilty', 32; Anon, 'Prisoners Allege Brutal Treatment', 11.
20 Anon, 'Prisoners on Diet', 19.
21 His barrister later told the court that the breakdown was the result of 'anguish and remorse because of his involvement in' armed robberies, but the timing suggests that it may have had more to do with the prisons 'brutal' punishment regime. Anon, 'Fewer Armed Robbery Cases Solved', 7; Anon, 'Prisoners Allege Brutal Treatment', 11.
22 Anon, *Annual Report 1972*, 38.
23 Department of Justice, Anon, *Annual Report 1973*, 41; Anon, *Annual Report 1971*, 33.
24 Department of Justice, *Annual Report 1972*, 17.
25 Anon, 'Garda Alert on Protests in Two Jails', 1.
26 O'Donnell, 'Portlaoise Prisoners' Union', 10.
27 Anon, 'Prisons Act, 1972 Statements pursuant to section 2(6) of the Act'.
28 Irish Press Reporter, 'Prisoners are Being Illtreated SF Charge Government', 4.
29 Anon, 'Prisoners Threaten to Strike', 5.
30 Dennehy, 'Portlaoise Prisoners' Union', 10.
31 Sweeney, 'Irish Hunger Strikes'; Grant, 'British Suffragettes', 114.
32 Sweeney, 'Irish Hunger Strikes', 421.
33 Anon, 'Prisoners in Mountjoy Protest', 1.
34 O'Donnell, 'Portlaoise Prisoners' Union', 10.
35 Department of Justice, *Memorandum for the Government: Proposed Bill to Amend the Prisons Act, 1972*.
36 O'Donnell, 'Portlaoise Prisoners' Union', 10.
37 Anon, 'Prisoners' Demands "Rejected"', 6.
38 O'Donnell, 'Portlaoise Prisoners' Union', 10.
39 Kearns, 'Prisoners' Rights', 8; Anon, 'Ex-Prisoner Attacks "Degrading" Life behind Bars', 6.
40 Prisoner Rights Organisation, 'Demands of the Portlaoise Prisoners' Union', 2.
41 Irish Independent Staff Reporter, 'Prison Protest', 1.
42 Anon, 'Cooney Hits As Prisoners' Union', 1.
43 'Letter from Portlaoise - Hoping for a New Deal', 6.
44 The other two prisoners were Dick Power and Tom Savage. Anon, 'Jail Roof Marathon', 1.
45 Anon, 'Jail Roof Marathon', 1.

46 Anon, 'Prisoners' Roof Protest', 24.

47 Anon, 'Jail Roof Marathon', 1.

48 Gibbons, 'Portlaoise Prison Protest', 8.

49 Anon, '"Bread and Water Diet" Allegation', 5.

50 Department of Justice, *Memorandum for the Government: Proposed Bill to Amend the Prisons Act, 1972.*

51 Anon, 'Knives Used in Jail', 3.

52 Anon, Knives Used in Jail', 3.

53 Anon, 'Prisoners to Stage Peaceful Protest', 6.

54 Anon, 'Prisoners Leaders Sent to Curragh', 12; Anon, 'Prison Union Leaders Moved', 12.

55 Anon, 'Plan to "Fix" Jail Officer Alleged', 3.

56 Kennedy, 'Attempt to Break Jail Union Alleged', 16.

57 Anon, 'Warders Victims of Organised Frame-Up Campaign', 6.

58 Anon, 'Portlaoise Prison Officers Found Not Guilty', 24; Anon, 'Justice Told Letters Were Never Posted', 4.

59 Anon, '"Libel" by Prisoners Alleged', 7.

60 Anon, 'Governor Remanded on Bail', 3.

61 Anon, 'Portlaoise Cases for Amnesty', 3.

62 'Portlaoise Cases for Amnesty', 3.

63 Anon, 'Court Told of Prison Brawl', 4; Anon, 'Convicted of Causing Bodily Harm', 5.

64 Anon, 'Provo Calls Off Hunger Strike', 4; Anon, '"Non Political" Fast May End Deadlock', 1; Anon, 'Lynch Calls for Facts on Death Threat', 4.

65 Anon, 'Relief at End of Protest', 16.

66 Anon, 'New Hunger Strike at Curragh', 1; Irish Press [Staff?] Reporter, 'Hunger Strike at Curragh', 4.

67 Anon, 'New Hunger Strike at Curragh', 1.

68 Anon, 'Jailed Man Convicted of Second Raid', 9.

69 Anon, 'Curragh Hunger Strike', 1.

70 Anon, 'New Hunger Strike at Curragh', 2; Anon, 'Curragh Hunger Strike', 1.

71 Anon, 'New Hunger Strike at Curragh', 2; Anon, 'Curragh Hunger Strike', 1.

72 Anon, 'New Hunger Strike at Curragh', 2; Anon, 'Curragh Hunger Strike', 1.

73 Anon, 'Four Still Fasting at the Curragh', 8.

74 Anon, 'Four Prisoners at Curragh End Hunger Strike', 14; MacGiolla Cear, 'Five Still on Strike at Curragh', 1.

75 Anon, 'Plea to Cooney on Behalf of Prisoners', 16; Anon, '"No Doctor" for Hunger Striker', 3.

76 Anon, 'Four Prisoners at Curragh End Hunger Strike', 14; Anon, 'Curragh', 6.

77 Secretary of the Prisoners Union in the Curragh, 'Curragh Incidents', 9.

78 Lynch and Redmond, 'Letter from Portlaoise', 6.

79 Secretary of the Prisoners Union in the Curragh, 'Curragh Incidents', 9.
80 Anon, 'Picket of Fifty on Mountjoy', 7.
81 Anon, 'Picket of Fifty on Mountjoy', 7.
82 Anon, 'Hunger Strike', 2.
83 Anon, 'Man Tells Court "12 on Hunger Strike"', 6.
84 Anon, 'Hunger Strike', 2.
85 Anon, 'Hunger Strike', 2.
86 Brophy and Farrelly, '6 Hurt in Mountjoy Jail Riot', 1; Anon, 'Prisoners Were Attacked, Claims Organisation', 4; Walsh, 'Several Hurt in Prison Clashes', 1.
87 'Jail Protest "a Publicity Stunt"', 3.
88 Brophy and Farrelly, '6 Hurt in Mountjoy Jail Riot', 1.
89 Anon, 'Prisoners Were Attacked, Claims Organisation', 4.
90 Anon, 'No Particular Reason for Mountjoy Disturbance', 1.
91 Anon, 'No Particular Reason for Mountjoy Disturbance', 1.
92 Anon, 'Public Enquiry Demanded', 9.
93 Anon, 'Public Enquiry Demanded', 9.
94 Anon, 'Plan to "Fix" Jail Officer Alleged', 3.
95 Department of Justice, *Annual Report 1977*, 33.
96 Department of Justice, *Annual Report 1977*, 33.
97 Anon, 'Prisons Act, 1972 as extended by Prisons Act, 1977: Statements pursuant to section 2(6) of the Act'.
98 Anon, 'Balance of 15-Year Jail Term Suspended by Judge', 8.
99 Anon, 'Prison "Mafia Bosses" Slated by Cooney', 3.

CHAPTER TWO

Chapter title found in Maher, 'A Voice for Prisoners', 6.
1 United Nations Office of Drugs and Crime, *United Nations Congress on Crime Prevention and Criminal Justice*, 3.
2 Anon, 'The GENEVA Demonstration', 9–10.
3 Prisoners' Rights Organisation, 'Untitled leaflet (Distributed in Geneva)'.
4 Prisoners' Rights Organisation, 'Untitled leaflet (Distributed in Geneva)'.
5 Prisoners' Rights Organisation, 'Untitled leaflet (Distributed in Geneva)'.
6 Prisoners' Rights Organisation, 'Untitled leaflet (Distributed in Geneva)'.
7 Anon, 'Geneva Defines Torture', 12; Anon, 'Terrorism Main Topic for Lawmen', 5.
8 Anon, 'Irish Protest at Geneva Conference', 4.
9 Costello, 'Press Release (Herrema)'.
10 Pat McCartan, interview with author, 14 August 2020.
11 Anon, 'Ex-prisoner Attacks "Degrading" Life behind Bars', 6.
12 Anon, 'Ex-prisoner Attacks "Degrading" Life behind Bars', 6.

13 Anon, 'New Group Seeking Prison Reform', 9; Anon, 'A Socialist Visionary and Trade Union Pragmatist'; White, 'Merrigan, Matthew Paul ('Matt')'.

14 Kearns, 'Prisoners' Rights', 8; Anon, 'Committee on Prison Reform', 3.

15 Prisoner Rights Organisation, 'Introduction', 2–3.

16 Prisoner Rights Organisation, 'Introduction', 2–3.

17 Prisoner Rights Organisation, 'Introduction', 2–3.

18 Prisoner Rights Organisation, 'Introduction', 2–3.

19 Prisoner Rights Organisation, 'Introduction', 2–3.

20 Prisoner Rights Organisation, 'Introduction', 2–3.

21 Prisoner Rights Organisation, 'Press Release 9 November 1973'.

22 Prisoner Rights Organisation, 'Introduction', 2–3; Fitzgerald, *Prisoners in Revolt*, 179–82.

23 Anon, 'Prison Reform Urged by Picket at Jail', 7.

24 Anon, 'Picket at Ministerial Function', 7.

25 Anon, 'Protest Over Prison Conditions', 4.

26 Anon, 'Prisoners to Stage Peaceful Protest', 6.

27 Anon, 'Daingean Reformatory', 6–7; Anon, 'Portlaoise Prison', 4–5; Anon, 'Dundrum', 6–7; Anon, 'Working Parole', 4–5.

28 Anon, 'Mountjoy Riots', 4–5; Anon, 'Prison Statements', 10–11; Anon, 'Reply to Prison Officers', 10–11.

29 Bofin, 'Coroner's Certificate'.

30 Anon, 'Death in Prison', 14.

31 Tully, 'Deposition of Garda Desmond A. Tully'.

32 Davis, 'Statement of Dr. Samuel Davis'.

33 Anon, 'Inquest Urges Jail "Medical"', 3.

34 Anon, 'Man Found Dead in Cell Inquest to Be Held', 11; Anon, 'Medical Examination Urged for Prisoners with Mental Illness', 18; Anon, 'Prison "Killed My Brother" Sister's Inquiry Call', 7.

35 Anon, 'Boy Burned – Father Hits Out at Dept.', 1.

36 Anon, 'Burned Convict. P.R.O. Demand Inquiry', 1; Anon, 'Inquiry Call over Burned Prisoner', 3.

37 Smith, 'Sudden Death'.

38 Callaghan, 'Statement of Evidence of Garda Michael John Callaghan'; Fitzgibbon, 'Statement of Edward Fitzgibbon'.

39 Donnellan, 'Statement of Mrs Nora Donnellan'.

40 Kennelly, 'Statement of Prison Officer John Kennelly'.

41 Kennelly, 'Statement of Prison Officer John Kennelly'.

42 Anon, 'Inquest Call for Public Inquiry into the Prison System', 3; Anon, 'Accident Verdict on Cell Death', 3.

43 Murphy, 'Sudden Death'.

44 McNamara, 'Statement of John McNamara'; Glasheen, 'Statement of Eugene Glasheen'; Quinn, 'Statement of Thomas Anthony Quinn'.

45 Donoghue, 'Statement of Denis Donoghue'.

46 Denieffe, 'Minister Hits at Pressure Groups', 5.

47 McCartan, 'Untitled Prisoner Rights Organisation Statement 7 May 1975'; Prisoner Rights Organisation, 'Untitled Prisoner Rights Organisation Statement 3 May 1975'; Prisoner Rights Organisation, 'Untitled Prisoner Rights Organisation Statement'.

48 Prisoners' Rights Organisation, 'Untitled Leaflet (Irish Law Year)'.

49 Prisoners' Rights Organisation, 'Untitled Leaflet (Irish Law Year)'.

50 Anon, 'Injunction Granted to Prevent Picket on Civil Servant's Home', 13.

51 Prisoner Rights Organisation, 'Untitled Prisoner Rights Organisation Statement 3 May 1975'; Prisoner Rights Organisation, 'Untitled Prisoner Rights Organisation Statement'.

52 Prisoner Rights Organisation, 'Untitled Prisoner Rights Organisation Statement'.

53 Anon 'Picketing Ban on Eight', 12.

54 Anon, 'Civil Servant Gets Picket Outlawed', 5.

55 Anon 'Picketing Ban on Eight', 12.

56 Anon, 'Order Bars Rights Group from Picketing', 3.

57 Anon, 'Picket on Civil Servant "Illegal"', 5; Anon, 'Picket on Home Again Barred', 7.

58 Denieffe, 'Minister Hits at Pressure Groups', 5.

59 Anon, 'Forum Discussion Group', 10.

60 Levine, 'Ex-prisoner Is Scourge of the Irish Penal System', 15.

61 Coghlan, 'Momentum Added to Prison Reform Campaign', 10.

62 Anon, 'Mothers Fear for Sons' Lives, Jail Needs Psychiatrists', 7.

63 Anon, 'Adjournment in Assault Case', 4; Anon, 'Accident Verdict on Cell Death', 3.

64 Anon, '12 Months for Picketing', 13–14.

65 Anon, '7 Picketers Held for Three Hours', 7.

66 Wladek Gaj, interview with author, 6 June 2019.

67 Anon, '7 Picketers Held for Three Hours', 7; Anon, '12 Months for Picketing', 13–14.

68 Anon, '12 Months for Picketing', 13–14.

69 Costello, 'Untitled Statement (Sentencing of Activists)'.

70 Anon, 'Court Picket Win Appeal', 5.

71 Anon, 'Court Picket Win Appeal', 5; Anon, 'Prisoner Swallows Metal', 1; Anon, 'Medical Profession Accused over Prison Psychiatric Treatment', 13.

72 Anon, 'Judge Rules on Special Care', 6; Anon, '"No Place" for Man Who Swallowed Spoon', 11; Anon, 'Republic's Institutions "Not Suitable"', 13.

73 The M'Naughten rules were established in England after an 1843 case in which a man, Daniel M'Naughten, assassinated the personal secretary of then prime minister Robert Peel. The rules determined that in order to plead insanity a

defendant must prove that they did not know the nature of the act or that the act was wrong. In the early decades of independence, the Irish courts also added the possibility of 'irresistible impulse' to this list (*Attorney General v Patrick Boylan* (1937). IR 499). Faye Boland, 'Insanity, The Irish Constitution', 261–2. McCaffery, 'Karl Alexander Crawley against Ireland, Exhibit 6'; Anon, 'Republic's Institutions "Not Suitable"', 13.

74 McCaffery, 'Karl Alexander Crawley against Ireland, Exhibit 6'.

75 McCaffery, 'Karl Alexander Crawley against Ireland Exhibit 10'.

76 Anon, 'Republic's Institutions "Not Suitable"', 13; Anon, '"No Place" for Man Who Swallowed Spoons', 11; Anon, 'No Place for This Prisoner', 7.

77 In the same year as Crawley's trial, McEntee went to pre-independence Namibia as an observer for the International Commission of Jurists, where he provided international oversight of a trial of political activists.

78 Finlay, 'Appendix 7: The State (at the Prosecution of C.) v. John Frawley', 374.

79 Finlay, 'Appendix 7: The State (at the Prosecution of C.) v. John Frawley', 373.

80 Anon, 'Man's Plea for Release Rejected', 11.

81 Anon, 'Judge Rules on Special Care', 6.

82 Anon, 'Man's Plea for Release Rejected', 11; Anon, 'Prisoner Refused Release Order', 7; Anon, 'Judge Rules on Special Care', 6.

83 Fardy, 'Open Letter to An Taoiseach'.

84 Mary Ellen Ring appeared as an ordinary member of the PRO committee in the minutes of a meeting in the early 1980s.

85 Central Statistics Office, 'Percentage Distribution of Males and Females at Each Year of Age'; Central Statistics Office, 'Percentage Distribution of Males and Females in Each Occupational Group'.

86 Davin et al. , *Report on Certain Aspects of Prison Conditions*.

87 Levine, 'Mairin, the Anti-Social Socialist', 4.

88 O'Carroll, 'Remembering Sue Richardson'.

89 Anon, 'Anti-Birth Devices Shop in City Centre', 4.

90 Anon, 'Booklet Sale Challenge to DPP', 3.

91 Anon, 'Restaurant Owner and Left-Wing Campaigner', 12.

92 Levine, 'Ex-prisoner Is Scourge of the Irish Penal System', 15.

93 Browne, 'Seeds of a Police State'.

94 Browne, 'Seeds of a Police State'.

95 Browne, 'Seeds of a Police State'.

96 Browne, 'Seeds of a Police State'.

97 Anon, 'Drivers of Raids Car Jailed', 4; Levine, 'Ex-prisoner Is Scourge of the Irish Penal System', 15.

98 Anon, '4 Years Jail for Theft', 3.

99 Levine, 'Ex-prisoner Is Scourge of the Irish Penal System', 15.

100 Michael Donnelly, interview with author, 4 August 2022.

101 Donnelly, *That's Life.*

102 Donnelly, *That's Life.*

103 Michael Donnelly, interview with author, 4 August 2022.

104 Michael Donnelly, interview with author, 4 August 2022.

105 Michael Donnelly, interview with author, 4 August 2022. 'Batings' and 'bet' are the noun and participle form of 'to beat' in the Dublin north inner city dialect.

106 Michael Donnelly, interview with author, 4 August 2022.

107 Michael Donnelly, Personal Communication with author, 18 January 2024.

108 Michael Donnelly, interview with author, 4 August 2022.

109 Michael Donnelly, interview with author, 4 August 2022.

110 Michael Donnelly, interview with author, 4 August 2022.

111 Michael Donnelly, interview with author, 4 August 2022.

112 Anon, 'Join Prisoners' Rights Organisation', 11; Anon, 'Balance Sheet at 14 May 1974', 15.

113 Anon, 'Treasurer's Report', 11.

114 Costello, 'Chairman's Address to the 1979 AGM', 3.

115 Anon, 'Sinn Fein Protest March', 1; Fanning, 'First Macra Protest March to the Dáil', 11; Anon, 'Internment Protest March', 1; Anon, '60 Plan Dublin Protest March', 11.

116 Gaj, *Untitled Photo.*

117 Prisoners' Rights Organisation, 'Untitled Draft Invitation'.

118 Anon, 'Editorial', 1.

119 Anon, 'Mountjoy Riots', 5.

120 Power, 'How to Win Friends', 3.

121 Anon, 'The Good Life', 12.

122 Anon, 'Daingean Reformatory', 6–7; Anon, 'Portlaoise Prison', 4–5.

123 Anon, 'Visiting Conditions: The Need for Change', 9.

124 Anon, 'Working Parole', 4–5

125 Anon, 'Working Parole', 4.

126 Anon, 'Sub-Citizens', 4.

127 Anon, 'Sub-Citizens', 5.

128 Prisoners' Rights Organisation, 'Prison and the Mentally Ill'.

129 Prisoners' Rights Organisation, 'Draft Statement by Prisoners' Rights Organisation'.

130 Levine, 'Ex-prisoner Is Scourge of the Irish Penal System', 15.

131 Anon, 'A Prisoner Remembers', 3; Anon, 'The Good Life', 12.

132 Anon, 'Death in Prison', 14.

133 Anon, 'Death in Prison', 14.

134 Anon, 'John Donnellan', 10.

135 Anon, 'John Donnellan', 11.

136 Anon, 'Prisons Exposed by Suicides', 5; Coghlan, 'Momentum Added to prison Reform Campaign', 10; Anon, 'Psychiatric Care "Needed in Jails"', 3; Kahn, 'Suicides Blamed on Conditions: Death-Wish Prisons Rapped', 1.

137 Fanning, 'When Home Is Behind Bars...', 9; Anon, 'Republic's Institutions "Not Suitable"', 13.

138 Fanning, 'When Home Is Behind Bars...', 9.

139 Fanning, 'When Home Is Behind Bars...', 9.

140 Anon, 'Republic's Institutions "Not Suitable"', 13.

141 Anon, 'Republic's Institutions "Not Suitable"', 13.

CHAPTER THREE

1 While many of these nineteenth century records have been destroyed or lost, enough has survived to offer some fascinating insights into nineteenth century prison life. For some recent examples, see the ongoing work of Catherine Cox and Hilary Marland: Cox and Marland, 'He Must Die or Go Mad in This Place'; Cox and Marland, 'We Are Recreating Bedlam'; Cox and Marland, 'Unfit for Reform or Punishment'.

2 Miscellaneous authors, 'Human Rights: Karl Crawley v Ireland'.

3 Smith, 'Karl Alexander Crawley v Ireland, Appendix 10', 18.

4 Anon, 'Mothers Fear for Sons' Lives, Jail Needs Psychiatrists', 7.

5 Anon, 'Court Picket Win Appeal', 5; Anon, 'Prisoner Swallows Metal', 1.

6 McCaffery, 'Karl Alexander Crawley against Ireland, Exhibit 6'.

7 Anon, 'The P.R.O. & Karl Crawley v The State', 3; Anon, 'Karl Crawley', 3; Anon, 'Appeal to Strasbourg', 1.

8 Anon, '12 Months for Picketing', 13.

9 McCaffery, 'Karl Alexander Crawley against Ireland, Exhibit 6', 11.

10 Anon, 'Karl Crawley', 3; Anon, 'Prison and Psychiatry', 10.

11 Anon, 'Memorandum: As to Fact'.

12 Fawcett, 'Decision of the Commission to the Application No. 8154/78', 23.

13 Fawcett, 'Decision of the Commission to the Application No. 8154/78', 19–21.

14 Fawcett, 'Decision of the Commission to the Application No. 8154/78', 13.

15 McCaffery, 'Karl Alexander Crawley against Ireland, Exhibit 6', 2.

16 McCaffery, 'Karl Alexander Crawley against Ireland, Exhibit 6', 3.

17 Kerrigan, 'Special Feature: A Necessary Respect'.

18 Kerrigan, 'Special Feature: A Necessary Respect'.

19 McCaffery, 'Karl Alexander Crawley against Ireland Exhibit 10', 3.

20 Crawley, 'Unpublished manuscript', 12.

21 McCaffery, 'Karl Alexander Crawley against Ireland, Exhibit 6', 3.

22 Kerrigan, 'Special Feature: A Necessary Respect'.

23 McCaffery, 'Karl Alexander Crawley against Ireland, Exhibit 6', 4.

24 McCaffery, 'Karl Alexander Crawley against Ireland, Exhibit 6', 5.

25 McCaffery, 'Karl Alexander Crawley against Ireland, Exhibit 6', 5.

26 McCaffery, 'Karl Alexander Crawley against Ireland, Exhibit 6', 5.

27 McCaffery, 'Karl Alexander Crawley against Ireland, Exhibit 6', 5; Crawley, 'Unpublished manuscript', 12.

28 McCaffery, 'Karl Alexander Crawley against Ireland, Exhibit 6', 5.

29 Commission to Inquire into Child Abuse, *Report of the Commission to Inquire into Child Abuse Volume I*, 72; Anon, 'Long Record of Work by Orphan Boys', 5; O'Sullivan 'Residential Child Welfare in Ireland', 335.

30 Kerrigan, 'Karl's Choices', 302.

31 Crawley, 'Unpublished manuscript', 16.

32 Crawley, 'Unpublished manuscript', 16.

33 McCaffery, 'Karl Alexander Crawley against Ireland, Exhibit 6', 6.

34 Crawley, 'Unpublished manuscript', 16.

35 McCaffery, 'Karl Alexander Crawley against Ireland, Exhibit 6', 6.

36 McCaffery, 'Karl Alexander Crawley against Ireland, Exhibit 6', 6.

37 Tommy Crawley, interview with author, 19 March 2024.

38 Tommy Crawley, interview with author, 19 March 2024.

39 McCartan, 'State (Karl Crawley) v Governor of Mountjoy, Case History'.

40 Wall, 'Brought in Dead'.

41 Kerrigan, 'Special Feature: A Necessary Respect'.

42 Anon, 'Karl Alexander Crawley v Ireland, Appendix 1', 1.

43 Anon, 'Karl Alexander Crawley v Ireland, Appendix 2', 1.

44 Daly, 'Letter from Liam Daly and John J. Smith to Secretary', 1.

45 Anon, 'Memorandum: As to Fact'.

46 Anon, 'Karl Alexander Crawley v Ireland, Appendix 2', 3.

47 'Karl Alexander Crawley v Ireland, Appendix 2', 3.

48 Anon, 'Memorandum: As to Fact', 7, 9.

49 'Memorandum: As to Fact', 4.

50 Anon, 'Karl Alexander Crawley v Ireland, Appendix 2', 1-7.

51 Anon, 'Memorandum: As to Fact', 4.

52 Kerrigan, 'Special Feature: A Necessary Respect'.

53 Kerrigan, *Hard Cases,* 302; Anon, 'Karl Alexander Crawley v Ireland, Appendix 2', 6.

54 Anon, 'Karl Alexander Crawley v Ireland, Appendix 2', 7.

55 Seán Reynolds, interview with author, 8 January 2018.

56 Anon, 'Karl Alexander Crawley v Ireland, Appendix 2', 2.

57 Anon, 'Karl Alexander Crawley v Ireland, Appendix 2', 4.

58 McCaffery, 'Karl Alexander Crawley against Ireland, Exhibit 6', 2.

59 Smith, 'Karl Alexander Crawley v Ireland, Appendix 10', 18; Crawley, 'Unpublished manuscript', 5.

60 McCaffery, 'Karl Alexander Crawley against Ireland, Exhibit 6', 8.

61 Kerrigan, 'Special Feature: A Necessary Respect'.

62 Kerrigan, 'Special Feature: A Necessary Respect'.

63 Anon, 'Karl Alexander Crawley v Ireland, Appendix 2', 4, 12.

64 'Karl Alexander Crawley v Ireland, Appendix 2', 2, 3.

65 Smith, 'Karl Alexander Crawley v Ireland, Appendix 10', 18.

66 Kerrigan, 'Special Feature: A Necessary Respect'.

67 Crawley, 'Unpublished manuscript', 15.

68 Anon, 'Memorandum: As to Fact', 6.

69 Anon, 'Karl Alexander Crawley v Ireland, Observations', 2.

70 Anon, 'Memorandum: As to Fact', 1.

71 Anon, 'Memorandum: As to Fact', 2; Anon, 'Karl Alexander Crawley v Ireland, Observations', 4.

72 Anon, 'Karl Alexander Crawley v Ireland, Observations', 4.

73 Anon, 'Memorandum: As to Fact', 1.

74 Anon, 'Karl Alexander Crawley v Ireland, Observations', 4.

75 Anon, 'Karl Alexander Crawley v Ireland, Observations', 4.

76 Anon, 'Memorandum: As to Fact', 2.

77 Anon, 'Memorandum: As to Fact', 2.

78 Anon, 'Karl Alexander Crawley v Ireland, Observations', 5.

79 Anon, 'Karl Alexander Crawley v Ireland, Observations', 5.

80 Anon, 'Karl Alexander Crawley v Ireland, Observations', 6; Anon, 'Memorandum: As to Fact', 2.

81 Anon, 'Karl Alexander Crawley v Ireland, Observations', 6.

82 McCaffery, 'Karl Alexander Crawley against Ireland Exhibit 10', 8.

83 Anon, 'Memorandum: As to Fact', 7.

84 My thanks to Dr. Harry Harvey for his expert advice about the effect of different combinations of medication.

85 Davis, 'Karl Alexander Crawley v Ireland, Appendix 10', 21.

86 McCartan, 'Karl Crawley against Ireland: Exhibit 4', 1; Kerrigan, 'Special Feature: A Necessary Respect'.

87 Kerrigan, 'Special Feature: A Necessary Respect'.

88 Thornberry, 'Karl Crawley against Ireland: Memorandum', 1.

89 Thornberry, 'Karl Crawley against Ireland: Memorandum', 1.

90 McCartan, 'Karl Crawley against Ireland: Exhibit 4', 1; Anon, 'Karl Alexander Crawley v Ireland, Observations', 7; McCartan, 'Karl Crawley against Ireland: Exhibit 1', 1–5.

91 McCartan, 'Karl Crawley against Ireland: Exhibit 4', 4.

92 Kerrigan, 'Special Feature: A Necessary Respect'.

93 McCaffery, 'Karl Alexander Crawley against Ireland, Exhibit 6', 7.

94 Anon, 'Karl Alexander Crawley v Ireland, Observations', 7.

95 Anon, 'Karl Alexander Crawley v Ireland, Appendix 2', 7.

96 Anon, 'Karl Alexander Crawley v Ireland, Appendix 2', 13.

97 Anon, 'Karl Alexander Crawley v Ireland, Appendix 2', 13.

98 Anon, 'Karl Alexander Crawley v Ireland, Appendix 2', 13; Kerrigan, 'Special Feature: A Necessary Respect'.

99 Anon, 'Karl Alexander Crawley v Ireland, Appendix 2', 13.

100 McCartan, 'Karl Crawley against Ireland: Exhibit 4', 5.

101 Illegible name, 'Letter from illegible name to Secretary, Department of Foreign Affairs', 1.

102 Tommy Crawley, interview with author, 19 March 2024.

103 Tommy Crawley, interview with author, 19 March 2024.

104 Tommy Crawley, interview with author, 19 March 2024.

105 Kerrigan, 'Karl's Choices', 137.

106 Kerrigan, 'Special Feature: A Necessary Respect'.

107 Kerrigan, 'Special Feature: A Necessary Respect'.

108 Crawley, 'Unpublished manuscript', 15.

109 McCaffery, 'Karl Alexander Crawley against Ireland Exhibit 10', 2, 10.

CHAPTER FOUR

1 Anon, 'Drugs: Quasi Intellectuals Pose Problem', 9; Maher, 'The New Drug Problem – 2', 12; Wall and Grannell, 'From "Opium Smoking Orgies" to "Junkie Babies"', 1.

2 McCarthy and Rogers, 'He's 12 – and He's a Heroin Addict', 1.

3 O'Mahony, *Drug Abusers in Mountjoy Prison*, 1. This is extrapolated from O'Mahony's claim that 8 per cent of the total prison population were regular drug users and the assumption that no political prisoners were regular drug users (an assumption based on the IRA's well-known animosity to recreational drug use).

4 O'Donnell, O'Sullivan, and Healy, *Crime and Punishment in Ireland*, 153.

5 O'Donnell, O'Sullivan, and Healy, *Crime and Punishment in Ireland*, 166–7.

6 O'Donnell, O'Sullivan, and Healy, *Crime and Punishment in Ireland*, 167.

7 O'Donnell, O'Sullivan, and Healy, *Crime and Punishment in Ireland*.

8 O'Donnell, O'Sullivan, and Healy, *Crime and Punishment in Ireland*.

9 O'Donnell, O'Sullivan, and Healy, *Crime and Punishment in Ireland*, 159–62.

10 Joe Costello, Interview with author, 13 August 2020.

11 Joe Costello, Interview with author, 13 August 2020.

12 Anon, 'Prison Officers Strike Threat', 1.

13 Anon, 'Officers in Prisons May Stop Work', 9.

14 Anon, 'Prison Men's Secretary Resigns', 4.

15 Broomfield, 'Prison Officers' Dismissal', 8.

16 Anon, 'Sacked Warder Attacks Prison System', 15.

17 Broomfield, 'Prison Officers' Dismissal', 8.

18 Anon, 'Dismissed Prison Office Loses Case', 4.

19 Anon, 'Prison Men's Secretary Resigns', 4.

20 Reddy, 'Bid to End Bitter Feud over Prison', 1.

21 Musgrave, '"Bury the Hatchet" Plea from New POA President', 9.

22 Foley, 'Senior Mountjoy Staff Angry at Officers', 9.

23 Department of Justice, *Annual Report on Prisons 1979*, 23.

24 Department of Justice, *Annual Report on Prisons 1979*, 23; Anon, '"Decision Soon" on Prison Probe', 3.

25 Department of Justice, *Annual Report on Prisons 1979*, 24.

26 Anon, 'Prison Officers Decide on Industrial Action', 6.

27 Anon, 'Warders Call Off Work Stoppages', 3.

28 Mulligan, 'Prisoners' Gifts to Pope', 1.

29 Costello, 'Protecting the Prisoner', 8.

30 Anon, 'Prison Officers Threaten Action', 1.

31 Anon, '30 Injured in Mountjoy Riot', 1.

32 Department of Justice, *Annual Report on Prisons 1979*, 31; Rogers et al., 'Warden Tells of Beating', 20; Rogers et al., '40 Hurt in Prison Battle', 1.

33 Anon, 'Prisoners Injured in Jail Clash', 1; Collins, 'Written Answer – Prison Riot'.

34 Collins, 'Written Answer – Prison Riot'; Anon, 'Prisoners Injured in Jail Clash', 1.

35 Anon, 'Prison Officers Threaten Action', 1.

36 Brady, 'Jail Riot Report with Minister', 3.

37 Brady, 'Jail Riot Report with Minister', 3.

38 Anon, 'Mountjoy Prison Riot', 1.

39 Anon, 'Mountjoy Jail Revenge Wave Feared', 4.

40 Anon, 'Jail Group "Has No Credibility"', 2.

41 Brady, 'Jail Riot Report with Minister', 3.

42 Brady, 'Jail Riot Report with Minister', 3.

43 Anon, 'New Prison Scheme Gets Mixed Reaction', 4.

44 Anon, 'New Prison Scheme Gets Mixed Reaction', 4.

45 Collins, 'Oral Answers – St. Patrick's Institution (Dublin) Over-Crowding'.

46 Anon, 'Prison Officers Threaten Action', 1.

47 Anon, 'Prison Officers Threaten Action', 1.

48 Anon, 'Prison Staff Backing for Jail Reforms', 3.

49 Brady, 'Jail Riot Report with Minister', 3; Anon, 'Jail Group "Has No Credibility"', 2.

50 Eddie Cahill, interview with author, 31 August 2022.

51 Yeats, 'Revenge Group Report to Be Investigated', 7.

52 Anon, 'Prison Officer – Guest at Sister's Wedding – Shot Dead at Clogher', 1; Brady, 'Threat to Ministers', 1.

53 MacHale, 'Gang Bet Up Couple after Jail Rioting', 5.

54 Anon, 'Savage Attack on ex-Prison Officer, Wife', 1.

55 Anon, 'Four Men Questioned after Attack', 23.

56 Anon, 'Mountjoy Jail Revenge Wave Feared', 4.

57 Anon, 'Mountjoy Jail Revenge Wave Feared', 4.

58 Boland, 'Arson Attacks Baffle Gardaí', 5; Anon, 'Slogans Found at Burned School', 11; Anon, '£36,000 Fire Award to UCD', 8.

59 Yeats, 'Revenge Group Report to Be Investigated', 7.

60 Anon, 'Warders May Ban Overtime', 1.

61 Anon, 'Prison Officers to Hit Back', 1.

62 Anon, 'Warders Ban Visits after Gang Attack', 1.

63 Managh, 'Attack on Two Prison Officers', 4.

64 Anon, 'Attacks on Homes of Warders', 4.

65 Ryan, 'Prisoners' Rights Deny Attacks Blame', 1; Molloy, 'Warders Claim PRO Supporters Were in Attacks', 3; Joe Costello, Interview with author, 13 August 2020.

66 Anon, 'High Court Bid to Block Irish Press Story Fails', 7.

67 Pat McCartan, interview with author, 14 August 2020.

68 Anon, 'Warder's Action Threat', 1.

69 Anon, 'Warders May Ban Overtime', 1.

70 Anon, 'Warders May Ban Overtime', 1.

71 Anon, 'Mountjoy Jail Riot Warning As Warders Start Overtime Ban', 3; Anon, 'Warders Call Off Prison Overtime Ban', 4.

72 Eddie Cahill, interview with author, 31 August 2022.

73 Anon, 'Prison Officer is Assaulted', 1.

74 Anon, 'Prison Officers Assaulted', 26.

75 Anon, 'Cars of Six Warders Vandalised', 8.

76 Anon, 'Petrol Bomb Thugs Strike', 1.

77 Anon, 'POA Seek Urgent Talks with Noonan on 'Hit-List', 18.

78 Anon, 'POA Seek Urgent Talks with Noonan on 'Hit-List', 18; Yeats, 'Revenge Group Report to Be Investigated', 7.

79 Anon, '"3 Hit Me with Bars" – Warder', 1.

80 Anon, 'Overtime Ban Threat over Prison Attack', 19.

81 Farrelly, 'Prison Group Claim Bombing', 1; Dowling, 'Petrol Bombers Got "Wrong" House', 1.

82 Anon, 'Warders' Families Now Face Attacks', 3.

83 Anon, 'Warders' Families Now Face Attacks', 3.

84 Anon, 'Stirring It Up', 7; Anon, 'Prison Staff May Seek Guns after Revenge Warning', 3.

85   Anon, 'Prison Staff May Seek Guns after Revenge Warning', 3.
86   Anon, 'Prison Revenge Group Identified', 3.
87   Anon, '"Sinister" Hit List of Jail Staff', 6.
88   Anon, 'Prison Attack – 2 Held', 5.
89   Whelan, 'Jail Officer Firebombed', 1.
90   Eddie Cahill, interview with author, 31 August 2022.
91   Reilly, 'Mountjoy Governor Condemns Assaults', 9.
92   Brady, 'Warders Threatened by Gunman', 1.
93   Brady, 'Thugs Plan Takeover of City Centre', 1.
94   Brady, 'Gardaí Find Gang's Guns', 7.
95   O'Keeffe, 'AIDS Prisoners Free after Riots', 3.
96   O'Keeffe, 'AIDS Prisoners Free after Riots', 3.
97   Anon, 'Strife Island', 1.
98   McClean, 'Jail Jab Cause of AIDS?', 5; Anon, 'Medical Check Urged for Jailed Drug Abusers', 3.
99   Weston and Berridge, 'AIDS Inside and Out', 256. This harsh prognosis, sadly, proved accurate and Hogg died nearly five years later in 1990. The Family of Peter Ben Hogg, 'Acknowledgements'; Cleary, 'Sculpture Recalls Heroin Victims'; RTÉ, *Today Tonight*.
100 Anon, 'Medical Check Urged for Jailed Drug Abusers', 3.
101 Anon, 'Medical Check Urged for Jailed Drug Abusers', 3.
102 Hennessy, 'AIDS-Hit Prisoners Cut Wrists in Protest', 1.
103 Lavery, 'AIDS Link Prisoners on the Roof', 1; Mara deLacy in Weston, *Positive in Prison*.
104 McDonagh, 'Why Me?', 8.
105 Weston and Berridge, 'AIDS Inside and Out'; Weston, *Positive in Prison*.
106 Mara deLacy in Weston, *Positive in Prison*.
107 John Lonergan in Weston, *Positive in Prison*.
108 Hennessy, 'AIDS-Hit Prisoners Cut Wrists in Protest', 1; Farrelly, 'Another Prison Suicide', 2; Anon, 'AIDS Unit Overdose by Pills', 4.
109 Sheehy, 'AIDS Unit Prisoner Unconscious', 26.
110 McDonagh, 'Why Me?', 8.
111 Brady, 'Move to End Row on AIDS Remark', 5; Brennan and Paterson, 'Gardai Hose Prison Rioters', 1.
112 McDonagh, 'Why Me?', 8; Malon, 'AIDS Scare and Suicides Spark Crisis in Prisons', 1; Farrelly, 'New Suicide at Prison', 1; Anon, 'Firemen Treated in Prison AIDS Scare', 1.
113 Anon, 'AIDS Unit Overdose by Pills', 4.
114 Brennan and Paterson, 'Gardai Hose Prison Rioters', 1.
115 Brennan and Paterson, 'Gardai Hose Prison Rioters', 1.
116 Mara deLacy in Weston, *Positive in Prison*.
117 Yeats, 'Revenge Group Report to Be Investigated', 7.

CHAPTER FIVE

1 Costello, 'PRO Address to United Nations Congress', 6.
2 Costello, 'Press Release and Leaflet, 31 August 1975'.
3 Costello, 'PRO Address to United Nations Congress', 6.
4 Central Statistics Office, *1971 Census, Volume 12: Education, Scientific and Technological Qualifications*, Table 3A.
5 Denieffe, '"Nighties in Mountjoy Sexy"', 24.
6 The Dublin Housing Action Committee was an activist group that, from 1966 to 1969, campaigned for housing for working-class people in Dublin. They organised a series of marches and squats in vacant buildings. McEneaney, 'Political Commemoration and Housing Protest in Ireland'. The Irish Women's Liberation Movement was a short-lived but highly influential feminist activist organisation in the early 1970s. The group was responsible for a number of very high profile events which helped to bring feminist issues into the public discourse. Connolly, *The Irish Women's Movement*, 111–29.
7 Treacy, *The IRA, 1956–69*, 136–7.
8 Anon, 'Derry Girl Sues for False Imprisonment', 6.
9 Anon, 'Eight More for Trial in Special Court', 4.
10 Anon, 'Court Protest over Prison Conditions', 4. The Garda Special Branch was the branch of the Irish police force tasked with counterintelligence and antisubversive activities throughout the mid- and late twentieth century. During the Troubles, it became increasingly controversial, as it was associated with 'heavy gang' tactics, including violence, intimidation, and forced confessions. Conway, *Policing Twentieth Century Ireland*, 138–51.
11 Pat McCartan, interview with author, 14 August 2020.
12 Anon, 'Prisoners Treated As Less Than Human', 10; Pat McCartan, interview with author, 14 August 2020.
13 Pat McCartan, interview with author, 14 August 2020.
14 Pat McCartan, interview with author, 14 August 2020.
15 Pat McCartan, interview with author, 14 August 2020.
16 Joe Costello, Interview with author, 13 August 2020.
17 Anon, 'New Group to Help Prisoners', 5.
18 Anon, 'New Group to Help Prisoners', 5.
19 Pat McCartan, interview with author, 14 August 2020.
20 Máirín De Búrca, interview with author, 27 July 2020; Pat McCartan, interview with author, 14 August 2020.
21 PRO Chairman, 'Resolutions Passed at AGM', 10.
22 Máirín De Búrca, interview with author, 27 July 2020.
23 Pat McCartan, interview with author, 14 August 2020.
24 Walsh et al., 'Prisoners' Representatives', 8.
25 Joe Costello, Interview with author, 13 August 2020.

26 Joe Costello, Interview with author, 13 August 2020.

27 Anon, 'Mothers Fear for Sons' Lives, Jail Needs Psychiatrists', 7.

28 Walsh et al., 'Prisoners' Representatives', 8.

29 Prisoners' Rights Organisation, *Loughan House*, 3.

30 Anon, 'Main Cause Is Lack of Parental Control', 2.

31 Quinn, 'Sorry, But We Have No Job For You!', 8.

32 Anon, 'Probation for Boys Who Fired House', 6.

33 Denieffe, 'Child Crime Move, Action Pledge by Minister', 1.

34 Collins, 'Questions. Oral Answers. – Places of Detention'.

35 Prisoners' Rights Organisation, *Loughan House*, front cover.

36 Prisoners' Rights Organisation, *Loughan House*, 3.

37 Prisoners' Rights Organisation, *Loughan House*, 7.

38 Prisoners' Rights Organisation, 'Draft Report on the Survey of over 200 Ex-prisoners'.

39 Prisoners' Rights Organisation, *Loughan House*, 4.

40 Prisoners' Rights Organisation, *Loughan House*, 4–5.

41 Prisoners' Rights Organisation, *Loughan House*, 5.

42 Prisoner Rights Organisation, 'Press Release 9 November 1973'; Fardy, 'Open letter to An Taoiseach'.

43 Prisoners' Rights Organisation, 'Untitled Leaflet (Christmas Presents)'.

44 Prisoners' Rights Organisation, 'Untitled Leaflet (Christmas Presents)'.

45 Collins, 'Oral Answers – Prison Library Facilities'.

46 Prisoners' Rights Organisation, 'Survey of over 200 Ex-prisoners'. Of the completed questionnaires, seven were recorded as 'spoiled', so the resultant statistics were based on the experiences of 195 people.

47 Prisoners' Rights Organisation, 'Survey of over 200 Ex-prisoners'.

48 Prisoners' Rights Organisation, 'Draft Report on the Survey of over 200 Ex-prisoners'.

49 Walsh, 'University Forum', 8.

50 Anon, 'Public Enquiry Petition Presented', 9.

51 Anon, 'Public Enquiry Petition Presented', 9.

52 Anon, 'Official Being Hounded: Collins', 1.

53 Anon, 'Official Being Hounded: Collins', 1.

54 Collins, 'Questions. Oral Answers. Prison Conditions'.

55 Anon, 'Why the Enquiry', 14.

56 Keane, 'MacBride, Seán'; Beckmann, 'Louk Hulsman: An Obituary'.

57 MacBride, *Report of the Commission of Enquiry into the Irish Penal System*, xiii.

58 MacBride, *Report of the Commission of Enquiry into the Irish Penal System*, xiii.

59 Taylor, Walton, and Young, *The New Criminology*, 296–7.

60 Prisoners' Rights Organisation, 'Draft Statement by Prisoners' Rights Organisation'.

61 Anon, 'Hussey Tops First Count in NUI', 4.
62 MacBride, *Report of the Commission of Enquiry into the Irish Penal System*, iv.
63 MacBride, *Report of the Commission of Enquiry into the Irish Penal System*, v.
64 MacBride, *Report of the Commission of Enquiry into the Irish Penal System*, 37.
65 MacBride, *Report of the Commission of Enquiry into the Irish Penal System*, 39, 40.
66 MacBride, *Report of the Commission of Enquiry into the Irish Penal System*, 46.
67 MacBride, *Report of the Commission of Enquiry into the Irish Penal System*, 44.
68 MacBride, *Report of the Commission of Enquiry into the Irish Penal System*, 54–5.
69 MacBride, *Report of the Commission of Enquiry into the Irish Penal System*, 58.
70 MacBride, *Report of the Commission of Enquiry into the Irish Penal System*, 60–4.
71 Anon, 'End Death Penalty', 8.
72 O'Donnell, *Justice, Mercy, and Caprice,* 133.
73 Clingan, 'Campaign Aims At Abolition of Death Penalty', 11.
74 Anon, 'Death Penalty Abolition Urged', 7. Noël Browne was best known as the Minister Health (1948–51) who introduced the 'Mother and Child Scheme' which gave free healthcare to new mothers and infants. Until the early 1980s, Browne was a vocal and often controversial advocate for various left-wing causes in the Dáil. Horgan, 'Browne, Noel Christopher'.
75 Anon, 'Call for End of Hanging Wins in Close Vote', 8.
76 Anon, 'Debate Refusal Regretted', 7.
77 Anon, 'Hanging Raises Loyalty Conflict', 8.
78 Anon, 'Nothing to Inquire Into, Says Cooney Rejecting Allegation', 5.
79 Department of Justice, *Memorandum for the Government: Proposed Bill to Amend the Prisons Act, 1972.*
80 Buckley, 'Published Reports Confirmed Inadequacy of Curragh Prison', 1.
81 Buckley, 'Published Reports Confirmed Inadequacy of Curragh Prison', 1.
82 Anon, 'Military Custody for Civilian Prisoners', 6.
83 Anon, 'Military Custody for Civilian Prisoners', 6.
84 MacBride, *Report of the Commission of Enquiry into the Irish Penal System,* 19–21.
85 Clingan, 'Campaign to Shut Curragh Jail Launched', 9.
86 Clingan, 'Campaign to Shut Curragh Jail Launched', 9.
87 Clingan, 'Campaign to Shut Curragh Jail Launched', 9.
88 Anon, 'Closure of Curragh Pledged', 11.
89 Anon, 'Closure of Curragh Pledged', 11.
90 Anon, 'MacBride Picks Senate Choice', 7.
91 Folley, 'Protest Over Use of Curragh', 11.
92 Kelly, 'Curragh Prison to Close by End of Year', 1.
93 Anon, 'Curragh Jail to Close', 4; Folley, 'Protest over Use of Curragh', 11.
94 Higgins, 'Supplementary Estimates, 1981'; Robinson, 'Prisons Bill, 1980'.

95 Noonan, 'Written Answers – Mountjoy Prison Unit'.
96 Murtagh, 'Prisoner Took Heroin Overdose', 6.
97 Anon, 'Curragh Prisoners Found Dead', 8.
98 Noonan, 'Written Answers – Curragh Military Detention Barracks'.
99 Joe Costello, Interview with author, 13 August 2020.
100 Prisoners' Rights Organisation, *Loughan House*, 3.
101 See, for example, Anon, 'Have You Been Mugged, Burgled, or Conned Yet?', 10; Anon, 'Nobody's Home is Safe – Judge', 11.
102 Anon, 'Ryan Attacks Demands by Prisoners for More Comfort', 7.
103 Anon, 'Ryan Attacks Demands by Prisoners for More Comfort', 7.
104 Costello, 'Prisoners' Rights', 9.
105 Anon, 'Statement by Mr. Joe Costello', 6; Anon, 'PRO Rejects Garda Claim on Subversion', 4.
106 Yeats, 'Revenge Group Report to Be Investigated', 7.
107 Richardson, 'Letter to Concerned Parents Against Drugs (1984)'.
108 Whitaker, 'Letter to Una O'Higgins O'Malley, 26 March 1984'.
109 Joe Costello, Interview with author, 13 August 2020.

CHAPTER SIX

1 Department of Justice, *Annual Report 1984*, 7; Conway, 'Inquiry Deal Ends Jail Row', 1.
2 Department of Justice, *Annual Report 1984*, 57.
3 Department of Justice, *Annual Report 1984*, 7.
4 Irish Council of Churches Board of Community Affairs, *Prisons in the Republic of Ireland*; The Council for Social Welfare, *The Prison System*.
5 Rogan, *Prison Policy in Ireland*, 167.
6 Heron, 'Do We Need to Lock Up Women?', 8.
7 Ryan, 'Prison Welfare Very Well Run, Says Collins', 7.
8 Power, 'Prisons Cannot Solve Crime – Bishops', 9.
9 Anon, 'Mountjoy Jail Death', 3; Anon, 'Inquiry Called', 2; Anon, 'Inquiry Call on Cell Death', 5.
10 Smith, 'Prison Staff Hit Dept. over Poor Conditions', 3.
11 Kilfeather, 'Gardaí, Army on Prison Standby', 16.
12 Kilfeather, 'Gardaí, Army on Prison Standby', 16.
13 Dillon, 'Jail Chaos Averted as Overtime Cuts Deferred', 1.
14 Chambers, *T.K. Whitaker*, 356, 340, 362.
15 Whitaker, 'Draft Letter to the Taoiseach, Undated'.
16 Henchy, 'Letter to TK Whitaker, 27 February 1984'.
17 Department of Finance, 'Appendix C,' in Department of Justice, 'Memorandum for the Government: Committee of Inquiry into the Prison System'.

18 Department of Justice, 'Memorandum for the Government: Committee of Inquiry into the Prison System', 2, 3.

19 Department of Justice, 'Memorandum for the Government: Committee of Inquiry into the Prison System', 5.

20 Department of Justice, 'Memorandum for the Government: Committee of Inquiry into the Prison System', 3.

21 Department of Justice, 'Memorandum for the Government: Committee of Inquiry into the Prison System', 7.

22 Department of Justice, 'Memorandum for the Government: Committee of Inquiry into the Prison System', 2, 3.

23 Thomas, 'Prison System "In Peril of Collapse"', 3.

24 Anon, '"Huge Saving" with Fewer in Jail', 1.

25 Anon, 'Prison Overhaul Plan Welcomed', 1.

26 Anon, 'Prison Governors Welcome Report', 16.

27 Anon, 'Prison Overhaul Plan Welcomed', 1; Anon, 'Welcome for Jail Report', 3; Anon, 'Penal Reform Plan Receives Wide Welcome', 5.

28 Dukes, 'Criminal Justice System: Motion (Resumed)'; Dukes, 'Ceisteanna – Questions Oral Answers – Whitaker Report on Penal System'; Dukes, 'Estimates, 1986 – Vote 24: Justice (Revised Estimate)'.

29 Anon, 'Jails Board "Should Be Independent"', 3.

30 Anon, 'Group Criticise Prisons Report', 3.

31 Anon, 'Prison Governors Welcome Report', 16.

32 McAleese, 'Our Prison Crisis', 8.

33 Irish Commission for Justice and Peace and Council for Social Welfare, *Response to the Report of the Committee of Inquiry into the Prison System*.

34 Whitaker, 'Letter to Alan Dukes, 22 July 1986'.

35 Whitaker, 'Letter to Alan Dukes, 14 May 1986'.

36 Dukes, 'Address to the POA Annual Conference'.

37 McVerry, 'Letter to TK Whitaker, 30 July 1986'.

38 Henchy, 'Letter to TK Whitaker, 7 October 1986'.

39 Mac Giolla, 'Written Answers – Report on the Penal System'.

40 Dukes, 'Ceisteanna – Questions Oral Answers – Whitaker Report on Penal System'.

41 Barry, 'Another Nail in the Coffin for the Whitaker Report'.

42 Anon, 'Women PO for First Time', 3.

43 McAuley, *Towards an Independent Prisons Agency*.

44 Brady, 'Row over Prisons Appointments', 3.

45 Prison Rules. S.I. No. 252 of 2007. Dublin: Stationary Office, 2007, Sections 79, 85.

46 United Nations Committee Against Torture, 'Forty-Sixth Session: Consideration of Reports Submitted by States Parties under Article 19 of the Convention', 3.

47 Reilly, *Report on an Inspection of St. Patrick's Institution*, 64.
48 Whitaker, *Report of the Committee of Inquiry into the Penal System*, 18.
49 Whitaker, *Report of the Committee of Inquiry into the Penal System*, 18.
50 O'Flynn, *Time for Change*, 3.
51 Irish Penal Reform Trust, *Progress in the Prison System*, 70.
52 Irish Penal Reform Trust, *Progress in the Prison System*, 66.
53 Whitaker, *Report of the Committee of Inquiry into the Penal System*, 57.
54 Whitaker, 'Welfare of Prisoners', 8.
55 Gavin and Kawałek, 'Viewing the Dublin Drug Treatment Court', 1–15.
56 Gallagher, 'Drug Treatment Court'; Collins, 'The Irish Experience'.
57 Department of Justice, Equality, and Law Reform, *Review of the Drug Treatment Court*, 18, 19, 24.
58 Whitaker, *Report of the Committee of Inquiry into the Penal System*, 9, 30.
59 Whitaker, *Report of the Committee of Inquiry into the Penal System*, 31.
60 Whitaker, *Report of the Committee of Inquiry into the Penal System*, 31.
61 Costello, *National Youth Policy Committee Final Report*, 22.
62 Whitaker, *Report of the Committee of Inquiry into the Penal System*, 9.
63 Costello, *National Youth Policy Committee Final Report*, 22.
64 Whitaker, 'Letter to Una O'Higgins O'Malley, 26 March 1984'.
65 Whitaker, 'Committee of Inquiry into the Prison System Discussion Paper'.
66 Whitaker, *Report of the Committee of Inquiry into the Penal System*, 64.
67 Whitaker, *Report of the Committee of Inquiry into the Penal System*, 67.
68 Joe Costello, interview with author, 13 August 2020.
69 Whitaker, *Report of the Committee of Inquiry into the Penal System*, 39.
70 Whitaker, *Report of the Committee of Inquiry into the Penal System*, 40.
71 Anon, 'PRO Chief Refused Access to Roof Men', 4.
72 Ní Chríodáin, 'Labour TD Calls for a New Body to Run Prisons', 4.

EPILOGUE

1 Anon, 'Dartmoor Convicts Join in Protest', 3; Anon, 'News in Brief', 3; Anon, 'Prisoners Threa
2 Anon, 'Cooney Hits at Prisoners' Union', 1.
3 O'Donnell, 'Portlaoise Prisoners' Union', 10.
4 Anon, 'Prison Reform', 16.
5 Levine, 'Ex-prisoner is Scourge of the Irish Penal System', 15.
6 Anon, 'Daingean Reformatory', 6–7; Anon, 'A Prisoner Remembers', 3; Anon, 'The Good Life', 12.
7 Anon, 'Prison Suicides', 8–9.
8 Yeats, 'Revenge Group Report to Be Investigated', 7.
9 Kerrigan, 'Special Feature: A Necessary Respect – The Small Legend of Karl Crawley'.

10 McCaffery, 'Karl Alexander Crawley against Ireland Exhibit 10: Transcript of Medical Evidence to High Court, 8 April 1976'.

11 Moore, 'Youth Set Fire to Cell to Get Out', 7.

12 Moore, 'Youth Set Fire to Cell to Get Out', 7.

13 Anon, 'Inquiry Call over Burned Prisoner', 3.

14 Anon, 'Boy Burned – Father Hits Out at Dept.', 1.

15 Anon, 'Boy Burned – Father Hits Out at Dept.', 1.

16 Anon, 'School Fire Averted by Alert Garda', 5.

17 Corry, 'Heroin Link to Prisoner's Suicide', 1.

18 Corry, 'Jail Shock that Led to Suicide', 3.

19 Rae, 'AIDS Baby Dad Hanged Himself', 1.

20 Anon, 'AIDS Baby Son of Jail Suicide', 1.

21 After this tragic event, the family disappeared from public view until 1991, when Paul's girlfriend Helen Spellman made a number of public appearances as a committee member of Body Positive, an activist group campaigning on behalf of HIV positive people.

Bibliography

Advisory Forum on Human Rights. *Prisoners in the Republic of Ireland.* Belfast: Irish Council of Churches, 1981.

Allen, Francis A. 'Criminal Justice, Legal Values and the Rehabilitative Ideal'. *Journal of Criminal Law and Criminality* 50, no. 3 (1959): 226–32.

Anonymous. 'Accident Verdict on Cell Death'. *Irish Press*, 20 June 1975, 3.

– 'Adjournment in Assault Case'. *Evening Herald*, 20 June 1975, 4.

– 'Agree of We Kill'. *Evening Echo*, 10 September 1971, 5.

– 'AIDS Baby Son of Jail Suicide'. *Sunday Press*, 2 February 1986, 1.

– 'AIDS Unit Overdose by Pills'. *Evening Press*, 18 January 1986, 4.

– 'Anti-Birth Devices Shop in City Centre'. *Evening Press*, 27 November 1978, 4.

– 'Appeal to Strasbourg'. *Jail Journal* 2, no. 4 (1978): 1.

– 'Attacks on Homes of Warders'. *Irish Press*, 1 September 1980, 4.

– 'Attica Hostages Shot Not Knifed: Doubt on Official Version'. *Irish Times*, 15 September 1971, 1.

– 'Balance of 15-Year Jail Term Suspended by Judge'. *Irish Times*, 26 November 1985, 8.

– 'Balance Sheet at 14 May 1974'. *Jail Journal* 1, no. 4 (1974): 15.

– 'Bomb Killed Escaper: Report'. *Evening Herald*, 18 March 1975, 1.

– 'Booklet Sale Challenge to DPP'. *Irish Press*, 9 December 1976, 3.

– 'Boy Burned – Father Hits Out at Dept.'. *Evening Herald*, 19 April, 1975, 1.

– '"Bread and Water Diet" Allegation'. *Munster Express*, 21 September 1973, 5.

– 'Burned Convict. P.R.O. Demand Inquiry'. *Irish Independent*, 21 April 1975, 1.

– 'Call for End of Hanging Wins in Close Vote'. *Irish Times*, 30 March 1981, 8.

– 'Cars of Six Warders Vandalised'. *Evening Press*, 9 July 1981, 8.

– 'Challenge on Curragh by Prisoners' Group'. *Irish Press*, 11 May 1978, 3.

- 'Civil Servant Gets Picket Outlawed'. *Irish Press*, 10 May 1975, 5.
- 'Closure of Curragh Pledged'. *Irish Times*, 18 December 1981, 11.
- 'Committee on Prison Reform Dossier for Minister'. *Irish Press*, 19 May 1973, 3.
- 'Convicted of Causing Bodily Harm'. *Nationalist and Leinster Times*, 14 December 1973, 5.
- 'Cooney Hits at Prisoners' Union'. *Cork Examiner*, 26 May 1973, 1.
- 'Court Picket Win Appeal, Sentences Quashed'. *Irish Press*, 12 November 1975, 5.
- 'Court Protest over Prison Conditions'. *Irish Press*, 9 January 1973, 4.
- 'Court Told of Prison Brawl'. *Irish Press*, 5 December 1973, 4.
- 'Curragh Hunger Strike'. *Nationalist and Leinster Times*, 28 February 1975, 1.
- 'Curragh Jail to Close'. *Irish Times*, 27 January 1983, 4.
- 'Curragh Prisoners Found Dead'. *Irish Times*, 9 March 1983, 8.
- 'Curragh'. *Nationalist and Leinster Times*, 7 March 1975, 6.
- 'Daingean Reformatory'. *Jail Journal* 1, no. 1 (1973): 6–7.
- 'Dartmoor Convicts Join in Protest'. *Irish Independent*, 1 September 1972, 3.
- 'Death in Prison'. *Jail Journal* 1, no. 1 (1973): 14–15.
- 'Death Penalty Abolition Urged'. *Irish Times*, 4 February 1981, 7.
- 'Debate Refusal Regretted'. *Irish Times*, 6 May 1981, 7.
- '"Decision Soon" on Prison Probe'. *Irish Press*, 25 May 1979, 3.
- 'Department Denies "Chaos at Joy"'. *Irish Independent*, 12 January 1973.
- 'Derry Girl Sues for False Imprisonment'. *Irish Press*, 1 November 1972, 6.
- 'Dismissed Prison Office Loses Case'. *Nationalist and Leinster Times*, 17 April 1981, 4.
- 'Drivers of Raids Car Jailed'. *Evening Herald*, 26 June 1979, 4.
- 'Drugs: Quasi Intellectuals Pose Problem'. *Cork Examiner*, 19 November 1969, 9.
- 'Dundrum'. *Jail Journal* 1, no. 3 (1974): 6–7.
- 'Editorial'. *Jail Journal* 1, no. 1 (1973): 1.
- 'Eight More for Trial in Special Court'. *Irish Press*, 13 June 1972, 4.
- '£8,648 Raid: Three Convicted'. *Irish Press*, 4 August 1972, 7.
- 'End Death Penalty'. *Irish Times*, 19 January 1980, 8.
- 'Ex-Prisoner Attacks "Degrading" Life behind Bars'. *Evening Herald*, 18 May 1973, 6.
- 'Fewer Armed Robbery Cases Solved'. *Irish Press*, 30 March 1973, 7.
- 'Firemen Treated in Prison AIDS Scare'. *Irish Press*, 17 January 1986, 1.
- 'Forum Discussion Group'. *Evening Herald*, 13 May 1974, 10.
- 'Four Men Questioned after Attack'. *Evening Press*, 7 November 1979, 23.
- 'Four Prisoners at Curragh End Hunger Strike'. *Irish Times*, 5 March 1975, 14.
- 'Four Still Fasting at the Curragh'. *Irish Times*, 3 March 1975, 8.

210 | Bibliography

- '4 Years Jail for Theft'. *Irish Press*, 18 February 1987, 3.
- 'Free Prison Hostages Bid Fails'. *Irish Press*, 11 September 1971, 5.
- 'Garda Alert on Protests in Two Jails'. *Irish Independent*, 8 January 1973, 1.
- 'Geneva Defines Torture'. *Irish Independent*, 11 September 1975, 12.
- 'Girls Beaten in Raids on Bookmakers'. *Irish Press*, 26 March 1966, 14.
- 'Governor Remanded on Bail'. *Irish Press*, 20 October 1973, 3.
- 'Group Criticise Prisons Report'. *Irish Independent*, 14 August 1985, 3.
- 'Hanging Raises Loyalty Conflict'. *Irish Times*, 26 October 1981, 8.
- 'Have You Been Mugged, Burgled, or Conned Yet?'. *Evening Press*, 1 April 1982, 10.
- 'High Court Bid to Block Irish Press Story Fails'. *Irish Press*, 4 September 1980, 7.
- 'Hostages Died from Gun Shot Wounds'. *Evening Echo*, 15 September 1971, 3.
- '"Huge Saving" with Fewer in Jail.' *Irish Independent*, 10 August 1985, 1.
- 'Hunger Strike'. *Jail Journal* 1, no. 12 (1977): 2.
- 'Hussey Tops First Count in NUI'. *Irish Press*, 13 August 1981, 4.
- 'Injunction for US Prisoners'. *Irish Times*, 11 September 1971, 1.
- 'Injunction Granted to Prevent Picket on Civil Servant's Home'. *Irish Times*, 17 May 1975, 13.
- 'Inquest Call for Public Inquiry into the Prison System'. *Irish Independent*, 17 May 1975, 3.
- 'Inquest Urges Jail "Medical"'. *Irish Press*, 16 October 1973, 3.
- 'Inquiry Call on Cell Death'. *Irish Press*, 9 March, 1983, 5.
- 'Inquiry Call over Burned Prisoner'. *Irish Press*, 21 April 1975, 3.
- 'Inquiry Called'. *Sunday Independent*, 6 February 1983, 2.
- 'Internment Protest March'. *Evening Herald*, 26 August 1971, 1.
- 'Introduction'. *Jail Journal* 1, no. 1 (1973): 1–3.
- 'Irish Protest at Geneva Conference'. *Irish Times*, 2 September 1975, 4.
- 'Jail Group "Has No Credibility"'. *Evening Herald*, 8 November 1979, 2.
- 'Jail Protest "a Publicity Stunt"'. *Irish Press*, 19 July 1977, 3.
- 'Jail Riot Riddle of Shot Hostages'. *Irish Press*, 15 September 1971, 1.
- 'Jail Roof Marathon: Portlaoise Protest Enters Second Day'. *Irish Press*, 15 September 1973, 1.
- 'Jailed Man Convicted of Second Raid'. *Cork Examiner*, 8 October 1974, 9.
- 'Jails Board "Should be Independent"'. *Irish Press*, 16 August 1985, 3.
- 'John Donnellan'. *Jail Journal* 1, no. 7 (1975): 8–11.
- 'Join Prisoners' Rights Organisation'. *Jail Journal* 1, no. 4 (1974): 11.
- 'Judge Rules on Special Care'. *Irish Press*, 14 April 1976, 6.
- 'Justice Told Letters Were Never Posted'. *Nationalist and Leinster Times*, 9 November 1973, 4.
- 'Karl Alexander Crawley v Ireland, Appendix 1: Sentences Served by the Applicant'. *National Archives of Ireland*, 2009/74/738.

- 'Karl Alexander Crawley v Ireland, Appendix 2: Curriculum Vitae'. *National Archives of Ireland*, 2009/74/738.
- 'Karl Alexander Crawley v Ireland, Observations of the Government of Ireland on the Admissibility of the Above Application'. *National Archives of Ireland*, 2009/74/738.
- 'Karl Crawley'. *Jail Journal* 1, no. 9 (1975): 3.
- 'Knives Used in Jail'. *Irish Independent*, 8 October 1973, 3.
- 'Letter from Portlaoise – Hoping for a New Deal'. *Evening Herald*, 8 September 1973, 6.
- '"Libel" by Prisoners Alleged'. *Irish Independent*, 4 January 1975, 7.
- 'Listowel's Golden Harvest Festival'. *Limerick Leader*, 26 September 1970, 3.
- 'Long Record of Work by Orphan Boys'. *Irish Independent,* 9 September 1963, 5.
- 'Lynch Calls for Facts on Death Threat'. *Irish Press*, 10 February 1975, 4.
- 'MacBride Picks Senate Choice'. *Irish Times*, 3 July 1981, 7.
- 'Main Cause Is Lack of Parental Control'. *Evening Echo*, 31 May 1977, 2.
- 'Man Found Dead in Cell Inquest to Be Held'. *Irish Independent,* 6 August 1973, 11.
- 'Man Freed, 2 Bailed in Raid Case'. *Irish Press*, 18 May 1972, 6.
- 'Man Tells Court "12 on Hunger Strike"'. *Evening Herald*, 10 March 1977, 6.
- 'Man Wanted Case Put to Rights Court'. *Irish Press*, 3 October 1972, 7.
- 'Man's Plea for Release Rejected'. *Irish Independent*, 14 April 1976, 11.
- 'Medical Check Urged for Jailed Drug Abusers'. *Irish Press*, 21 November 1985, 3.
- 'Medical Examination Urged for Prisoners with Mental Illness'. *Irish Times*, 16 October 1973, 18.
- 'Medical Profession Accused over Prison Psychiatric Treatment'. *Irish Times*, 16 October 1975, 13.
- 'Memorandum: As to Fact'. *National Archives of Ireland*, 2009/74/738.
- 'Military Custody for Civilian Prisoners'. *Jail Journal* 2, no. 5 (1978): 4–7.
- 'Minister Hits at Pressure Groups'. *Sunday Independent*, 18 May 1975, 5.
- 'Mothers Fear for Sons' Lives, Jail Needs Psychiatrists'. *Irish Press*, 4 June 1975, 7.
- 'Mountjoy Jail Death'. *Irish Press*, 5 February 1983, 3.
- 'Mountjoy Jail Revenge Wave Feared'. *Irish Press*, 7 November 1979, 4.
- 'Mountjoy Jail Riot Warning as Warders Start Overtime Ban'. *Belfast Telegraph*, 9 September 1980, 3.
- 'Mountjoy Prison Riot'. *Jail Journal* 3, no. 3 (1979): 1–2.
- 'Mountjoy Riots'. *Jail Journal* 1, no. 1 (1973): 4–5.
- 'New Group Seeking Prison Reform'. *Nationalist and Leinster Times,* 23 May 1973, 9.

- 'New Group to Help Prisoners'. *Irish Times*, 25 July 1977, 5.
- 'New Hunger Strike at Curragh'. *Evening Herald*, 24 February 1975, 2.
- 'New Hunger Strike at Curragh'. *Irish Independent*, 24 February 1975, 1.
- 'New Prison Scheme Gets Mixed Reaction'. *Irish Press*, 10 November 1979, 4.
- 'News in Brief'. *Irish Independent*, 9 August 1972, 3.
- 'Nobody's Home Is Safe – Judge'. *Drogheda Independent*, 4 November 1983, 11.
- '"No Doctor" for Hunger Striker'. *Irish Press*, 3 March 1975, 3.
- '"Non Political" Fast May End Deadlock'. *Irish Press*, 12 February 1975, 1.
- 'No Particular Reason for Mountjoy Disturbance, Says Department'. *Irish Times*, 19 July 1977, 1.
- '"No Place" for Man Who Swallowed Spoons'. *Cork Examiner,* 9 April 1976, 11.
- 'No Place for This Prisoner'. *Irish Independent*, 9 April 1976, 7.
- 'Nothing to Inquire into, Says Cooney Rejecting Allegation'. *Irish Times*, 18 April 1977, 5.
- 'Obduracy on Both Sides'. *Kerryman*, 7 February 1975, 8.
- 'Officers in Prisons May Stop Work'. *Irish Independent*, 25 September 1973, 9.
- 'Official Being Hounded: Collins'. *Irish Press*, 27 October 1977, 1.
- 'Order Bars Rights Group from Picketing'. *Evening Herald*, 16 May 1975, 3.
- 'Overtime Ban Threat over Prison Attack'. *Irish Press*, 6 August 1984, 19.
- 'Parting Kiss for Her £143,000'. *Evening Herald*, 12 May 1970, 9.
- 'Penal Reform Plan Receives Wide Welcome'. *Irish Independent*, 10 August 1985, 5.
- 'Petrol Bomb Thugs Strike'. *Evening Herald*, 20 August 1981, 1.
- 'Picket at Ministerial Function'. *Irish Examiner*, 29 August 1973, 7.
- 'Picket of Fifty on Mountjoy'. *Evening Herald*, 17 March 1977, 7.
- 'Picket on Civil Servant "Illegal"'. *Irish Press*, 17 May 1975, 5.
- 'Picket on Home Again Barred'. *Irish Independent*, 17 May 1975, 7.
- 'Picketing Ban on Eight'. *Cork Examiner*, 10 May 1975, 12.
- 'Plan to "Fix" Jail Officer Alleged'. *Irish Independent*, 4 February 1977, 3.
- 'Plea to Cooney on Behalf of Prisoners'. *Irish Independent*, 3 March 1975, 16.
- 'POA Seek Urgent Talks with Noonan on 'Hit-List'. *Irish Press*, 30 April 1984, 18.
- 'Portlaoise Cases for Amnesty'. *Irish Press*, 13 December 1972, 3.
- 'Portlaoise Prison Officer Found Not Guilty'. *Nationalist and Leinster Times*, 3 May 1974, 32.
- 'Portlaoise Prison'. *Jail Journal* 1, no. 2 (1973): 4–5.
- 'Portlaoise Worse Than Long Kesh'. *Irish Press*, 10 September 1974, 4.
- 'Prison "Killed My Brother" Sister's Inquiry Call'. *Irish Press*, 24 October 1973, 7.
- 'Prison "Mafia Bosses" Slated by Cooney'. *Irish Press*, 26 May 1973, 3.
- 'Prison and Psychiatry'. *Jail Journal* 3, no. 3 (1979): 10.

- 'Prison Attack – 2 Held'. *Evening Press*, 8 September 1985, 5.
- 'Prison Back to Normal in Portlaoise'. *Nationalist and Leinster Times*, 17 November 1972, 1.
- 'Prison Governors Welcome Report'. *Cork Examiner*, 20 August 1985, 16.
- 'Prison Men's Secretary Resigns'. *Irish Press*, 19 January 1977, 4.
- 'Prison Officer – Guest at Sister's Wedding – Shot Dead at Clogher'. *Ulster Herald*, 21 April 1979, 1.
- 'Prison Officer Is Assaulted'. *Evening Herald*, 13 October 1980, 1.
- 'Prison Officers Decide on Industrial Action'. *Irish Press*, 9 June 1979, 6.
- 'Prison Officers Strike Threat'. *Irish Press*, 19 September 1973, 1.
- 'Prison Officers Threaten Action'. *Irish Press*, 7 November 1979, 1.
- 'Prison Officers to Hit Back'. *Evening Press*, 8 September 1980, 1.
- 'Prison Overhaul Plan Welcomed'. *Irish Independent*, 10 August 1985, 1.
- 'Prison Reform Urged by Picket at Jail'. *Irish Independent*, 30 July 1973, 7.
- 'Prison Reform'. *Irish Independent*, 13 June 1973, 16.
- 'Prison Revenge Group Identified'. *Irish Press*, 24 January 1985, 3.
- 'Prison Rioters: No Surrender'. *Irish Independent*, 11 September 1971, 3.
- 'Prison Staff Backing for Jail Reforms'. *Irish Press*, 12 November 1979, 3.
- 'Prison Staff May Seek Guns after Revenge Warning'. *Irish Press*, 15 January 1985, 3.
- 'Prison Statements'. *Jail Journal* 1, no. 1 (1973): 10–11.
- 'Prison Suicides'. *Jail Journal* 1, no. 7 (1975): 7–12.
- 'Prison Union Leaders Moved'. *Irish Independent*, 12 November 1973, 12.
- 'Prisoner Refused Release Order'. *Cork Examiner*, 14 April 1976, 7.
- 'A Prisoner Remembers'. *Jail Journal* 1, no. 7 (1975): 3.
- 'Prisoner Swallows Metal'. *Irish Press*, 24 September 1975, 1.
- 'Prisoners Allege Brutal Treatment'. *Irish Times*, 8 December 1972, 11.
- 'Prisoners in Mountjoy Protest'. *Cork Examiner*, 8 January 1973, 1.
- 'Prisoners Injured in Jail Clash'. *Cork Examiner*, 6 November 1979, 1.
- 'Prisoners Leaders Sent to Curragh'. *Irish Independent*, 14 November 1973, 12.
- 'Prisoners on Diet'. *The Nationalist*, 24 November 1972, 19.
- 'Prisoners Threaten to Strike'. *Irish Press*, 21 February 1973, 5.
- 'Prisoners Threaten "Tougher Action"'. *Evening Echo*, 5 August 1972, 1.
- 'Prisoners to Stage Peaceful Protest'. *Evening Herald*, 26 October 1973, 6.
- 'Prisoners Treated as Less Than Human'. *Irish Independent*, 8 September 1973, 10.
- 'Prisoners Were Attacked, Claims Organisation'. *Irish Times*, 20 July 1977, 4.
- 'Prisoners' Demands "Rejected"'. *Irish Press*, 3 February 1973, 6.
- 'Prisoners' Roof Protest'. *Irish Independent*, 15 September 1973, 24.
- 'Prisons Act, 1972 as Extended by Prisons Act, 1977: Statements Pursuant to Section 2(6) of the Act'. Oireachtas Library, Collection DL015352, Document ID 4597.

214 | Bibliography

- 'Prisons Act, 1972 Statements Pursuant to Section 2(6) of the Act: 31 May 1972'. Oireachtas Library, Collection DL021182, Document ID 102660.
- 'Prisons Act, 1972 Statements Pursuant to Section 2(6) of the Act'. Oireachtas Library, Collection DL06645, Document ID 6449.
- 'Prisons Exposed by Suicides'. *Irish Press*, 26 May 1975, 5.
- 'The P.R.O. & Karl Crawley v The State'. *Jail Journal* 1, no. 8 (1975): 3.
- 'PRO Chief Refused Access to Roof Men'. *Irish Press*, 7 May 1990, 4.
- 'PRO Rejects Garda Claim on Subversion'. *Irish Press*, 12 April 1983, 4.
- 'Probation for Boys Who Fired House'. *Evening Herald*, 24 June 1977, 6.
- 'Protest over Prison Conditions'. *Irish Press*, 26 September 1973, 4.
- 'Provo Calls Off Hunger Strike'. *Irish Press*, 11 February 1975, 4.
- 'Provos End 36-Hours Prison Fast'. *Irish Independent*, 3 January 1976, 3.
- 'Psychiatric Care "Needed in Jails"'. *Cork Examiner*, 24 May 1975, 3.
- 'Public Enquiry Demanded'. *Jail Journal* 2, no. 3 (1977): 9–10.
- 'Public Enquiry Petition Presented'. *Jail Journal* 2, no. 3 (1977): 8–9.
- 'Relief at End of Protest'. *Irish Independent*, 17 February 1975, 16.
- 'Remanded in Robbery with Violence Case'. *Evening Herald*, 8 September 1964, 1.
- 'Reply to Prison Officers'. *Jail Journal* 1, no. 2 (1973): 10–11.
- 'Republic's Institutions "Not Suitable" for Man Whose Release Is Sought'. *Irish Times*, 9 April 1976, 13.
- 'Restaurant Owner and Left-Wing Campaigner'. *Irish Times*, 2 July 2011, 12.
- 'Review: The Liberty Suit'. *Jail Journal* 2, no. 4 (1978): 9–11.
- 'Riot Jail Deaths Riddle'. *Irish Independent*, 15 September 1971, 6.
- 'Robber Protests at 7-Year Sentence'. *Irish Times*, 4 August 1972, 9.
- 'Ryan Attacks Demands by Prisoners for More Comfort'. *Irish Times*, 24 August 1984, 7.
- 'Sacked Warder Attacks Prison System'. *Irish Independent*, 17 April 1974, 15.
- 'Savage Attack on Ex-prison Officer, Wife'. *Evening Press*, 6 November 1979, 1.
- 'School Fire Averted by Alert Garda'. *Evening Herald*, 6 September 1980, 5.
- '7 Picketers Held for Three Hours'. *Irish Press*, 9 July 1975, 7.
- '"Sinister" Hit List of Jail Staff'. *Irish Independent*, 6 September, 1985, 6.
- 'Sinn Féin Protest March'. *Evening Herald*, 4 March 1972, 1.
- '60 Plan Dublin Protest March'. *Cork Examiner*, 14 September 1968, 11.
- 'Slogans Found at Burned School'. *Irish Times*, 23 September 1980, 11.
- 'A Socialist Visionary and Trade Union Pragmatist'. *Irish Times*, 17 June 2000.
- 'Solicitor Cleared of Obstructing Sergt.'. *Nationalist and Leinster Times*, 14 March 1975, 6.
- 'Statement by Mr. Joe Costello'. *Irish Times*, 26 July 1984, 6.
- 'Stirring It Up'. *Irish Press*, 6 September 1985, 7.
- 'Strife Island'. *Cork Examiner*, 2 September 1985, 1.

- 'Sub-Citizens'. *Jail Journal* 1, no. 6 (1974): 4–5.
- 'Terrorism Main Topic for Lawmen'. *Evening Echo*, 1 September 1975, 5.
- 'The GENEVA Demonstration'. *Jail Journal* 1, no. 8 (1975): 9–10.
- 'The Good Life'. *Jail Journal* 1, no. 1 (1973): 12.
- '30 Injured in Mountjoy Riot'. *Irish Press*, 6 November 1979, 1.
- '37 Killed as Police Quell Prison Revolt'. *Irish Times*, 14 September 1971, 1.
- '£36,000 Fire Award to UCD'. *Irish Times*, 19 December 1984, 8.
- 'Three Charged with £8,864 Robbery Raid'. *Evening Herald*, 2 August 1972, 4.
- '"3 Hit Me with Bars" – Warder'. *Evening Press*, 9 June 1986, 1.
- 'Treasurer's Report'. *Jail Journal* 2, no. 3 (1977): 11.
- 'Tribute Paid to Fermoy's Patriot Soldier'. *The Corkman*, 23 October 1971, 1, 16.
- '12 Months for Picketing'. *Jail Journal* 1, no. 7 (1975): 13–14.
- 'Visiting Conditions: The Need for Change'. *Jail Journal* 1, no. 6 (1974): 9—10.
- 'Wants His Case to Go to Human Rights Court'. *Irish Independent*, 3 October 1972, 4.
- 'Warder's Action Threat'. *Cork Examiner*, 7 November 1979, 1.
- 'Warders Call Off Prison Overtime Ban'. *Irish Press*, 11 September 1980, 4.
- 'Warders Call Off Work Stoppages'. *Irish Press*, 18 June 1979, 3.
- 'Warders May Ban Overtime'. *Evening Press*, 1 September 1980, 1.
- 'Warders Victims of Organised Frame-Up Campaign'. *Evening Herald*, 8 September 1973, 6.
- 'Warders' Families Now Face Attacks'. *Irish Independent*, 14 January 1985, 3.
- 'Welcome for Jail Report'. *Irish Press*, 14 August 1985, 3.
- 'Why the Enquiry'. *Jail Journal* 2, no. 4 (1978): 12–14.
- 'Women PO for First Time'. *Irish Independent*, 9 January 1986, 3.
- 'The Women's Prison: The Facts of the Horror'. *Jail Journal* 1, no. 2 (1973): 6.
- 'Working Parole'. *Jail Journal* 1, no. 4 (1974): 4–5.

Arnold, Bruce. 'Reconstruction or Progress?'. *Irish Independent*, 4 June 1977, 6.

Bailey, Victor. *The Rise and Fall of the Rehabilitative Ideal, 1895–1970*. London: Routledge, 2019.

Ball, Stephen. *Education Policy and Social Class: The Selected Work of Stephen J. Ball*. London: Routledge, 2006.

Barkley, L.D. 'The Attica Liberation Faction Manifesto of Demands and Anti-Depression Platform (1971)'. *Race and Class* 53, no. 2 (2011): 28–35.

Barry, Gerald. 'Another Nail in the Coffin for the Whitaker Report'. *Sunday Tribune,* 21 September 1986.

Beckmann, Andrea. 'Louk Hulsman: An Obituary'. *Criminal Justice Matters* 76 (2009): 52.

Behan, Cormac. *Citizen Convicts: Prisoners, Politics and the Vote*. Manchester: Manchester University Press, 2016.

- 'The Prisoners' Rights Organisation and Penal Reform in the Republic of Ireland'. In *The Carceral Network in Ireland: History, Agency and Resistance*, edited by Fiona McCann, 91–112. Basingstoke: Palgrave, 2020.
- 'Putting Penal Reform on the Map: Prisoners' Rights Movement and Penal History'. *Contention et Subversion en Prison* 21 (2020): 1–17.
- '"We Are All Convicted Criminals?" Prisoners, Protest, and Penal Politics in the Republic of Ireland'. *Journal of Social History* 52, no. 2 (2018): 501–26.

Beresford, David. *Ten Dead Men: The Story of the 1981 Irish Hunger Strike*. London: Grafton Books, 1987.

Bofin, P.J. 'Coroner's Certificate, 1973'. National Archives of Ireland, CC/Coroners Inquest Dublin 244/1973.

Boland, Colm. 'Arson Attacks Baffle Gardaí'. *Irish Times*, 22 August 1980, 5.

Boland, Faye. 'Insanity, The Irish Constitution and the European Convention on Human Rights'. *Northern Ireland Legal Quarterly* 47, no. 3 (1996): 260–80.

Bosworth, Mary. *Encyclopedia of Prisons and Correctional Facilities*. Thousand Oaks, CA: SAGE Publications, 2004.

Brady, Tom. 'Gardaí Find Gang's Guns'. *Evening Press*, 4 April 1986, 7.
- 'Jail Riot Report with Minister'. *Irish Press*, 8 November 1979, 3.
- 'Move to End Row on AIDS Remark'. *Irish Press*, 12 February 1986, 5.
- 'Row over Prisons Appointments'. *Irish Independent*, 10 December, 1998, 3.
- 'Threat to Ministers'. *Irish Press*, 8 April 1977, 1.
- 'Thugs Plan Takeover of City Centre'. *Evening Press*, 18 October 1985, 1.
- 'Warders Threatened by Gunman'. *Evening Press*, 31 March 1986, 1.

Brennan, Steve, and Gordon Paterson. 'Gardaí Hose Prison Rioters'. *Evening Herald*, 11 March 1986, 1.

Briscoe, Ben. 'Private Members' Business – Crime and Vandalism in Dublin: Motion (Resumed)'. *Dáil Éireann Debate* 334, no. 2 (5 May 1982).

Broomfield, Arthur. 'Prison Officers' Dismissal'. *Irish Press*, 17 April 1974, 8.

Brophy, Michael, and Jim Farrelly. '6 Hurt in Mountjoy Jail Riot'. *Irish Independent*, 18 July 1977, 1.

Browne, Vincent. 'Seeds of a Police State'. *Magill,* 31 August 1983.

Buckley, Don. 'Published Reports Confirmed Inadequacy of Curragh Prison'. *Irish Times*, 29 September 1978, 1.

Butler, Richard J. *Building the Irish Courthouse and Prison: A Political History, 1750–1850*. Cork: Cork University Press, 2020.

Byrne, Raymond, Gerard W. Hogan, and Paul McDermott. *Prisoners' Rights: A Study in Irish Prison Law*. Dublin: Co-op Books, 1981.

Callaghan, Michael John. 'Statement of Evidence of Garda Michael John Callaghan, 14847D, Bridewell Garda Station, Dublin'. National Archives of Ireland, CC/Coroners Inquest Dublin 113/1975.

Carroll-Burke, Patrick. *Colonial Discipline: The Making of the Irish Convict System*. Dublin: Four Courts Press, 2000.

Central Statistics Office. 'Percentage Distribution of Males and Females at Each Year of Age by Highest Type of Educational Establishment Attended Full-Time,' In *Census 1971 Volume 12: Education, Scientific and Technological Qualifications.* Dublin: Stationery Office, 1971.

Central Statistics Office. 'Percentage Distribution of Males and Females in Each Occupational Group Classified by Highest Level of Educational Establishment Attended Full Time,' In *Census 1981 Volume 10: Education, Scientific and Technological Qualifications.* Dublin: Stationery Office, 1981.

Chambers, Anne. *T.K. Whitaker: Portrait of a Patriot.* London: Random House, 2014.

Cleary, Catherine. 'Sculpture Recalls Heroin Victims'. *Irish Times*, 1 February 1997.

Clingan, Willy. 'Campaign Aims at Abolition of Death Penalty'. *Irish Times*, 9 January 1981, 11.

– 'Campaign to Shut Curragh Jail Launched'. *Irish Times*, 10 December 1981, 9.

Coghlan, Denis. 'Momentum Added to Prison Reform Campaign'. *Irish Times*, 26 May 1975, 10.

Colley, Zoe. *Ain't Scared of Your Jail: New Perspectives on the History of the South.* Gainesville: University Press of Florida, 2013.

– 'War without Terms: George Jackson, Black Power and the American Radical Prison Rights Movement, 1941–1971'. *History* 101, no. 2 (2016): 265–86.

Collins, Gerry. 'Oral Answers: Intensive Supervision Scheme'. *Dáil Éireann Debate* 307, no. 7, 14 June 1978.

– 'Oral Answers – Places of Detention'. *Dáil Éireann Debate* 302, no. 8, 13 December 1977.

– 'Oral Answers – Prison Conditions'. *Dáil Éireann Debate* 302, no. 8, 13 December 1977.

– 'Oral Answers – Prison Library Facilities'. *Dáil Éireann Debate* 303, no. 7, 14 February 1978.

– 'Oral Answers – St. Patrick's Institution (Dublin) Over-Crowding'. *Dáil Éireann Debate* 320, no. 3, 1 May 1980.

– 'Written Answer – Prison Riot'. *Dáil Éireann Debate* 318, no. 2, 21 February 1980.

Collins, John. 'The Irish Experience: Policy Transfer from US Drug Courts'. In *Rethinking Drug Courts: International Experiences of a US Policy Export*, edited by John Collins, Winifred Agnew-Pauley, and Alexander Soderholm, 51–74. London: LSE International Drug Policy Unit, 2019.

Commission to Inquire into Child Abuse. *Report of the Commission to Inquire into Child Abuse Volume I.* Dublin: Stationary Office, 2009.

Connolly, Linda. *The Irish Women's Movement: From Revolution to Devolution.* London: Palgrave, 2002.

Conway, Michael. 'Inquiry Deal Ends Jail Row'. *Irish Press*, 12 March 1983, 1.

Conway, Vicky. *Policing Twentieth Century Ireland: A History of An Garda Síochána*. London: Routledge, 2014.

Cooney, Patrick. 'Committee on Finance – Vote 20'. *Dáil Éireann Debate* 270, no. 3, 12 February 1974.

– 'Prisons Bill, 1974: Second Stage'. *Dáil Éireann Debate*, 271, no. 12, 21 May 1974.

Corry, Eoghan. 'Heroin Link to Prisoner's Suicide'. *Sunday Press*, 19 January 1986, 1.

– 'Jail Shock That Led to Suicide'. *Sunday Press*, 19 January 1986, 3.

Costello, Declan. *National Youth Policy Committee Final Report'*. Dublin: Stationary Office, 1984.

Costello, Joe. 'Chairman's Address to the 1979 AGM'. *Jail Journal* 3, no. 3 (1979): 3.

– 'Press Release and Leaflet, 31 August 1975'. Dublin: Prisoners' Rights Organisation, 1975. Private Archive of Máirín de Búrca.

– 'Press Release (Herrema)'. October 1975. Private Archive of Máirín de Búrca.

– 'Prisoners' Rights'. *Irish Times*, 17 September 1984, 9.

– 'PRO Address to United Nations Congress'. *Jail Journal* 4, no. 1 (1980): 6–8.

– 'Protecting the Prisoner'. *Irish Press*, 16 October 1979, 8.

– 'Untitled AGM Report, 17 June 1976'. Private Archive of Máirín de Búrca.

– 'Untitled Statement (Sentencing of Activists)'. 19 July 1975. Private Archive of Máirín de Búrca.

Council for Social Welfare. *The Prison System*. Dublin: The Council for Social Welfare, 1983.

Cox, Catherine, and Fiachra Byrne. '"Straightening Crooked Souls:" Psychology and Children in Custody in 1950s and 1960s Ireland'. In *Histories of Punishment and Social Control in Ireland: Perspectives from a Periphery*, edited by Lynsey Black, Louise Brangan, and Dierdre Healy, 37–54. Leeds, UK: Emerald Publishing, 2022.

Cox, Catherine, and Hilary Marland. 'Broken Minds and Beaten Bodies: Cultures of Harm and the Management of Mental Illness in Mid- to Late-Nineteenth century English and Irish Prisons'. *Social History of Medicine* 31, no. 4 (2018): 688–710.

– '"He Must Die or Go Mad in This Place": Prisoners, Insanity, and the Pentonville Model Prison Experiment, 1842–52.' *Bulletin of the History of Medicine* 92, no. 1 (2018): 78–109.

– '"Unfit for Reform or Punishment": Mental Disorder and Discipline in Liverpool Borough Prison in the Late Nineteenth Century'. *Social History* 44, no. 2 (2019): 173–201.

– '"We Are Recreating Bedlam": A History of Mental Illness and Prison Systems in England and Ireland'. In *Mental Health in Prisons: Critical Perspectives on Treatment and Confinement*, edited by Alice Mills and Kathleen Kendall, 25–47. London: Palgrave, 2018.

Crawley, Karl. 'Unpublished Manuscript'. Private Archive of Tommy Crawley.

Cummins, Eric. *The Rise and Fall of California's Radical Prison Movement.* Stanford, CA: Stanford University Press, 1994.

Daly, Liam, and John J. Smith. 'Letter from Liam Daly and John J. Smith to Secretary, Department of Justice, 24 April 1978'. National Archives of Ireland, 2009/74/738.

Daly, Martin. 'Another Striker Takes Food'. *Irish Press*, 20 April, 1977, 1.

Davin, William, Marin O'Sullivan, L.J. Duffy, and James Larkin Jr. *Report on Certain Aspects of Prison Conditions in Portlaoighise Convict Prison.* Dublin: The Labour Party, 1946.

Davis, Samuel. 'Karl Alexander Crawley v Ireland, Appendix 10: Transcript of Medical Evidence to High Court, 8 April 1976'. National Archives of Ireland, 2009/74/738.

– Statement of Dr. Samuel Davis, M.B. Medical Officer Attached to Mountjoy Prison, 1973'. National Archives of Ireland, CC/Coroners Inquest Dublin 244/1973.

de Búrca, Máirín. 'Press Release, 22 November 1973'. Private Archive of Máirín de Búrca.

Denieffe, Michael. 'Child Crime Move, Action Pledge by Minister'. *Sunday Independent*, 10 July 1977, 1.

– 'Minister Hits at Pressure Groups'. *Sunday Independent*, 18 May 1975, 5.

– '"Nighties in Mountjoy Sexy" says Máirín de Búrca'. *Sunday Independent*, 31 July 1977, 24.

Dennehy, Denis. 'Portlaoise Prisoners' Union'. *Irish Press*, 30 May 1973, 10.

Department of Finance. 'Memorandum for the Government: Committee of Inquiry into the Prison System'. Unpublished memorandum. University College Dublin Archives [UCD Archives], TK Whitaker Collection, P175/133, C3.

Department of Justice. *Annual Report on Prisons for 1963.* Dublin: Stationary Office, 1964.

– *Annual Report on Prisons for the Year 1967.* Dublin: Stationary Office, 1968.

– *Annual Report on Prisons for 1968.* Dublin: Stationary Office, 1970.

– *Annual Report on Prisons for the year 1971.* Dublin: Stationary Office, 1973.

– *Annual Report on Prisons and Detention Centres for the year 1972.* Dublin: Stationary Office, 1974.

– *Annual Report on Prisons and Places of Detention for the Year 1973.* Dublin: Stationary Office, 1976.

– *Annual Report on Prisons and Places of Detention for the Year 1975.* Dublin: Stationary Office, 1977.

- *Annual Report on Prisons and Places of Detention for the Year 1977.* Dublin: Stationary Office, 1977.
- *Annual Report on Prisons and Places of Detention for the Year 1978.* Dublin: Stationary Office, 1979.
- *Annual Report on Prisons, and Places of Detention for the Year 1979.* Dublin: Stationary Office, 1979.
- *Annual Report on Prisons and Places of Detention for the Year 1984.* Dublin: Stationary Office, 1985.
- 'Memorandum for the Government: Committee of Inquiry into the Prison System'. Unpublished Memorandum. UCD Archives, TK Whitaker Collection, P175/133.
- *Memorandum for the Government: Proposed Bill to Amend the Prisons Act, 1972 (April 1974).* Unpublished memorandum. National Archives of Ireland, Jus/2008/156/2 1/3.
- 'Memorandum to the Government, 30 January 1974'. National Archives of Ireland, TAOIS/2003/16/317.

Department of Justice, Equality, and Law Reform. *Review of the Drug Treatment Court.* Dublin: Department of Justice, Equality, and Law Reform, 2010.

Dillon, Willie. 'Jail Chaos Averted as Overtime Cuts Deferred'. *Irish Independent*, 12 March, 1983, 1.

Donnellan, Nora. 'Statement of Mrs Nora Donnellan, Ballyconnoe North, Lisdoonvarna, Co. Clare, Housewife, Aged 40 Years Since 11th February, 1935'. National Archives of Ireland, CC/Coroners Inquest Dublin 134/1975.

Donnelly, Michael. Interviewed by Tony Mac Newton and Gerard De Fenton. *That's Life.* Dublin City Fm, 18 February, 2021.

Donoghue, Denis. 'Statement of Denis Donoghue, Governor St. Patrick's Institution Dublin to Inspector Murphy on 22/5/1975'. National Archives of Ireland, CC/Coroners Inquest Dublin 154/1975.

Dowling, Noeleen. 'Petrol Bombers Got "Wrong" House'. *Irish Press*, 24 December 1984, 1.

Dukes, Alan. 'Address to the POA Annual Conference'. UCD Archives, TK Whitaker Collection, P175/133.

- 'Ceisteanna – Questions Oral Answers – Whitaker Report on Penal System'. *Dáil Éireann Debate* 366, no. 10, 22 May 1986.
- 'Criminal Justice System: Motion (Resumed)'. *Seanad Éireann Debate* III, no. 9, 26 February 1986.
- 'Estimates, 1986 – Vote 24: Justice (Revised Estimate)'. *Dáil Éireann Debate* 368, no. 7, 27 June 1986.

Dunne, Frank. *Prisons and Places of Detention – Survey of Objectives.* Dublin: Stationary Office, 1981.

Dunne, Paul. 'Nineteen Portlaoise Escapees Still Free Massive Manhunt'. *Irish Press*, 19 August 1974, 1.

Dwyer, T. Ryle. *Haughey's Forty's Years of Controversy.* Cork: Mercier Press, 2005.

Family of Peter Ben Hogg. 'Acknowledgements – Hogg'. *Evening Herald,* 13 March 1990, 32.

Fanning, Aengus. 'First Macra Protest March to the Dáil'. *Irish Independent,* 23 October 1975, 11.

– 'When Home Is Behind Bars…'. *Sunday Independent,* 24 October 1971, 9.

Fardy, Michael. 'Open Letter to an Taoiseach, Mr Liam Cosgrave; an Taniste, Mr Brendan Corish and Mr Jack Lynch T.D.'. 22 May 1975. Private Archive of Máirín de Búrca.

Farrelly, Brendan. 'Another Prison Suicide'. *Evening Herald,* 17 January 1986, 2.

– 'New Suicide at Prison'. *Evening Herald,* 17 January 1986, 1.

– 'Prison Group Claim Bombing'. *Irish Independent,* 24 December 1984, 1.

Fawcett, J.E.S. 'Decision of the Commission to the Application No. 8154/78 by Karl Alexander Crawley against Ireland'. National Archives of Ireland, 2009/74/738.

Finlay, Thomas. 'Appendix 7: The State (at the Prosecution of C.) v. John Frawley'. National Archives of Ireland, 2009/74/738.

Fitzgerald, Mike. 'Prisoners in Revolt: The Origin and Development of Preservation of the Rights of Prisoners (PROP), the British Prisoners Union'. PhD diss., University of Leicester, 1975.

Fitzgibbon, Edward. 'Statement of Edward Fitzgibbon, 1 Chancery Place, Dublin 7 Taken by Inspector Patrick Daly on the 21st April, 1975'. National Archives of Ireland, CC/Coroners Inquest Dublin 113/1975.

Fitzpatrick, David. *Harry Boland's Irish Revolution.* Cork: Cork University Press, 2003.

Folley, Michael. 'Protest over Use of Curragh'. *Irish Times,* 24 February 1983, 11.

– 'Senior Mountjoy Staff Angry at Officers'. *Irish Times,* 8 November 1983, 9.

Foucault, Michel. *Discipline and Punish: The Birth of the Prison.* Translated by Alan Sheridan. London: Penguin Books, 1991.

– *Untitled Photo.* Private archive of Wladek Gaj.

Gallagher, Conor. 'Drug Treatment Court: A Failed Experiment Imported from the US'. *Irish Times,* 24 June 2019.

Garland, David. *Punishment and Welfare: A History of Penal Strategies.* Louisiana: Quid Pro, 2018.

Gavin, Paul, and Anna Kawałek. 'Viewing the Dublin Drug Treatment Court through the Lens of Therapeutic Justice'. *International Journal for Court Administration* 11, no. 1 (2020): 1–15.

Geiran, Vivian. 'The Development of Social Work in Probation'. In *Social Work in Ireland: Historical Perspectives,* edited by Noreen Kearney and Caroline Skehill, 77–107. Dublin: Institute of Public Administration, 2005.

Gibbons, Conal. 'Portlaoise Prison Protest'. *Irish Independent*, 25 September 1973, 8.

Glasheen, Eugene. 'Statement of Eugene Glasheen, 16 years, St. Patrick's Institution (Inmate) to Inspector Murphy on 21/5/75'. National Archives of Ireland, CC/Coroners Inquest Dublin 154/1975.

Gramsci, Antonio. *Selections from The Prison Notebooks of Antonio Gramsci.* Edited and translated by Quintin Hoare and Geoffrey Nowell Smith. New York: International Publishers, 1932.

Grant, Kevin. 'British Suffragettes and the Russian Method of Hunger Strike'. *Comparative Studies in Society and History* 53, no. 1 (2011): 113–43.

Hall, Stuart. 'Encoding and Decoding in the Television Discourse'. Discussion paper. Birmingham: University of Birmingham, 1973.

– 'Encoding Decoding'. In *Media and Cultural Studies: Keyworks,* edited by Meenakshi Gigi Durham and Douglas M. Kellner, 163–73. Hoboken: John Wiley & Sons, 2009.

Henchy, Séamus. 'Letter to TK Whitaker, 27 February 1984'. UCD Archives, TK Whitaker Collection, P175/133.

– 'Letter to TK Whitaker, 7 October 1986'. UCD Archives, TK Whitaker Collection, P175/133.

Hennessy, Mark. 'AIDS-Hit Prisoners Cut Wrists in Protest'. *Cork Examiner*, 17 January 1986, 1.

Heron, Marianne. 'Do We Need to Lock Up Women?'. *Irish Independent*, 27 November 1980, 8.

Heylin, Greg. *Evaluating Prisons, Prisoners, and Others.* Dublin: The Policy Institute, 2001.

Higgins, Michael D. 'Supplementary Estimates, 1981,' *Dáil Éireann Debate* 330, no. 8, 5 November 1981.

Horgan, John. 'Browne, Noel Christopher'. In *Dictionary of Irish Biography*, edited by James McGuire and James Quinn. Cambridge, UK: Cambridge University Press, 2018.

Illegible name. 'Letter from [illegible name] to Secretary, Department of Foreign Affairs'. National Archives of Ireland, 2009/74/738.

Irish Commission for Justice and Peace and Council for Social Welfare. *Response to the Report of the Committee of Inquiry into the Prison System.* Dublin: Irish Commission for Justice and Peace and Council for Social, 1986.

Irish Council of Churches Board of Community Affairs. *Prisons in the Republic of Ireland.* Belfast: Irish Council of Churches, 1981.

Irish Independent Staff Reporter. 'Prison Protest'. *Irish Independent*, 24 May 1973, 1.

Irish Penal Reform Trust. *Progress in the Prison System: A Framework for Penal Reform.* Dublin: Irish Penal Reform Trust, 2019.

- *Progress in the Prison System: A Framework for Penal Reform.* Dublin: Irish Penal Reform Trust, 2020.

Irish Press Reporter. 'Hunger Strike at Curragh'. *Irish Press*, 24 February 1975, 4.

- 'Prisoners Are Being Illtreated SF Charge Government'. *Irish Press*, 2 February 1973, 4.

Jackson, George. *Soledad Brother: The Prison Letters of George Jackson.* New York: Lawrence Hill Books, 1994.

Joint Working Party. *Punishment & Imprisonment: With Special Reference to Prisons and Places of Detention in the Republic of Ireland.* Dublin: Dominican Publications, 1985.

Kahn, Frank. 'Suicides Blamed on Conditions: Death-Wish Prisons Rapped'. *Irish Independent*, 17 May 1975, 1.

Kantorwicz, Ernst Hartwig. *The King's Two Bodies: A Study in Mediaeval Political Theology.* Princeton, NJ: Princeton University Press, 1997.

Keane, Ronan. 'MacBride, Seán'. In *Dictionary of Irish Biography*, edited by James McGuire and James Quinn. Cambridge, UK: Cambridge University Press, 2018.

Kearns, John. 'Prisoners' Rights'. *Irish Press*, 7 July 1973, 8.

Kelly, Niall. 'Curragh Prison to Close by End of Year'. *Irish Times*, 20 November 1982, 1.

Kennedy, Geraldine. 'Attempt to Break Jail Union Alleged'. *Irish Times*, 22 September 1973, 16.

Kennelly, John. 'Statement of Prison Officer John Kennelly, 618 Kilnamanagh Estate, Tallaght, Co. Dublin, Made to Inspector Michael Walsh, on 29th April, 1975'. National Archives of Ireland, CC/Coroners Inquest Dublin 134/1975.

Kenney, Padraic. '"I Felt a Kind of Pleasure in Seeing Them Treat Us Brutally." The Emergence of the Political Prisoner, 1865–1910'. *Comparative Studies in Society and History* 54, no. 4 (2012): 863–89.

Kerrigan, Gene. *Hard Cases: True Stories of Irish Crime.* Dublin: Gill and Macmillan, 1996.

- 'Karl's Choices.' In *With Trust in Place: Writing from the Outside*, edited by Alice Leahy, 129–38. Dublin: Town House, 2003.

- 'Special Feature: A Necessary Respect – The Small Legend of Karl Crawley'. *Magill*, 31 May 1982.

Kilcommins, Shane, Ian O'Donnell, Eoin O'Sullivan, and Barry Vaughan. *Crime, Punishment and the Search for Order in Ireland.* Dublin: Institute of Public Administration, 2004.

Kilfeather, Vivion. 'Gardaí, Army on Prison Standby'. *Cork Examiner*, 10 March 1983, 16.

Klienrichert, Denise. *Republican Internment and the Prison Ship Argenta, 1922.* Dublin: Irish Academic Press, 2004.

Kraft, Joseph. 'Attica: Parallel with the Blacks in Army?'. *Sunday Independent*, 26 September 1971, 9.

Lavery, Don. 'AIDS Link Prisoners on the Roof'. *Irish Press*, 12 March 1986, 1.

Lentin, Louis (Dir.). *Dear Daughter*, 1996. Produced by Louis Lentin. Irish Film Institute, Louis Lentin Collection. Video, 55 minutes.

Levine, June. 'Ex-Prisoner Is Scourge of the Irish Penal System'. *Sunday Independent*, 4 May 1975, 15.

– 'Máirín, the Anti-Social Socialist'. *Sunday Independent*, 17 September 1972, 4.

Lewis, Anthony. 'The Corruption of Officially Condoned Violence'. *Irish Times*, 20 September 1971, 7.

Lynch, Noel, and Daniel Redmond. 'Letter from Portlaoise– Hoping for a New Deal'. *Evening Herald*, 8 September 1973, 6.

MacBride, Seán. *Crime and Punishment.* Dublin: Ward River Press, 1982.

– *Report of the Commission of Enquiry into the Irish Penal System.* Ireland: Commission of Enquiry into the Irish Penal System, 1980.

Mac Giolla Cear, Peadar. 'Five Still on Strike at Curragh'. *Irish Times*, 27 February 1975, 1.

Mac Giolla, Tomás. 'Written Answers – Report on the Penal System,' *Dáil Éireann Debate* 361, no. 1, 23 October 1985.

MacHale, John. 'Gang Beat Up Couple after Jail Rioting'. *Evening Herald*, 6 November 1979, 5.

Maher, Mary. 'The New Drug Problem – 2'. *Irish Times*, 22 October 1969, 12.

– 'A Voice for Prisoners'. *Irish Times*, 28 August 1973, 6.

Malon, Charles. 'AIDS Scare and Suicides Spark Crisis in Prisons'. *Sunday Independent*, 19 January 1986, 1.

Managh, Ray. 'Attack on Two Prison Officers'. *Evening Herald*, 13 September 1980, 4.

Martin, Jimmy. *Prisoner Population and Trends – Discussion Paper.* Dublin: Department of Justice and Equality, 2016.

McAleese, Mary. 'Our Prison Crisis'. *Irish Independent*, 22 January 1986, 8.

McAuley, Dan. *Towards an Independent Prisons Agency.* Dublin: Stationary Office, 1997.

McCaffery, B. 'Karl Alexander Crawley against Ireland, Exhibit 6: Psychiatric Reports of Dr. B McCaffery'. National Archives of Ireland, 2009/74/738.

– 'Karl Alexander Crawley against Ireland Exhibit 10: Transcript of Medical Evidence to High Court, 8 April 1976'. National Archives of Ireland, 2009/74/738.

McCartan, Patrick. 'State (Karl Crawley) v Governor of Mountjoy, Case History'. Private archive of Tommy Crawley.

– 'Karl Crawley against Ireland: Exhibit 1: Affidavit of Patrick McCartan'. National Archives of Ireland, 2009/74/738, 1–5.

- 'Karl Crawley against Ireland: Exhibit 4: Instructing Solicitor's Notes'. National Archives of Ireland, 2009/74/738.
- 'Untitled Prisoner Rights Organisation Statement 7 May 1975'. National Archives of Ireland, CC/Coroners Inquest Dublin 154/1975.

McCarthy, Kerry, and Helen Rogers. 'He's 12 – and He's a Heroin Addict'. *Evening Herald*, 31 July 1981, 1.

McCaughren, Tom. *Escape by Helicopter*. Dublin: RTÉ, 1973.

McClean, Denis. 'Jail Jab Cause of AIDS?'. *Evening Press*, 20 November 1985, 5.

McConville, Seán. *Irish Political Prisoners 1848–1922: Theatres of War*. London: Routledge, 2003.

- *Irish Political Prisoners, 1920–62: Pilgrimage of Desolation*. London: Routledge, 2014.
- *Irish Political Prisoners, 1860–2000: Braiding Rage and Sorrow*. London: Routledge, 2021.

McDiarmid, Lucy. 'Comradeship: Feminists and Revolutionaries in Holloway Prison, 1918–1919'. In *Women and the Irish Revolution*, edited by Linda Connolly, 33–46. Newbridge, IE: Irish Academic Press, 2020.

McDonagh, Marese. 'Why Me?'. *Irish Independent*, 1 December 1986, 8.

McNamara, John. 'Statement of John McNamara, 19 Years, 55 St. Ita's Street Limerick Made to Sergeant John Kerrigan at St. Patrick's Institution Dublin'. National Archives of Ireland, CC/Coroners Inquest Dublin 154/1975.

McVerry, Peter. 'Letter to TK Whitaker, 30 July 1986'. UCD Archives, TK Whitaker Collection, P175/133.

Miller, Ian. *A History of Force Feeding: Hunger Strikes, Prisons and Medical Ethics, 1909–1974*. London: Palgrave, 2016.

Miscellaneous authors. 'Human Rights: Karl Crawley v Ireland'. National Archives of Ireland, 2009/74/738.

Mitchell, Jim. 'Criminal Justice Bill, 1981: Committee and Final Stages'. *Seanad Éireann Debate* 96, no. 7, 12 November 1981.

Molloy, Philip. 'Warders Claim PRO Supporters Were in Attacks'. *Irish Press*, 2 September 1980, 3.

Moore, Kevin. 'Youth Set Fire to Cell to Get Out'. *Sunday Independent*, 20 April 1975, 7.

Moore, Niamh. 'The Politics and Ethics of Naming: Questioning Anonymisation in (Archival) Research'. *International Journal of Social Research Methodology* 15 (2012): 331–40.

Mulligan, Gerry. 'Prisoners' Gifts to Pope'. *Evening Herald*, 25 September 1979, 1.

Murphy, D. 'Sudden Death: John McCarthy, Statement by Inspector D. Murphy'. National Archives of Ireland, CC/Coroners Inquest Dublin 154/1975.

Murphy, William. *Political Imprisonment and the Irish, 1912–1921*. Oxford: Oxford University Press, 2014.

Murtagh, Peter. 'Prisoner Took Heroin Overdose'. *Irish Times*, 15 October 1983, 6.

Musgrave, Donal. '"Bury the Hatchet" Plea from New POA President'. *Cork Examiner*, 25 May 1985, 9.

Naughton, Lindie. *Markievicz: A Most Outrageous Rebel*. Newbridge, IE: Merrion Press, 2016.

Ní Chríodáin, Louise. 'Labour TD Calls for a New Body to Run Prisons'. *Irish Press*, 10 August 1993, 4.

Noonan, Michael. 'Written Answers – Curragh Military Detention Barracks'. *Dáil Éireann Debate* 342, no. 11, 25 May 1983.

– 'Written Answers – Mountjoy Prison Unit'. *Dáil Éireann Debate* 340, no. 8, 2 March 1983.

O'Carroll, Aileen. 'Remembering Sue Richardson'. Workers Solidarity Movement, 2012. http://www.wsm.ie/c/anarchist-sue-richardson-sarah-fenwick-owen.

O'Donnell, Ian. *Justice, Mercy, and Caprice: Clemency and the Death Penalty in Ireland*. Oxford: Oxford University Press, 2017.

O'Donnell, Ian, Eoin O'Sullivan, and Deirdre Healy. *Crime and Punishment in Ireland 1922 to 2003: A Statistical Sourcebook*. Dublin: Institute of Public Administration, 2005.

O'Donnell, Simon. 'Portlaoise Prisoners' Union'. *Irish Press*, 24 May 1973, 10.

O'Flynn, Alice. *Time for Change: A Research Study on Begging in Dublin City Centre*. Dublin: Dublin City Council, 2016.

O'Hearn, Denis. 'Bobby Sands: Prison and the Formation of a Leader'. In *The Palgrave Handbook of Auto/Biography*, edited by Julie M. Parsons and Anne Chappell, 433–55. London: Palgrave, 2020.

O'Keeffe, Alan. 'AIDS Prisoners Free after Riots'. *Irish Independent*, 2 March 1986, 3.

O'Mahony, Paul. *Drug Abusers in Mountjoy Prison: Five Years On*. Dublin: Department of Justice, 1982.

O'Mahony, Seán. *Frongoch: University of Revolution*. Dublin: FDR Teoranta, 1987.

O'Malley, Desmond. 'Committee on Finance – Prisons Bill, 1972: Second Stage (Resumed)'. *Dáil Éireann Debate* 261, no. 1, 23 May 1972.

O'Sullivan, Eoin. 'Residential Child Welfare in Ireland, 1965–2008'. In *Report of the Commission to Inquire into Child Abuse Volume IV*, by Commission to Inquire into Child Abuse, 245–430. Dublin: Stationary Office, 2009.

Parker, Stewart. 'Prison Prophet'. *Irish Press*, 1 May 1971, 12.

– 'School for Revolution'. *Irish Times*, 7 April 1970, 11.

Parle, Julie. *States of Mind: Searching for Mental Health in Natal and Zululand, 1868–1918*. Scottsville, SA: University of KwaZulu-Natal Press, 2007.

Power, Joseph. 'Prisons Cannot Solve Crime – Bishops'. *Irish Independent*, 23 February, 1983, 9.

Power, Richard. 'How to Win Friends'. *Jail Journal* 1, no. 2 (1973): 3.

Prison Study Group. *An Examination of the Irish Penal System*. Dublin: Prison Study Group, 1972.

Prisoner Rights Organisation. 'Demands of the Portlaoise Prisoners' Union (Smuggled Out on 8/5/'73)'. *Jail Journal* 1, no. 5 (1974): 2.

– 'Draft Report on the Survey of over 200 Ex-prisoners'. Unpublished. Private Archive of Wladek Gaj.

– 'Draft Statement by Prisoners' Rights Organisation: May 16th 1975'. Draft Statement. 16 May 1975. Private Archive of Máirín de Búrca.

– 'Introduction'. *Jail Journal* 1, no. 1 (1974): 1–3.

– *Loughan House: A Survey of Fifty 12–16 Year-Old Male Offenders from the Sean McDermot Street–Summerhill Area of Dublin's Inner-City*. Dublin: Prisoners' Rights Organisation, 1978.

– 'Press Release, 9 November 1973'. Private Archive of Máirín de Búrca.

– 'Prison and the Mentally Ill'. Press Release 15 October 1975. Private Archive of Máirín de Búrca.

– 'Survey of over 200 Ex-prisoners'. Unpublished. Private Archive of Wladek Gaj.

– 'Untitled Draft Invitation'. 1976–1977. Private Archive of Máirín de Búrca.

– 'Untitled Leaflet (Christmas Presents)'. January 1978. Private Archive of Máirín de Búrca.

– 'Untitled Leaflet (Distributed in Geneva)'. August 1975. Private Archive of Máirín de Búrca.

– 'Untitled Leaflet (Irish Law Year)'. Undated, probably October 1975. Private Archive of Máirín de Búrca.

– 'Untitled Prisoner Rights Organisation Statement'. National Archives of Ireland, CC/Coroners Inquest Dublin 154/1975.

– 'Untitled Prisoner Rights Organisation Statement 3 May 1975'. National Archives of Ireland, CC/Coroners Inquest Dublin 154/1975.

Prisoners' Rights Organisation Chairman. 'Resolutions Passed at AGM'. *Jail Journal* 2, no. 3 (1977): 10–14.

Quinn, Brian. '"Sorry, But We Have No Job for You!"'. *Irish Independent*, 18 June 1977, 8.

Quinn, Thomas Anthony. 'Statement of Thomas Anthony Quinn, Prison Officer, St. Patrick's Institution, Dublin to Inspector Murphy on 21/5/1975'. National Archives of Ireland, CC/Coroners Inquest Dublin 154/1975.

Rae, Stephen. 'AIDS Baby Dad Hanged Himself'. *Sunday Independent*, 2 February 1986, 1.

Raidió Teilifís Éireann. *Central Mental Hospital Dundrum*. Dublin: Raidió Teilifís Éireann, 1971.

– *Today Tonight.* Dublin: Raidió Teilifís Éireann, 1986.

Reddy, Tom. 'Bid to End Bitter Feud over Prison'. *Irish Press*, 8 November 1983, 1.

Reilly, Jerome. 'Mountjoy Governor Condemns Assaults'. *Irish Independent*, 10 September 1985, 9.

Reilly, Michael. *Report on an Inspection of St. Patrick's Institution by the Inspector of Prisons Judge Michael Reilly.* Dublin: Office of the Inspector of Prisons, 2012.

Reinisch, Dieter. 'The Fight for Political Status in Portlaoise 1973–7: Prologue to the H-Blocks Struggle'. *War & Society* 40, no. 2 (2021): 134–54.

Richardson, Sue. 'Letter to Concerned Parents against Drugs (1984)'. Unpublished. Private archive of Wladek Gaj.

Robinson, Mary. *Everybody Matters: A Memoir.* London: Hodder, 2013.

– 'Prisons Bill, 1980,' *Seanad Éireann Debate* 94, no. 3, 14 May 1980.

Rogan, Mary. *Prison Policy in Ireland: Politics, Penal Welfarism, and Political Imprisonment.* London: Routledge, 2011.

– 'Rehabilitation, Research and Reform: Prison Policy in Ireland'. *Irish Probation Journal* 9, no. 1 (2012): 6–32.

Rogers, Helen, Brendan Farrelly, Jim Farrelly, Gerry O'Regan, and Katherine Donnelly. '40 Hurt in Prison Battle'. *Irish Independent*, 6 November 1979, 1.

– 'Warden Tells of Beating'. *Irish Independent,* 6 November 1979, 20.

Rowley, Tom. 'Drink – A Mass Killer Stalking the Roads'. *Irish Independent*, 8 February 1978, 1 & 22.

Ruesch, Jurgen, and Gregory Bateson. *Communication: The Social Matrix of Psychiatry.* New York: W.W. Norton & Company, 1951.

Ryan, Liam. 'Prison Welfare Very Well Run, Says Collins'. *Irish Independent*, 20 June 1981, 7.

– 'Prisoners' Rights Deny Attacks Blame'. *Irish Independent*, 2 September 1980, 1.

Secretary of the Prisoners Union in the Curragh. 'Curragh Incidents'. *Jail Journal* 1, no. 9 (1976): 8–9.

Seddon, Toby. *Punishment and Madness: Governing Prisoners with Mental Health Problems.* London: Glasshouse Books, 2007.

Sheehy, Clodagh. 'AIDS Unit Prisoner Unconscious'. *Cork Examiner*, 18 January 1986, 26.

Sheridan, Peter. *The Liberty Suit.* Dublin: Co-op Books, 1978.

Smith, John J. 'Karl Alexander Crawley v Ireland, Appendix 10: Transcript of Medical Evidence To High Court, 8 April 1976'. National Archives of Ireland: 2009/74/738.

Smith, Noel. 'Prison Staff Hit Dept. over Poor Conditions'. *Irish Independent*, 14 January 1983, 3.

Smith, Vincent. 'Sudden Death: Leo Byrne, Statement by Inspector Vincent Smith'. National Archives of Ireland, CC/Coroners Inquest Dublin 113/1975.

Sweeney, George. 'Irish Hunger Strikes and the Cult of Self-Sacrifice'. *Journal of Contemporary History* xxviii (1993): 421–37.

Taylor, Ian, Paul Walton, and Jock Young. *The New Criminology: For a Social Theory of Deviance*. London: Taylor & Francis, 2013.

Thomas, Paul. 'Prison System "in Peril of Collapse"'. *Evening Herald*, 9 August 1985, 3.

Thornberry, Cedric. 'Karl Crawley against Ireland: Memorandum 30 June 1978'. National Archives of Ireland, 2009/74/738.

Treacy, Matt. *The IRA, 1956–69: Rethinking the Republic*. Manchester: Manchester University Press, 2011.

Tully, Desmond A. 'Deposition of Garda Desmond A. Tully 16C29, Newtownmountkennedy Station, 1973'. National Archives of Ireland, CC/Coroners Inquest Dublin 244/1973.

United Nations Committee Against Torture. 'Forty-Sixth Session: Consideration of Reports Submitted by States Parties under Article 19 of the Convention'. UN Treaty Body Database, CAT/C/IRL/CO/1, 3.

United Nations Office of Drugs and Crime. *United Nations Congress on Crime Prevention and Criminal Justice 1955–2010: 55 Years of Achievement*. Austria: United Nations Office of Drugs and Crime, 2010.

Useem, Bert, and Peter Kimball. *States of Siege: US Prison Riots, 1971–1986*. Oxford: Oxford University Press, 1991.

Walker, C.P. 'Irish Republican Prisoners – Political Detainees, Prisoners of War or Common Criminals'. *Irish Jurist* 19, no. 2 (1984): 189–225.

Wall, Oisín. '"Brought in Dead": Post-Mortem Glimpses of the Early "Heroin Epidemic" in Ireland, 1971–1983'. *Social History of Medicine* (forthcoming).

– '"Embarrassing the State": The "Ordinary" Prisoner Rights Movement in Ireland, 1972–6'. *Journal of Contemporary History* 55, no. 2 (2020): 388–410.

Wall, Oisín, and James Grannell. 'From "Opium Smoking Orgies" to "Junkie Babies": Representations of Heroin-Use in Ireland, 1915–90'. *Cultural & Social History* 20, no. 1 (2023): 95–116.

Walsh, Brendan, Michael Finn, John Lawlor, Joseph Fagan, and Gerard Flynn. 'Prisoners' Representatives'. *Irish Press*, 18 November 1977, 8.

Walsh, Caroline. 'Several Hurt in Prison Clashes'. *Irish Times*, 18 July 1977, 1.

Walsh, Thomas. 'Prisons Bill, 1956 – Second and Subsequent Stages'. *Seanad Éireann Debate* 45, no. 16, 15 March 1956.

Walshe, John. 'University Forum'. *Irish Independent*, 23 February 1973, 8.

Weston, Janet. *Positive in Prison*. Dublin: Digital Drama, 2017.

Weston, Janet, and Virginia Berridge. 'AIDS Inside and Out: HIV/AIDS and Penal Policy in Ireland and England & Wales in the 1980s and 1990s'. *Social History of Medicine* 33, no. 1 (2020): 247–67.

Whelan, Ken. 'Jail Officer Firebombed'. *Evening Press*, 5 September 1985, 1.

Whitaker, T.K. 'Committee of Inquiry into the Prison System Discussion Paper'. UCD Archives, TK Whitaker Collection, P175/133.

– 'Draft Letter to the Taoiseach, Undated'. UCD Archives, TK Whitaker Collection, P175/133.

– 'Letter to Alan Dukes, 14 May 1986'. UCD Archives, TK Whitaker Collection, P175/133.

– 'Letter to Alan Dukes, 22 July 1986'. UCD Archives, TK Whitaker Collection, P175/133.

– 'Letter to Una O'Higgins O'Malley, 26 March 1984'. UCD Archives, TK Whitaker Collection, P175/133.

– *Report of the Committee of Inquiry into the Penal System.* Dublin: Stationary Office, 1985.

– 'Welfare of Prisoners'. *Irish Independent*, 24 January 1986, 8.

White, Lawrence William. 'Merrigan, Matthew Paul ('Matt')'. In *Dictionary of Irish Biography*, edited by James McGuire and James Quinn. Cambridge: Cambridge University Press, 2018.

Wright, David, and Renée Saucier. 'Madness in the Archives: Anonymity, Ethics, and Mental Health History Research'. *Journal of Canadian Historical Association* 23, no. 2 (2012): 65–90.

Yeats, Padraig. 'Revenge Group Report to Be Investigated'. *Irish Times*, 14 January 1985, 7.

Yeats, Síle. 'Freed PRO Man Pledges to Fight On'. *Irish Press*, 5 August 1987, 5.

Index

abortion, 145–6
Ad Hoc Committee for Prison Reform (now PRO), 55, 68, 132
"AIDS Inside and Out" (Weston and Berridge), 126
Amnesty International, 24–5, 51, 145–6, 149
An Chomhairle Oiliúna, 62–3
Angry Brigade, 80
annual reports on prisons and places of detention, 15–16, 28, 31, 33, 36–7. *See also* Visiting Committees
anti-death penalty campaign, 145–6
Arbour Hill Prison, *32*, 34, 114, 125–8, 184n82
Artane Industrial School, 89–90
assault, sexual, 58, 83, 96, 105
asymmetric communication, 13–14, 15–19
Attica Prison Rebellion, US, 43–6
Auld Triangle (ballad), *The*, 19

Bailey, Victor, 35
Ball, Stephen, 11–12
Bates, Maura, 68

Bateson, Gregory, 6–7, 12, 15
Behan, Cormac, 21–2
Beirnes, Patrick, 56, 58, 59
Beresford, David, 21
Berridge, Virginia, 21, 26, 39, 126
Bird's Nest orphanage, 94–5
black power activists, 42, 44
Boland, Harry, 20
Bourke, Tom, 68
Briscoe, Ben, 38
British and Irish Communist Organisation, 53
British prisoners' organisation (PROP), 69–70
Brixton Prison, London, England, 126
Broomfield, Arthur, 112–13
Browne, Noël, 140, 146, 149, 203n74
Browne, Vincent, 81
Buckley, Christine, 26
Byrne, Fiachra, 21
Byrne, Henry, 145
Byrne, Leo, 72
Byrne, Raymond, 38

Cahill, Anthony, 150
Cahill, Eddie, 118–19
Canada, correctional system, 143
Carroll-Burke, Patrick, 21
Catholic Bishops' Conference, 34, 67, 156, 161, 169
Central Mental Hospital (CMH) in Dundrum, 39–40, 51, 71, 83, 97–8
Chains or Change (IWLM), 69
Children's Act, 136
Clondalkin, prison in, 117, 156
coded communication, 13–14
Collins, Gerry, 38, 136–7
Collins, Michael, 20
Committee of Inquiry into the Penal System. *See* Whitaker Report
communication, 6–7, 13–14, 15–19. *See also* protests
Concerned Parents Against Drugs (CPAD), 17–18, 153
Concern of Prisoners (COP), 81
confessions, forced, 81, 182n42, 201n10
Coogan, Tim Pat, 121
Cooney, John G., 157–8
Cooney, Patrick, 16, 37, 52, 55, 70, 73
Cork Prison, 30, *32*, 34, 114, 155, 184n82
Cosgrave, Liam, 48
Costello, Declan, 168
Costello, Joe: about, 79; on amnesty at Pope visit, 115; and anti-death penalty campaign, 146; and Curragh reports, 148; as editor of *Jail Journal* (PRO), 135; elected to office, 171–2; on HIV prisoners' needs, 127; and petition to the Dáil, 140; picketing for PRO, 74; on prison officer attacks, 121; on PRO, 111, 129; response to attack by Richie Ryan on PRO, 152–3; run

for office, 142; at UN congress for PRO, 130
Cox, Catherine, 21
Crawley, Bernadette, 75, 92, 106
Crawley, Karl Alexander, 91–108; about, 24, 48, 89, 107; description in *Jail Journal*, 76; early life, 94–7; photo of, 99; and PRO, 76, 92–4, 105–7, 133; punishment of, 77, 102–7; resistance strategies, 97–101
crime wave, 151–2, 160
Criminal Justice Acts, 10, 30, 136, 145, 146
Crowe, Richard, 73–5
Crummy, Frank, 74, 80
culchies, 11, 27, 182n23
Curragh Military Detention Barracks: about, 34, 53; closure recommended, 144, *147*, 148–50; for disruptive prisoners, 10, 41–2, 148; hunger strikes and the PU, 58–60, 70

Daingean Reformatory, 71, 87
Davis, Samuel, 104, 107
de Búrca, Máirín, 28, 68–9, 74, 76, 79–80, 106, 131–5
Delaney, Stephen, 113, 117, 121
demands/campaigns/manifestos: Amnesty International anti-prison torture campaign, 51; Attica rebellion with list of demands, 44–6; *Chains or Change* (IWLM), 69; CPAD campaign against heroin dealing, 17–18, 153; Dublin Housing Action Committee, 80, 132, 201n6; POA campaign for better working conditions, 112–14; political prisoners' campaigns, 40, 58–9; PRO

234 | Index

campaign for Karl Crawley, 92–4, 107; PRO campaign for penal reform, 68–70, 78, 154, 160, 173, 176; PRO campaign to abolish the death penalty, 145–7; PRO campaign to close Curragh, 25, 147–50, 176; PRO campaign to humanize prisoners, 23–4; PRO demands and Whitaker Report, 169–71; PRO demands for public inquiries, 71–4, 139–40, 173, 176; PRS campaign of violence against prison officers, 24, 119–25, 153; publicity for, 59–60, 71, 73–5, 89, 175; PU campaigns for improved prison conditions, 50–7, 59–61, 169, 173; Saoirse campaign for release of OIRA prisoners, 53
De Rossa, Proinsias, 20
De Valera, Éamon, 66
Dóchas Centre, 165
Doherty, Sean, 38
Donnellan, John, 72–3, 75
Donnellan, Nora, 75
Donnelly, Michael, 82–4
Downey, Peter Anthony, 58
Doyle, Declan, 158
Doyle, Patricia, 71
drugs: Concerned Parents Against Drugs (CPAD), 17–18, 153; Crawley use of, 97–8, 104–7, 176; Dublin Drugs Treatment Court, 167; from medical to police issue, 12; PRO on, 17, 153–4; and shift in prison population, 110–11; use in prison population, 109–10, 197n3; war-on-drugs approach, 36; and the Whitaker Report, 161, 166–7. *See also* heroin
Dublin Drugs Treatment Court, 167
Dublin Housing Action Committee, 80, 132, 201n6
Dukes, Alan, 162

Dundalk Prison, 29–30
Dwyer, T. Ryle, 36

education, 39, 68, 137–8
escapes, 40–3
European Commission of Human Rights (ECHR), 92, 93, 102

family planning, 137
Fardy, Michael, 42, 48, 74, 75, 81–2, 88
Fianna Fáil, 36, 38, 123, 136, 149, 161, 172–3
Fine Gael party, 37, 38, 48, 117, 146, 161
Finlay, Thomas, 77–8, 94
Fitzgerald, Garret, 150
Fitzgerald, Michael, 45
Fitzpatrick, David, 20
Flynn, Mannix, 18
forced confessions, 81, 182n42, 201n10
Fort Mitchell (prison), *32*, 34, 114, 125, 127, 164, 184n82
Foucault, Michel, 9–10

Gaj, Margaret, 28, 69, 75, 76, 80, 121
Gaj, Wladek, 74, 75, 76
Galway Prison, 29–30
Gaol of Clonmel (ballad), *The*, 19
Gardaí/Garda: assaults on, 49, 75, 82, 101, 132, 145; forced confessions, 81, 182n42, 201n10; Garda Special Branch, 80, 124, 201n10; physical violence, 48, 153; Prisoners' Revenge Squad/Group (PRS, later PRG), 119–25; recommendations for reform, 144; as reinforcements in prisons, 54, 115, 125; as strike-breaking labour, 157; submissions to the Whitaker Report, 159

Index | 235

Gibbons, Conal, 68, 79
Gibbons, Jo Ann, 74
Gladstone Committee on Prisons (1895), 35
Gramsci, Antonio, 14
Gregory, Tony, 149

Hall, Stuart, 6, 12, 13–15, 111
hardmanship, 48, 102
hards, 11, 182n23
Haughey, Charles, 36–7, 149
Hayes, Patrick, 123, 124
helicopter, for escape, 40–1
Henchy, Séamus, 157, 163
heroin: change in prison population, 33, 176; Concerned Parents Against Drugs (CPAD), 17–18, 153; epidemic in Dublin, 24, 109–10; and loss of community, 109; use of, 82, 104, 125, 150, 179
Higgins, Michael D., 79, 141, 149, 150
HIV in prisons, 21, 107, 125–8, 176, 179, 207n21
Hogan, Gerard, 38
Hogg, Peter 'Ben', 125–6, 200n99
Holden, Thomas, 58, 59
Holloway Women's Prison, 20
Howard League (UK), 130
Hulsman, Louk, 141
hunger strikes: about, 4, 16, 45, 52–3; in Curragh, 23, 58–60; in Mountjoy, 55, 60–2; in Portlaoise, 50–1, 56, 58; as resistance, 6, 21, 40, 50–1, 56
Hussey, Gemma, 142

imprisonment, approaches to, 34–40
independent prison authorities, 144, 161, 163–4, 169
International Police Association, 70
Irish Council for Civil Liberties (ICCL), 80, 145–6

Irish Council of Churches, 34, 38, 156, 161
Irish Family Planning Association (IFPA), 80
Irish Penal Reform Trust (IPRT), 166, 172
Irish Political Prisoners (McConville), 20
Irish prison history, 19–22, 29–34, 183–4nn73–4
Irish Prison Service (IPS), 164
Irish Republic Socialist Party, 182n42
Irish Women's Liberation Movement (IWLM), 69, 80, 132, 201n6

jackeens, 11, 182n23
Jackson, George, 44
Jail Journal (PRO): about, 85, 133; initial issues on experiences and conditions in jails, 70–1, 86, 135, 175; mentions, 28, 54, 60–1, 66, 76, 106, 130; on prisoners' lack of agency, 87–9, 93; shift in language, 86–7, 135
John Paul II, Pope, 115
Joint Working Party, report on prison system, 34, 38
juveniles in prison: campaigns, committees, or commissions on, 36, 165, 172; Children's Act, 136; Daingean Reformatory, 71, 87; Loughan House, 136–7, 152; Marlborough House juvenile detention centre, 82; Ryan Report on institutional child abuse, 96. *See also* St Patrick's Institution

Kantorwicz, Ernst, 4
Kavanagh, James, 172
Kavanagh, Joseph, 71, 88–9
Keane, Colm, 124
Kearns, John, 68

Kelly, Christy, 59–60
Kelly, Nicky, 17, 182n42
Kemmy, Jim, 149
Kenna, Christina, 75
Kenna, Kevin and Paul, 72, 75, 177–80
Kerrigan, Gene, 95, 96, 105, 107
Kinsella, Desmond, 49
Kleinrichert, Denise, 20
Kraft, Joseph, 45

Law Students Union for Action
  (LSUA, UCD), 68, 131, 139–40
League of Nations' International
  Penal and Penitentiaries
  Commission, 65
legitimacy of prisoner's voices:
  about, 5; communication, 11–13;
  distortion of, 15; lack of, 16, 56,
  65–6; in this book, 19, 27; through
  prisoners' organizations, 22;
  through the Whitaker Report, 160
Lenihan, Brian, 37
Levine, June, 75
Lewis, Anthony, 45
Liberty Suit (Sheridan), The, 9
lick-ups, 11, 182n23
Limerick Prison: armed soldiers
  as sentries, 43; children in, 136;
  education at, 39; picketing at,
  113; population, 28, 32; prisoners'
  submissions to Whitaker Report,
  159; women held there, 28, 30, 165
Loneliness of the Long Distance
  Runner (Sillitoe), The, 10
Lonergan, John, 126
Loughan House (prison), 32, 34, 120,
  136–7, 151–2
Lynch, Noel, 53, 55, 58, 59, 91

MacBride Commission Report,
  135–45, 148–9, 154, 155–6
MacBride, Seán, 24, 140–1, 149

Mac Giolla, Tomás, 163
Mac Uardain, Seamus, 113
Magill Magazine, 84
Markievicz, Constance, 20
Marland, Hilary, 21
Marlborough House juvenile deten-
  tion centre, 82
McAleese, Mary, 141, 161
McAuley, Dan / McAuley Report, 164
McCaffery, Brian, 77, 93, 94, 96, 97,
  98, 105
McCartan, Pat: about, 79; central
  figure in PRO, 131–5; on connec-
  tion between PRS and PRO, 121;
  founder of IPRT, 172; founder of
  LSUA, 68, 139–40; picketing, 74;
  protest at UN Congress, 66; solici-
  tor of Crawley, 105–7
McCarthy, John, 72–3
McConville, Seán, 20
McDermott, Paul, 38
McDiarmid, Lucy, 20
McEntee, Patrick, 77, 104, 192n77
McGrath, Denis, 113
McKee Army Barracks, 132
McMahon, J.P., 153
McMahon, Thomas, 42
McNally, Brian, 81
McVerry, Peter, 157, 163
Meath Hospital, 76, 93, 98
medical treatment, 8, 39, 59–60, 83
Meenan, Hugh, 52, 53
mental illness, 21, 39–40, 148, 169
Merrigan, Matt, 68, 140
Miller, Ian, 21
Mitchell, Jim, 38, 149
M'Naughten, Daniel, 191n73
Mother and Child Scheme, 203n74
Mountjoy Prison: about, 30, 33;
  annual Visiting Committee
  reports, 62, 114; children in, 136;
  education, 39; and Karl Crawley,

Index | 237

102; population, 28, *32*, 155; PRO donation of educational books, 138; protests, 16, 55, 60, 61–2, 70, 114–18, *116*; union established, 23; women held there, 28, 165

Murphy, William, 21

National Civil Liberties League, 68

National Council for Crime and Delinquency (US), 130

National Youth Policy Committee Report (D. Costello), 168–9

Naughton, Lindie, 20

New Criminology (Taylor, Walton, and Young), *The*, 141–2

newspaper publicity, 59, 77, 89, 151, 156, 160–1, 171

Nicky Kelly case, 17, 182n42

Noonan, Michael, 150, 161

Oberstown Detention School, 165

O'Callaghan, Gerry, 18

O'Donnell, Simon, 52, 53

O'Donoghue, Breege, 158

Official Irish Republican Army (OIRA), 50, 53

Official Secrets Act, 3

Official Sinn Féin / Workers' Party, 53, 133–4, 136, 161, 172–3. *See also* de Búrca, Máirín

O'Hearn, Denis, 20

O'Mahony, Paul, 172, 197n3

O'Mahony, Seán, 20

O'Malley, Dessie, 37

O'Malley, O'Higgins, 169

O'Malley, Tom, 172

ordinary prisoners: about, 4–5, 21, 152; *versus* political prisoners, 40–3, 52–3, 58; submissions to the Whitaker Report, 159. *See also* prisoners

O'Reilly, Anthony, 89

overcrowding: as alleged reason for movement of prisoners, 55; cause for riots, 115–18, 127; from heroin epidemic, 24; solutions, 34, 42, 115, 155

Owen, Nora, 164

Portlaoise Prison: about, 30, 185n110; armed soldiers as sentries, 43; education, 39, 68; picketing by PRO, 70; political prisoners *versus* ordinary, 14, 41–2, 50, 52; population of, *32*, 155; punishments, resistance, and the PU, 50–8, 62, 169

Poulikos, Sarah (now Sue Richardson), 17–18, 80

Power, Richard, 56, 59, 86

Preservation of the Rights of Prisoners (PROP), 69–70

prisoners: education, 39, 68, 137–8; lack of agency, 87–9, 93, 144; ordinary prisoners *versus* political, 40–3, 52–3, 58; Preservation of the Rights of Prisoners (PROP), 69–70; Prisoners' Committee, 133–5; Prisoners' Revenge Squad/Group (PRS, later PRG), 119–25, 153; women in prison, 20, 27–9, 30, 156, 165. *See also* drugs; Gardaí/Garda; juveniles in prison; legitimacy of prisoner's voices; ordinary prisoners; Prisoners' Rights Organisation (PRO); Prisoners' Union (PU); prisons; protests

Prisoners' Rights Organisation (PRO), 65–90, 130–54; Ad Hoc Committee for Prison Reform (now PRO), 55, 68, 132; blamed for prison-worker attacks, 121; campaign for penal reform, 68–70, 78, 154, 160, 173, 176; campaign to

238 | Index

abolish the death penalty, 145-7; campaign to close Curragh, 25, *147*, 147-50, 176; campaign to humanize prisoners, 23-4; change in messaging, 135-42, 175-6; and Crawley, 76, 92-4, 105-7, 133; de Búrca, Máirín, 28, 68-9, 74, 76, 79-80, 106, 131-5; decline and end of, 150-4, 171-2; demands for public inquiries, 71-4, 139-40, 173, 176; legitimacy/respectability of, 25, 67, 71-2, 78-9, 135-42, 146-7, 175; MacBride Commission, 140-1, 142-5; names of members and types, 78-85; and Official Sinn Féin, 133-4, 136; picketing, 69-76, 92-3; and the PPU/PU, 54, 56; PRO demands and Whitaker Report, 169-71; surveys prisoners, 137-9; at the UN Congress, 65, 70, 133, 142; Walsh, Brendan, 18, 66, 68, 74, 131-5; on the Whitaker Report, 161; and women in prison, 28. *See also* demands/campaigns/manifestos; *Jail Journal* (PRO)

Prisoners' Union (PU): campaigns for improved prison conditions, 50-7, 59-61, 169, 173; final protest, 109; formation at Mountjoy, 55; hunger strikes in Mountjoy, 60-2; hunger strikes in the Curragh, 58-60; as part of Ad Hoc Committee for Prison Reform, 68

prison officers: Prison Officers' Association (POA), 4-5, 37, 55, 112-14, 156-7, 159, 161; prison workers as targets of PIRA, 119-23

prisons: independent prison authorities, 144, 161, 163-4, 169; Irish history of, 19-22; as last resort, 144, 166-7; legislation, 7, 9-10, 41-2, 164; population, 28, 31-3,

32, 110-11, 125-8, 155, 167-8, 176; *Prisons and Places of Detention; Survey of Objectives* (Department of Justice), 34; as sites of radicalization, 45-6. *See also* Gardaí/ Garda; overcrowding; prisoners; prison officers; reports; Visiting Committees; individual prisons

Prison Study Group (UCD), 39, 40, 79

protests, 109-29; picketing, 70-6, 113, 133; Prisoners' Revenge Squad, 119-25, 153; riots, 16, 114-19, 125-8; rooftop protests, 16, 115, *116*, 125; self-harm, 51, 83, 92, 100-1; sit-ins, 16, 50, 52, 54, 63, 174. *See also* hunger strikes; strikes

Provisional IRA (PIRA), 17-18, 40-1, 52, 55, 79, 119-23

Provisional Sinn Féin, 20

Quinn, Ruairi, 146

Red Mass, 73

Redmond, Daniel, 47-64; development as activist, 49-50; early convictions, 48-9; later convictions and release, 62-3; punishments, resistance, and the PU in Curragh, 58-60; punishments, resistance, and the PU in Mountjoy, 60-2; punishments, resistance, and the PU in Portlaoise, 50-8

Redmond, Kevin, 49, 51, 58, 187n21 [51]

Reform, anti-corporal punishment organisation, 80

rehabilitation, 31, 33-40, 43, 68, 113, 136, 143, 167, 170

Reinisch, Dieter, 20

reports: annual reports on prisons and places of detention, 15-16, 28,

Index | 239

31, 33, 36–7; European Commission of Human Rights (ECHR), 92, 93, 102; Joint Working Party, report on prison system, 34, 38; League of Nations' International Penal and Penitentiaries Commission, 65; MacBride Commission Report, 135–45, 148–9, 154, 155–6; McAuley Report, 164; Prison Study Group (UCD), 39, 40, 79; *Response to the Report of the Committee of Inquiry into the Penal System* (Catholic Bishops' Council and Irish Council of Churches), 161. *See also* Whitaker Report

Response to the Report of the Committee of Inquiry into the Penal System (Catholic Bishops' Council and Irish Council of Churches), 161

revenge squad, 119–25

Reynolds, Seán, 43, 100

Richardson, Sue (was Sarah Poulikos), 17–18, 80

Ring, Mary Ellen, 79, 192n84

riots, 16, 114–19, 125–8

Robinson, Mary, 79, 150

Rock, James, 124

Rogan, Mary, 21, 36

rooftop protests, 16, 115, *116*, 125

Royale, George, 60–1, 81–2

Ruesch, Jurgen, 6–7, 12, 13, 15

Rules for the Government of Prisons (1947), 7–9, 11

Ryan, Brendan, 149

Ryan, Richie, 152–3

Ryan Report on institutional child abuse, 96

Sallins train robbery, 182n42

Sands, Bobby, 20

Saor Éire, 53, 132

self-harm, 51, 83, 92, 100–1

sexual assault, 58, 83, 96, 105

Shanganagh Castle (prison), *32*, 34

Shelton Abbey (prison), *32*, 34

Sillitoe, Alan, 10

Sinn Féin/Provisional Sinn Féin, 20. *See also* Official Sinn Féin / Workers' Party

sit-ins, 16, 50, 52, 54, 63, 174

Soledad Brother (Jackson), 44

Spellman, Helen, 207n21

Spike Island, prison on. *See* Fort Mitchell (prison)

Stack, Brian, 122, 124

St Patrick's Institution, 30, *32*, 97–8, 114, 136, 144, 165

St Philomena's Home (orphanage), 95–6

strikes: labour, 16; thirst, 16. *See also* hunger strikes

St Vincent's in Glasnevin, 96

suicides, 51, 60, 71–2, 92, 126, 169

Sweeney, George, 21, 53

Taylor, Ian, 141

Teachtaí Dála, Members of Parliament, 19–20

the Troubles, 40–3

Thornley, David, 42

toilet facilities, 164

torture, 70, 77, 81

United Nations (UN) Committee Against Torture, 164–5

United Nations (UN) Congress on the Prevention of Crime and the Treatment of Offenders, 65, 70, 133

United States, 44, 130, 143

University College Dublin (UCD), 23, 68, 120, 131, 139–40

Vagrancy Act, 166
Valera, Éamon de, 66
Visiting Committees: abolition recommended, 54; about, 8–9; annual reports on prisons and places of detention, 15–16, 28, 31, 33, 36–7; documents as source material, 15; minimization of prisoner disruption, 16, 115–16; punishment of prisoners, 50–1; reports on Curragh, 148; reports on Mountjoy Prison, 62, 114; submissions to Whitaker Report, 159

Walsh, Brendan, 18, 66, 68, 74, 131–5
Walton, Paul, 141
Waterford Prison, 29–30
Weldon, Michael, 120, 124
Weston, Janet, 21, 26, 39, 126
What is Policy? (Ball), 11–12
Wheatfield Prison, *32*, 117
Whelan, Sean, 50–1

Whitaker, T.K., 25, 154, 157
Whitaker Report, 155–73; brought prisoners' rights to mainstream, 172–3; on drugs, 161, 166–7; establishment of the Whitaker Inquiry, 157–60; and legitimacy of prisoner's voices, 160; and the MacBride Report, 169; POA on, 161; prisoners' rights movements, 169–72; *PRO* on, 161; reception of the report, 160–2; recommendations and implementation of the report, 162–9; submissions to, 159
women: Irish Women's Liberation Movement (IWLM), 69, 80, 132, 201n6; in prison, 20, 27–9, 30, 156, 165; as prison officers, 163–4; and PRO, 28; suffragettes, 21
Workers' Party. *See* Official Sinn Féin / Workers' Party

Young, Jock, 141